To Scott

From Bill Sievers + Family

NEW EVERY MORNING

MEDITATIONS
FROM YOUR FAVORITE
CHRISTIAN WRITERS

NEW EVERY MORNING

366 DAILY
DEVOTIONAL GEMS FROM
BILLY GRAHAM,
PHILLIP KELLER,
DALE EVANS ROGERS,
BRUCE LARSON,
LLOYD OGILVIE,
CHARLES SWINDOLL
AND MORE!

COMPILED BY

Al Bryant

WORD BOOKS
PUBLISHER
WACO, TEXAS

A DIVISION OF
WORD, INCORPORATED

NEW EVERY MORNING

567898   RRD   987654321

Library of Congress Cataloging in Publication Data
Main entry under title:

New every morning.

Bibliography: p.
Includes index.
1.   Devotional calendars.   I. Bryant, Al, 1926–
BV4810.N46   1985   242'.2   85–20372
ISBN 0–8499–0507–9

Printed in the United States of America

For

NATHAN
(Nathaniel Barton Townsend)

the grandson whom God sent
into my life to season it with joy.
Fittingly, his name means "gift of God."

Preface

Nearly thirty years ago, in the excitement of youthful enthusiasm, I compiled a book called *Climbing the Heights* (Zondervan, 1956). At the time I was only standing in the doorway of the Christian life, and even though I had experienced some difficult as well as triumphant days, much of what I said and quoted in that book I did not know *experientially*. Today, past the halfway point as far as my physical life is concerned, I'm still learning some spiritual lessons. I have changed in those thirty years. I hope I have grown spiritually. But this I know—the God whom I knew and loved then at the threshold of life is still the same today. *He* has not changed!

This book, *New Every Morning*, has grown out of my personal pilgrimage over these last thirty years. Like most Christians, I have experienced life's high points (on the *heights*), but I have also plodded through the valleys. During the last couple of years, especially, I have had to live with a certain amount of physical impairment (a "first" for me, who always used to boast that I was "disgustingly" healthy), but even that problem is slowly passing. And there has been

Preface

suffering of other kinds as well. But God has always been there! With the writer of Lamentations I can exult:

> But this I call to mind,
>   and therefore I have hope:
> The steadfast love of the LORD never ceases,
>   his mercies never come to an end;
> they are *new every morning*;
>   great is thy faithfulness.
> "The LORD is my portion," says my soul,
>   "therefore I will hope in him."
>
> (3:21–24, RSV, italics mine)

I have learned, indeed, that God's mercies are *new every morning.* If they were not, we frail "children of dust" would never survive! In this book I have selected widely from favorite authors of the past and present, and their names appear at the end of their respective meditations. I have also listed in the back of the book, the titles from which I have excerpted the works of modern-day authors, and I acknowledge with deep appreciation their kind permission to quote them in this way. The titles appearing over each meditation are my suggestions—and in many cases I have also selected what I felt was an appropriate Scripture verse. The unsigned meditations are my own. It is my prayer this book will enrich your life and bless your year.

January

1

IN THE BEGINNING

In the beginning was the Word, and the Word was with God, and the Word was God.

John 1:1

Plato said that "the beginning is the most important part of the work." Life is full of beginnings. Every day offers us a new beginning. Though we are now at the beginning of a year, this verse talks about a beginning that goes back beyond all the years, all the dates of history, before time began, beyond the beginnings of creation. Even then Christ *was*. What a sublime stretch of being these words give to Him who is our Savior! We cannot begin to grasp the thought, but we *can find* security and comfort in it when we think of Christ and rest in Him as our hope and salvation. We trust in human friends, and it's a comfort to us on the way. Yet we should never forget that human friends are transient creatures. We cannot be sure of having them even for tomorrow. But we can trust in Christ and know that from eternity to eternity He is the same and therefore our confidence is forever sure and strong.

2

EXCEEDING RICHNESS

But God, who is rich in mercy, for his great love wherewith he loved us . . . hath raised us up together, and made us sit together in heavenly places in Christ Jesus: that in the ages to come he might show the exceeding riches of his grace in his kindness toward us through Christ Jesus.

Ephesians 2:4–7

January

This is one of those Scripture promises that comes to us Christians "new every morning." And it sometimes takes a rather homely illustration to drive home the truth of a vast promise such as this. A story comes out of the long war of invasion as Great Britain sought to subdue the rugged Scots to its rule. Because of their overwhelming forces the British were inclined to think nothing could stand in their way. They could overcome any enemy by sheer force of numbers—or so they thought.

A British force lay siege to a solitary Scottish castle, thinking they would be able to starve the Scottish garrison simply by "waiting them out." They sent in a message demanding the unconditional surrender of the small defending force. The answer came back over the wall to them—a string of fresh fish still dripping from their watery home. The answer? A subterranean passage to the sea supplied the defenders of the castle with an unlimited supply of fresh fish. In a small way, this illustrates the truth of the "exceeding richness" available to the believer no matter what the circumstances.

3

Living the Lord's Way

That ye be not slothful, but followers of them who through faith and patience inherit the promises.

Hebrews 6:12

Laxity in our Christian lives has, without doubt, something to do with our past failures. As long as the bright summer sun shines into the forest, the fungus has no chance to flourish; but when the sunshine wanes, in the months of autumn, the woods are filled with these strange products of decay. It is because we drift from God that our lives are the prey of numberless and nameless ills. Make the best of all new starts, and return to the more earnest habits of earlier days, or beginning from them now, give yourself to God, believing that He will receive and welcome you, without a word of condemnation or delay.

Form habits of morning and evening prayer, especially in the morning, taking time for deep communion with God. Live in His Word until He speaks to you. Join with His people in worship, and find a place of Christian service there. Depend upon the Holy Spirit to enable you, keeping you true to your new resolves, causing you to be steadfast, immovable, and set on maintaining life at a higher level. In all these ways, let the beginning of this new year witness a new start for you.

F. B. Meyer

4

THE NATURE OF TRUE PRAYER

We lift up our heart and hands toward God in heaven.
Lamentations 3:41, NASB

Prayer was never intended to make us feel guilty. It was never intended to be a verbal marathon for only the initiated . . . no secret-code talk for the clergy or a public display of piety. None of that. Real prayer—the kind of prayer Jesus mentioned and modeled—is realistic, spontaneous, down-to-earth communication with the living Lord that results in a relief of personal anxiety and a calm assurance that our God is in full control of our circumstances.

I encourage you to start over. Form some brand new habits as you fight off the old tendency to slump back into meaningless jargon. Get a fresh, new grip on prayer. It is essential for survival.

Many years ago I decided to do that very thing. I was fed up with empty words and pharisaical phrases. In my search for new meaning, I came across this brief description of prayer, which I set on my desk and carried in the front of my Bible for years. I cannot locate the book from which it was taken, but I do know the author, a seventeenth-century Roman Catholic Frenchman named François Fenelon. Although written centuries ago, it has an undeniable ring of relevance:

> Tell God all that is in your heart, as one unloads one's heart, its pleasures and its pains, to a dear friend. Tell Him your troubles, that He may comfort you; tell Him your joys, that He may sober them; tell Him

January

your longings, that He may purify them; tell Him your dislikes, that He may help you to conquer them; talk to Him of your temptations, that He may shield you from them; show Him the wounds of your heart, that He may heal them . . . .

Charles R. Swindoll (SYG)

5

GOD'S WILL

Howbeit when he, the Spirit of truth, is come, he will guide you into all truth . . . .

John 16:13

I asked the New Year for some motto sweet,
Some rule of life by which to guide my feet,
I asked and paused; it answered soft and low,
    "God's will to *know*."

Will knowledge then suffice? New Year, I cried,
But ere the question into silence died
The answer came, "No, this remember too,
    God's will to *do*."

Once more I asked, is there still more to tell?
And once again the answer sweetly fell;
"Yes, this one thing all other things above,
    God's will to *love*."

Author Unknown

6

THE GREATNESS OF GOD

God said, "Let the waters bring forth . . . and let the birds fly . . . ." So God created the great sea monsters and every living creature that moves . . . and every winged bird.

Genesis 1:20–21, RSV

How great is God! His Word made not only the giant whale, but also the tiny, delicate humming bird. Should I hesitate to entrust my life to such a One as this? The One with whom we have to do is far greater than our limited concept of Him—and He is far more capable of keeping His children than the most loving earthly parent.

Someone asked a little child: "Why is there but one God?" Promptly he answered: "Because God fills every place and there's no room for another one." That's the kind of simple faith I should have as I confront the problems of my day!

7

THE MINISTRY OF ADVERSITY

Everything on the dry land in whose nostrils was the breath of life died. . . . Only Noah was left and those with him in the ark.

Genesis 7:22–23, RSV

It is important to remember that the flood waters which drowned the wicked were the very waters which bore Noah and his family to safety. In the providence of God what may seem to be tragedies are often the very means which God uses to lead His children into a higher place of service or surrender. Just as Noah must have thanked God for deliverance *through* the flood, God's children today should remember to give thanks to Him for their deliverance *through* adversity.

That tree which survives the greatest beating from wind and weather is the tree that becomes the hardiest and most rugged. This is true in the life of the Christian as well. God chastens those whom He loves. Seen in this light, difficulties become stepping stones to greater heights of Christian service.

Norman B. Harrison writes: "It is in the furnace of affliction that our Savior watches for Christlikeness to be brought out in us. He is pictured as a purifier and refiner of silver, and we are told that He counts the process complete only when He can see His likeness in the molten metal."

January

8

A Cloud of Blessing

I do set my bow in the cloud . . . .   Genesis 9:13

How often the soul that is frightened by trial sees nothing but a confused and repulsive mass of broken expectations and crushed hopes! But if that soul, instead of fleeing away into unbelief and despair, would only draw up near to God, it would soon discover that the cloud was full of angels of mercy. In one cherub-face it would see "Whom I love I chasten." Another angel would say, "All things work together for good to them that love God." In still another sweet face the heavenly words are coming forth, "Let not your heart be troubled; you believe in God, believe also in me. In my Father's house are many mansions . . . . Where I am there shall ye be also."

No cloud can be big enough to shut out heaven if we keep the eye toward the Throne. And when we reach heaven and see the cloud from God's side, it will be blazing and beaming with the illuminations of His love.

Theodore L. Cuyler

The world's fierce winds are blowing
Temptations sharp and keen;
I feel a peace in knowing,
My Savior stands between.

Author Unknown

9

The God of Seeing

So she (Hagar) called the name of the Lord who spoke to her, "Thou art a God of seeing . . . ."

Genesis 16:13, RSV

Hagar was fleeing from an uncomfortable and disagreeable situation. Abraham's wife, Sarah, jealous of Hagar, had virtually told Abraham, "It's either Hagar or me—take your choice!" But Hagar could not flee from the sight of God, nor His care for her. In fact, in her flight she learned submission to the will of God. She returned to Abraham's tent where she remained with her son, Ishmael, until after Isaac's birth.

No, fleeing a disagreeable situation does not help. The Lord Jesus did not flee Gethsemane or the cross—even though He knew what torture and terrible death awaited Him. We believers can rest in the promise, "Thou God seest me," (KJV) realizing that no matter what befalls us, our heavenly Father sees and cares.

10

GOD MEANT IT FOR GOOD

And now do not be grieved or angry with yourselves, because you sold me here; for God sent me before you to preserve life. For the famine has been in the land these two years, and there are still five years in which there will be neither plowing nor harvesting. And God sent me before you to preserve for you a remnant in the earth, and to keep you alive by a great deliverance.
Genesis 45:5–7, NASB

Eventually Jacob and all his sons were settled permanently in Egypt. After Jacob died, Joseph's brothers came to him asking forgiveness for what they had done to him. His response was filled with the wisdom and greatness that his own suffering and hardship had produced. What he said gives us the key to understanding God's providence in our own lives. "Do not be afraid," Joseph said, "for am I in God's place? And as for you, you meant evil against me, but God meant it for good in order to bring about this present result, to preserve many people alive" (Gen. 50:19–20). Those words plunge us into the deep waters of God's sovereignty, our free will, man's fallen inhumanity to himself and others, and yet God's power to use it all to eventually accomplish his ultimate purposes.

Joseph refused to take God's place. He would not play God over his brothers or judge what they had done to him. All that he had been through had broken his pride and enabled him to praise God. He trusted God unreservedly and was able to give him glory.

God knows today what he's doing with you and me. If we can say with Joseph in life's calamities, "Men meant it for evil, but God meant it for good," then we have discovered the secret of living with freedom and joy.

Lloyd J. Ogilvie (AHA)

11

FEAR NOT!

Fear not to go down into Egypt; for I will there make of thee a great nation: I will go down with thee into Egypt; and I will also surely bring thee up again.

Genesis 46:3-4

Jacob must have shuddered at the thought of leaving the land of his fathers and dwelling among heathen strangers. It was a new scene, and likely to be a trying one. Who shall venture among strangers without anxiety? Yet the way was evidently appointed for him, and therefore he resolved to go.

This is frequently the position of believers today. They are called upon to change jobs, to face situations new and untried: at such times let them imitate Jacob's example by offering sacrifices of prayer to God, and seeking His direction; let them not take a step until they have waited upon the Lord for His blessing. Then they will have Jacob's Companion to be their friend and helper. . . .

Let us exercise Jacob's confidence. "Fear not" is the Lord's command and His divine encouragement to those who at His bidding are launching upon new seas and new ways; the divine presence and preservation forbid so much as one unbelieving fear. Without our God we should fear to move; but when He bids us go, it would be dangerous to delay. Reader, go forward and fear not!

C. H. Spurgeon

January

12

DEPENDABLE AND DEPENDENT

I know him, that he . . . [and] his children . . . after him . . . shall keep the way of the Lord.

Genesis 18:19

God wants people whom He can depend upon. He could say of Abraham, "I know him, that the Lord may bring upon Abraham all that He hath spoken." God can be depended upon; He wants us to be just as decided, as reliable, as stable. This is just what faith means. God is looking for people on whom He can put the weight of all His love, and power, and faithful promises. When God finds such a person there is nothing He will not do for that one. God's engines are strong enough to draw any weights we attach to them. Unfortunately the cable which we fasten to the engine is often too weak to hold the weight of our prayer. Therefore, God is drilling us, disciplining us, and training us to stability and certainty in the life of faith.

A. B. Simpson

The circus showman, P. T. Barnum, had an interesting comment on the subject of faith: "On the whole, more people are cheated by believing nothing than by believing too much."

13

THE ROPE OF FAITH

But Joseph said to them, "Fear not . . . (though) you meant evil against me . . . God meant it for good, to bring it about that many people should be kept alive, as they are today."

Genesis 50:19–20, RSV

Because the upper surface of a plane's wing is greater than the lower surface, the differential between pressures of the air passing over these top and bottom surfaces, whisks a 630,000-pound airliner into the sky and keeps it there. That's simplifying it a bit, but it's the

January

general idea. In any case, gravity is in the picture and it can't be turned off. Somewhere between being earthbound by gravity and nullifying it, there is a way to use it to fly.

So it is with apocalyptic events. While the clock ticks, God keeps on working. And it is helpful to remember that he works not only through Joseph, but through Joseph's brothers and even Potiphar's wife.

As with Joseph, all that God requires of us is faithfulness in the circumstances. At the end of our rope, we will find God waiting. He knows exactly when the rope will give out.

It is then we discover that not only we, but the rope are his.

Stan Mooneyham

14

BURDENS CAN BE BLESSINGS

. . . I am the Lord, and I will bring you out from under the burdens . . . .
Exodus 6:6

If some people made this promise, we would take it "with a grain of salt." But notice that God prefaces this promise with the statement, "I am the Lord." That is all the qualification He needs to supply to convince us of His ability. Wherever we look in the Word of God we are impressed with the "all powerfulness" of our God. So, we can take Him at His Word and then proceed without fear on the basis of His promise. If we have burdens, He has promised to bring us out from under them. In other words, He will take over the burden and leave us with the blessing. Perhaps others could take over our burden for a while, but eventually they would have to give it back to us. Not so with God. He is the only One with "what it takes" to assume our burden permanently and conclusively.

A biologist watched an ant carrying a piece of straw—what seemed a huge burden to the tiny creature. The ant came to a wide crack too broad for it to cross. It stood for a time as if pondering the problem. Then it laid the straw over the crack and walked over it! That ant teaches us all a lesson. A person's burden can become a bridge over the problem. Burdens are sometimes blessings in disguise.

15

MY LORD KNOWS THE WAY

But God led the people round by the way of the wilderness toward the Red Sea. And the people of Israel went up out of the land of Egypt equipped for battle.

Exodus 13:18, RSV

You can't appreciate the full meaning of these words without a map of that ancient region. Suffice it to say, the most logical journey would have been "by the way of the land of the Philistines" (v. 17). The other route was farther, less comfortable, more threatening, and included a dead end at the Red Sea. But since when did human logic dictate to divine leading?

By the way, are you going through a few surprises these days? Are you being led away from familiar turf and into a "wilderness" journey? There's nothing to fear so long as you know God is in it. He's good at surprises, you know.

Charles R. Swindoll (DYG)

16

GOD'S GUIDANCE

And the Lord went before them by day in a pillar of a cloud, to lead them the way . . . .

Exodus 13:21

How perfectly safe at all times the children of Israel were, for "the Lord went before them by day in a pillar of a cloud to lead them the way, and by night in a pillar of fire to give them light." Thus they had the continual presence of the Lord God Almighty. He was with them as a guide by day, as a light by night, and as a shield or protection by both day and night. But what has that to do with me? May I expect God's presence to be with me, both for protection and direction, even as it was with the children of Israel? Yes, praise God! I may. Solomon has said: "In all thy ways acknowledge Him, and He shall direct thy paths." The psalmist declared: "Thy word is a lamp to my feet and a light unto my path." The words of the Lord Jesus are: "The Father shall give you another Comforter, that He may abide with you for ever, even the Spirit of truth." And the apostle Paul has taught us that our "body is the temple of the Holy Ghost." Therefore, if I honor and obey Him I may with confidence expect continued guidance by God's Word, and His Holy Spirit, and His providence, both from day to day and all the days of my life.

John Roberts

17

Stand Still

And Moses said unto the people, Fear ye not, stand still, and see the salvation of the Lord, which he will shew to you today: for the Egyptians whom ye have seen today, ye shall see them again no more for ever.
Exodus 14:13

These words contain God's command to the believer when he is reduced to great straits and brought into extraordinary difficulties. He cannot retreat; he cannot go forward; he is shut up on the right hand and on the left; what is he now to do? The Master's word to him is, "Stand still." It will be well for him if at such times he listens only to his Master's word, for other and evil advisers come with their suggestions.

Despair whispers, "Lie down and die; give it all up." But God would have us put on a cheerful courage, and even in our worst times, rejoice in His love and faithfulness.

Cowardice says, "Retreat; go back to the worldling's way of action; you cannot play the Christian's part, it is too difficult. Relinquish your

January

principles." But, however much Satan may urge this course upon you, you cannot follow it if you are a child of God.

Precipitancy cries, "Do something. Stir yourself; to stand still and wait is sheer idleness." We must be doing something at once—we must do it, so we think—instead of looking to the Lord, who will not only do something but will do everything.

Presumption boasts, "If the sea be before you, march into it and expect a miracle." But Faith listens neither to Presumption, nor to Despair, nor to Cowardice, nor to Precipitancy, but it hears God say, "Stand still," and immovable as a rock it stands.

"*Stand* still"—keep the posture of an upright man, ready for action, expecting further orders, cheerfully and patiently awaiting the directing voice; and it will not be long ere God shall say to you, as distinctly as Moses said it to the people of Israel, "Go forward."

C. H. Spurgeon

18

The Divine Gardener

Thou in thy mercy hast led forth the people which thou hast redeemed: thou hast guided them in thy strength unto thy holy habitation.

Exodus 15:13

God is love in its highest degree. He is love rendered more than love. Love is not God, but God is love; He is full of grace, He is the plentitude of mercy—He delights in mercy.

I believe that every flower in a garden, which is tended by a wise gardener, could tell of some particular care that the gardener takes of it. He does for the dahlia what he does not for the sunflower; somewhat is wanted by the rose that is not required by the lily; and the geranium calls for an attention which is not given to the honeysuckle. Each flower wins from the gardener a special culture.

He loves us better than we love ourselves.

C. H. Spurgeon

January

19

THE NEED FOR QUIET OBEDIENCE

(The Lord said:) Now therefore, if ye will obey my voice indeed, and keep my covenant, then ye shall be a peculiar treasure unto me above all people (people special to me): for all the earth is mine.

Exodus 19:5

We are activists. We look for sensory satisfaction and become easily bored. When something does not happen immediately, if we do not give up entirely, we continue in half-hearted fashion. We forget the way of the cross is not always easy.

Often we use times of quietness and prayer to try to convince God to want what we want. We see him in our perspective rather than seeing ourselves in his perspective. Few of us like the word *surrender* when the surrender of our every wish to him should become the most important part of our quiet time. Until we are entirely his, to do with as he pleases, he can do very little with us or for us.

Harold Rogers

20

TRUE OBEDIENCE

Thou shalt have no other gods before me.   *Exodus 20:3*

This is the first of the ten commandments God gave to Moses and, significantly, if it were obeyed, all of the other commandments would be kept in this one. If we put nothing before God, our obedience would be complete. But how many times we put other "gods" in God's place—money, ambition, pleasure, recreation, etc.—and so often we put ourselves first. But the only way to true peace and heart satisfaction is the way of obedience to God.

The English poet, Francis Quarles, put obedience at the top of the list when he wrote, "Let the ground of all religious action be obedience; examine not why it is commanded, but observe it because it is commanded. True obedience neither procrastinates nor questions."

21

THE PLACE OF REST

At the commandment of the Lord they rested in the tents, and at the commandment of the Lord they journeyed.

Numbers 9:23

This is the secret of peace and calm elevation. If an Israelite, in the desert, had taken it into his head to make some movement independent of Jehovah; if he took it upon him to move when the crowd was at rest, or to halt while the crowd was moving, we can easily see what the result would have been. And so it will ever be with us. If we move when we ought to rest, or rest when we ought to move, we shall not have the divine presence with us.

C. H. MacIntosh

22

GO TO GOD FIRST

Thou wast a servant in the land of Egypt, and . . . the Lord thy God brought thee out . . . through a mighty hand and by a stretched out arm.

Deuteronomy 5:15

It is important that we cry for grace from God to see His hand in every trial, and then for grace, seeing His hand, to submit at once to it—not only to submit, but to rejoice in it. "It is the Lord, let him do what seemeth him good." I think there is generally an end to troubles when we get to that, for when the Lord sees we are willing that He should do what He wills, then He takes back His hand and says: "I need not chasten My child; he submits himself to Me. What would have been worked out by My chastisement is worked out already, and therefore I will not chasten him."

January

There are two ways of getting help. One is to go around to all your friends, be disappointed, and then go to God at last. The other is to go to God first. That is the shortest way. God can make your friends help you afterwards. Seek first God and His righteousness. Out of all troubles the surest deliverance is from God's right hand. Don't go to friends, but pour out your story to God:

> Were half the breath that's vainly spent,
> To heaven in supplication sent;
> Our cheerful song would oftener be,
> Hear what the Lord hath done for me.

C. H. Spurgeon

23

GOD'S GRACE IS ALWAYS TIMELY

As your days, so shall your strength be.   *Deuteronomy 33:25,* NASB

God does not give His grace as He gives His sunshine—pouring it out on all alike. He discriminates in spiritual blessings. He gives strength according to our need. His eye is ever on us in tender, watchful love, and what we need He supplies. He gives us grace for grace. When one grace is exhausted another is ready. The grace is always timely. It is not given in large store in advance of the need, but it is ready always on time. It may not always be what we wish, but it is always what we really need.

There is in the Bible no promise of grace in advance of the soul's need. God does not say He will put strength into our arm for the battle while we are in quiet peace and the battle is yet far off. When the conflict is at hand the strength will be given. He does not open the gates for us, nor roll away the stones, until we have come up to them. He did not divide the Jordan's waters while the people were yet in their camps, nor even as they began their march toward the river.

The wild stream continued to flow as the host moved down the banks, even until the feet of the priests had been dipped in the water. This is the constant law of divine help. It is not given in advance. As we come up to the need the supply is ready, but not before. Yet many Christians worry because they cannot see the way opened and the needs supplied far in advance of their steps. Shall we not let God provide and have faith in Him?

J. R. Miller

24

INCREASING STRENGTH

As thy days, so shall thy strength be.   *Deuteronomy 33:25*

There are two ways of reading these words. According to the common interpretation, they contain an assurance of strength proportioned to the need. Each day has its trials, difficulties, and demands; so for each day there is God's provision of strength. That strength will come as the day comes. Whatever kind of strength is wanted, that kind of strength shall be given. "As thy days, so shall thy strength be."

But we may see another thought in the words. Observe that it is not written, "As thy day is . . . " but, "As thy days." That is, as your days increase, according to the number of your days, as you grow older. Now, what is the promise here given? It is an assurance of strength that brings out the contrast between the natural and the supernatural. According to natural experience, age brings with it weakness and infirmity. After a certain point in one's life, the older we are the feebler we become. But in the divine life, God promises that if our days are many, our strength shall be great. In other words, He promises that our spiritual strength shall increase with our days.

Evan H. Hopkins

25

WILLING OBEDIENCE

And they answered Joshua, saying, "All that you have commanded us we will do, and wherever you send us we will go.

January

"Just as we obeyed Moses in all things, so we will obey you; only may the Lord your God be with you, as He was with Moses."

Joshua 1:16–17, NASB

That's abandonment! "All . . . wherever . . . ." And talk about willing obedience! " . . . we will do . . . we will go . . . we will obey . . . ." And how do you think Joshua felt when they promised him the same loyalty they had given to Moses? How could they have been so willing? What prompted such wholesale commitment? Aren't these the offspring of that mob of independent, stubborn, and spoiled nomads who struck out against Moses and resisted the Lord in the wilderness? Indeed they are! Then, how can we explain the change? What could possibly be powerful enough to turn the hearts of these people? Their eyes were fully on the Lord. He was now in focus. They saw Him at work. As a result, their entire perspective had changed. He was giving the drumbeat, and they were marching in step with the cadence. There was no reluctance; they now wanted Him and His will. With that mindset, phenomenal adjustments and adaptations are possible. But let us all be warned—without it, forget about being drawn closer. Operation assimilation becomes a distant dream, abandonment becomes a joke, and unity, an impossibility. Trite though it may sound, it's true—not until our eyes are on the Lord will we be big enough to overlook differences and open enough to adapt and adjust.

Charles R. Swindoll (DYG)

26

EXHORTED TO ENCOURAGE

Be strong and of a good courage . . . be thou strong and very courageous . . . .

Joshua 1:6–7

As Christians one of our hallmarks should be that of courage and fortitude. All through God's Word He gives us enormous encouragement (read Joshua 1). He exhorts us to take heart, to be strong, to be courageous.

January

Our late twentieth-century society is notorious for its despair, its cynicism. The media is in the control of skeptics. Gloom and doom are dispensed in large doses from books, magazines, newspapers, radio, and T.V. programs.

As God's people we are to encourage those around us. We are to show them there can be purpose, direction, and fulfillment in life. Let us draw alongside the weak and faltering to lift their hearts, fire their hopes, and transfer their attention from failing to our Father's faithfulness.

W. Phillip Keller (SS)

27

SAUL'S LACK OF SURRENDER

And Samuel said to Saul, "You have done foolishly; you have not kept the commandment of the Lord your God . . . for now the Lord would have established your kingdom forever. But now your kingdom shall not continue; the Lord has sought out a man after his own heart; and the Lord has appointed him to be prince over his people because you have not kept what the Lord commanded you.

1 Samuel 13:13–14, RSV

What Saul had demonstrated at Gilgal was a stubborn, impetuous, strong self-will that insisted on asserting itself. He was obviously not suited to serve under the sovereignty of God. Again and again this trait would lead to his downfall. He was a man incapable of coming under divine control.

The principle is an all-important one for each of us. Will we wait patiently and comply with Christ's wishes? Or must we push ahead with our own ideas and insist on using our own initiative? Are we the ones who will "call the shots," or are we ready to respond in hearty good will to what heaven's royalty arranges for us?

To have our own way is to end up in disarray.

To quietly do our Father's will is to know strength and security!

W. Phillip Keller (D)

January

28

The Enemy Envy

Vexation kills the fool and jealousy slays the simple. Job 5:2, RSV

"Envy shoots at others," the wise man said, "and wounds itself."

One of the early church fathers, Chrysostom, once commented, "As a moth gnaws a garment, so does envy consume a man." The temptation to be envious of others is one of the most subtle pitfalls into which a person, believer or unbeliever, can fall. This is a problem many Christian people must face. And this jealousy can be as destructive and annihilating as a full-fledged attack on a woolen garment by a cloud of moths. How does one overcome this natural human tendency? In verse 8 of Job 5, Job's friend Eliphaz admonishes, " . . . as for me, I would seek God and I would commit my cause to God . . . ." The secret of victory over this temptation, then, is to yield it along with all of our other problems to our all-powerful God.

29

Faith in Action

And Elijah said unto her, Fear not . . . For thus saith the Lord God of Israel, The barrel of meal shall not waste, neither shall the cruse of oil fail. . . .

1 Kings 17:13–14

God does not indulge in embarrassing those who put their confidence in Him. He honors those who honor Him. He vindicates the faith of any man or woman who invests their trust in His capacity to meet His commitments to them. He is pleased to find those who recognize His sterling character.

It is to such people that Christ comes and fills their lives to overflowing, not only with spiritual benefits, but also with moral and material resources beyond their fondest dreams.

The powerful prophet looked calmly and quietly at the distraught widow. His words were soothing, healing ointment to her tempestuous fears. *"Don't be afraid. Don't worry. Don't panic. The Lord can and will supply all the flour and oil we shall ever require."*

This was faith in action.

This was Elijah's powerful, positive response to the word spoken by God.

It demonstrated that he had an unshakable confidence in the character of Jehovah, God. He would come through. He would supply flour and oil, bread and butter, for all of them throughout the famine.

This was to exercise faith not only for himself, but also on behalf of others. His God was alive! His God was active! His God would deliver them out of their dilemma!

This was faith without fear.

It was straightforward obedience to the declared will and wishes of the Lord. It was the secret of Elijah's success, the key to the prophet's power.

W. Phillip Keller (E)

30

BEATING BURNOUT

But he [Elijah] went a day's journey into the wilderness, and came and sat down under a juniper tree: and he requested for himself that he might die; and said, "It is enough; now, O Lord, take away my life . . . ."

1 Kings 19:4

In this day of great pressure, high stress, constant demands, and little leisure, more and more of God's people are dropping through the cracks as victims of burnout and fatigue. It is not uncommon to meet those in the Lord's business who have worked themselves into a frenzy, burning the proverbial candle at both ends until there is neither candle nor wick left to burn. They find themselves weary and dreary souls greatly in need of rest—time to repair and heal—not at all interested in programs or projects that require energy and more time. Those folks need to be respected, not harassed. They need time to work through and silence "the tyranny of the urgent."

Periodically, we'll have folks slip into our church who are in need of inner healing. They are spent. Hungry for a place to repair, they long for the freedom to be still and to gain renewed perspective. Such folks are to be respected and allowed some room to recover. They don't need somebody to corner them and "put 'em to work." In such cases, assimilation and involvement need to be put on hold. Their greater need (as in the case of Elijah) is to be allowed the freedom to relax. In due time, the energy and perspective will return. Burnout isn't a terminal disease in most cases.

Charles R. Swindoll (DYG)

31

Freedom from Fear

They feared the Lord, but also served their own gods, after the manner of the nations from among whom they had been carried away.
2 Kings 17:33, RSV

People today, as they did back in King Hezekiah's time, still *fear* one God, and *serve* another. What does it mean to "fear God"? In our Scripture passage, the fear is merely a counterfeit, it does not ring true. It is only a superficial showing of outward respect, like the little boy who, after repeatedly being made to sit in a corner, finally told his mother, "I may be sitting down on the outside, but I'm still standing up inside!" The real fear of God is not lip service but heart homage, an attitude of spirit in which one's inner soul is continually on its knees before God.

Some anonymous wise man has put it well: "To be free from all fear, we must have but one fear—the fear of God."

February

1

OF STARS AND MUD

Is not God in the height of heaven? and behold the height of the stars, how high they are!

Job 22:12

God's people are realists. We recognize we are in a decadent society. We see corruption and decay everywhere. Yet amid the mayhem our spirits soar in hope. For our confidence is not in the community of man but in the goodness and graciousness of our God.

We are acutely aware of increasing anarchy. Yet we are intensely excited about the redemptive work of Christ rescuing men and women from the chaos.

We can challenge others to follow the Master. We can inspire them to serve God and serve men. We can look up and see the stars when others only look down and see the mud.

W. Phillip Keller (SS)

2

BIGNESS OF SPIRIT

. . . man is born to trouble as the sparks fly upward.   *Job 5:6*, RSV

One of the great paradoxes of the Christian faith is that we learn and grow through difficulties and hard times. Yet we resist them in our passion to live safely and avoid hurt. But Bernard Baruch, a wise and brilliant counselor to several United States presidents, cut through so much of the superficial thinking of his day and ours with this perceptive comment, "The art of living lies not in eliminating but in growing with troubles." And a great Jewish thinker has given us this profound sentence, "Mature people are not made out of good times but out of bad times." I'd like to suggest that you take those two statements and write them out on a small card that can be tucked into the corner of your mirror where you can see them every morning. These are attitude-changers that can give new meaning and understanding and zest to life.

Jeremy Taylor, that great eighteenth-century man of God, said on one occasion, "It is usually not so much the greatness of our trouble as the littleness of our spirit which makes us complain." I think he hit on something very important for each of us. The Christian life has always called for us to be people with "bigness of spirit." After all, it is "bigness of spirit" that will help us handle life's rough places and hard times. It is this spirit that will give us the capability to be "more than conquerors through him that loved us" (Rom. 8:37, KJV). And it is this spirit that will give us the strength and power to handle adversity, to risk and face danger in the name of Jesus, and to grow and mature in our Christian walk.

Dale Evans Rogers (GHT)

3

QUIETNESS

When he giveth quietness, who then can make trouble?   Job 34:29

These are the words of Elihu to Job, and are, perhaps, the best utterance that ever escaped his lips. Whatever Elihu might have meant by them when he spoke thus to the suffering patriarch, they are most comforting and cheering to every true saint of God today. "When He [God] giveth quietness [perfect rest and peace], who then can make trouble?" Can my circumstances? No! Can my associations? No! Can my difficulties? No! Can my enemies? No! For in all these things we are more than conquerors if God giveth quietness.

But does God give to men today His quietness, this perfect rest and peace? Yes, He certainly does. But, you ask, to whom does He bestow this great blessing? Then our answer is: First, to those who are pre-

pared to leave all and wholly follow Jesus. And then to those consecrated souls who will dare to trust God their heavenly Father to do
right, and to do right for them under all circumstances and at all
times. To such persons "He giveth quietness," and "who then can
make trouble" for them? Not any, either on earth or in hell. Oh, to
learn more and more to trust in God at all times!

John Roberts

4

THE DWELLINGPLACE OF GOD

*Behold, God is mighty, and despiseth not any: he is mighty in strength
and wisdom.*

Job 36:5

Each of God's saints is sent into the world to prove some part of
the divine character. In heaven we shall read the great book of the
experience of all the saints, and gather from that book the whole of
the divine character as having been proved and illustrated. Each
Christian is a manifestation and display of some position or other of
God; a different part may belong to each of us, but when the whole
shall be combined, when all the rays of evidence shall be brought, as
it were, into one great sun, and shine forth with meridian splendor,
we shall see in Christian experience a beautiful revelation of our God.

Wherever the church is, there is God. God is pleased, in His mercy
and condescension, to stoop from the highest heavens to dwell in
this lower heaven—the heaven of His church. It is here, among the
household of faith, He deigns—let me say it with sacred reverence—
to unbend Himself, and be familiar with those round about Him
whom He has adopted into His family. He may be a consuming fire
abroad, but when He comes into His own house He is all mercy,
mildness, and love. Abroad He does great works of power; but at
home in His own house He does great works of grace.

C. H. Spurgeon

February

5

THE WEAVER

He that is perfect in knowledge is with thee . . . He is mighty in strength and wisdom.

Job 36:4–5

My life is but a weaving
　Between my Lord and me;
I cannot choose the colors
　He works on steadily.

Ofttimes He weaves sorrow
　And I in foolish pride,
Forget that He sees the upper,
　And I the under side.

Not till the loom is silent
　And the shuttles cease to fly,
Shall God unroll the canvas
　And explain the reason why.

The dark threads are as needful
　In the Weaver's skillful hand,
As the threads of gold and silver
　in the pattern He has planned.

Author Unknown

6

THE GOOD ROAD

The Lord knows the way of the righteous, but the way of the wicked shall perish.

Psalm 1:6, RSV

Have you ever seen how a road "breaks up" in the spring after a hard winter? This happens even down here in Texas where the winters are relatively mild—and it happens even more often in Michigan where I grew up. But there always seemed to be certain stretches of road that were not disturbed by the changing seasons. The secret lay in the foundation or preparation of the roadbed. That is the difference between a "good" and a "bad" road—the foundation. That is the way it is with the ungodly. Their road is a poorly prepared one. Its very foundations are rotten, built, as Jesus says, of "wood, hay and stubble." But Christ said, "I am the way!" And that is the good road, the road whose builder and maker is God. Changing circumstances cannot affect its condition, for it remains the only perfectly prepared way, a way down which believers may walk side by side in equal peace and happiness.

7

THE HEAVENLY GIVER

Ask of me, and I shall give thee the heathen for thine inheritance, and the uttermost parts of the earth for thy possession.

Psalm 2:8

The Father holds Himself in the attitude of Giver. "Ask of Me"—that petition to God the Father empowers all agencies, inspires all movements. The gospel is divinely inspired. Back of all its inspirations is prayer. "Ask of Me" lies back of all movements. Standing as the endowment of the enthroned Christ is the oath-bound covenant of the Father, "Ask of me, and I will give thee the nations for thine inheritance, and the uttermost parts of the earth for thy possession."

We can do all things by God's aid, and can have the whole of His aid by asking. The gospel, in its success and power, depends on our ability to pray. The dispensations of God depend on man's ability to pray. We can have all that God has. *Command ye Me.*

E. M. Bounds

He who has learned to pray has learned the greatest secret of a holy and happy life.

William Law

February

8

THE LORD OUR LIFTER

Thou, O Lord, art a shield for me; my glory, and the lifter up of mine head.

Psalm 3:3

This short psalm is the song of a sorrowful soul who found help and comfort in the Lord. David says, "How are they increased that trouble me!" But then he thanks the Lord for being a shield between him and his tormentors. God is the only One sufficiently strong to "stand off" the adverse circumstances of life. David then adds, "my glory," the glory which cannot be touched by the dirt of the world, the glory which cannot be dimmed by the actions of the godless. With such a God, and such a glory, how can the child of God be anything but "lifted up"? "I will lift up mine eyes unto the hills, from whence cometh my help," says David in another psalm, fully realizing that even in such a simple act as "looking upward" God has the decisive part.

Evangelist Merv Rosell explained the presence of God in the life of the believer thus: "God could have kept Daniel out of the lion's den . . . He could have kept Paul and Silas out of jail—He could have kept the three Hebrew children out of the fiery furnace . . . But God has never promised to keep us out of hard places . . . What he has promised is to go with us through every hard place, and to bring us through victoriously."

9

CONFIDENCE IN PRAYER

. . . for unto thee will I pray.

Psalm 5:2

Robert Louis Stevenson tells a vivid story of a storm at sea. The passengers below were greatly alarmed, as the waves dashed over the vessel. At last one of them, against orders, crept to the deck and came to the pilot, who was lashed to the wheel which he was turning without flinching. The pilot caught sight of the terror-stricken man, and gave him a reassuring smile. Below went the passenger, and comforted the others by saying, "I have seen the face of the pilot, and he smiled. All is well."

That is how we feel when through the gateway of prayer we find our way into the Father's presence. We see His face, and we know that all is well, since His hand is on the helm of events, and "even the winds and the waves obey him." When we live in fellowship with Him, we come with confidence into His presence, asking in the full confidence of receiving and meeting with the justification of our faith.

E. M. Bounds

He who prays fervently knows not whether he prays or not, for he is not thinking of the prayer which he makes, but of God, to whom he makes it.

St. Francis of Sales

10

STAND AND STARE

When I look at thy heavens, the work of thy fingers, the moon and the stars which thou hast established; what is man that thou art mindful of him, and the son of man that thou dost care for him?

Psalm 8:3–4, RSV

The greatness of God is revealed in his creation. The vastness of his universe engenders a sense of wonder. Think of it! If we were to drive a car day and night at top speed without stopping it would take us nine years to reach the moon, three hundred years to reach the sun, eighty-three hundred years to reach the planet Neptune, seventy-five million years to reach Alpha Centauri, and seven hundred million years to reach the Pole Star. . . .

When we are startled by the wonder of the created universe, in which God has boldly written his signature, we are amazed that he knows each of us and has a plan for our lives. That led the psalmist to say in a later psalm, "Thou hast made me to drink of the wine of astonishment" (Psalm 60:3). We are astonished by his creation, but even more by our own creation. W. H. Davies was right: "What is life if, full of care, we have no time to stand and stare?"

Lloyd J. Ogilvie (AHA)

11

WHAT IS MAN?

What is man, that thou art mindful of him?　　　　*Psalm 8:4*

In 1 John 4:8 the apostle says, "God is love. . . ." That sums it up for me. With Henry Drummond I marvel that "God's love for poor sinners is very wonderful, but God's patience with ill natured saints is a deeper mystery."

I stand at the foot of the mountain which lifts its head beyond the cloud and catches on its summit the first gleam of the King of Day in his rising and I say, "What am I?" That mountain has been there through the passing of the ages and I am here and shall be gone before the sun melts the snow upon its summit. "What is man?" But the psalmist has another point of observation: "Thou art mindful of him; thou visitest him."

G. Campbell Morgan

12

LINCOLN THE THEOLOGIAN

Righteousness exalteth a nation; but sin is a reproach to any people.
Proverbs 14:34

Today is the birthday of one of the greatest Americans who ever lived—Abraham Lincoln. Yet Lincoln was a very humble man, not seeking greatness but finding it because of his outspoken reliance upon God and his commitment to excellence. In the crisis periods of his life, he turned to God for guidance and counsel. His deep faith in God and the Word was revealed time and time again during his term as President. And he has left our country a spiritual heritage which continues strong more than a hundred years after his death.

As long as Lincoln is remembered and revered, this country will have, at its heart, the right relationship to God. If the day ever comes, however, when this country turns its back upon Lincoln and his God, history will record the downfall of a once mighty nation.

William J. Wolfe has called Abraham Lincoln, "one of the greatest theologians of America." He adds that Lincoln's theology was profound, "not in the technical meaning of producing a system of doctrine, certainly not as the defender of some one denomination, but in the sense of seeing the hand of God intimately in the affairs of nations."

13

THE SECRET OF PURITY

The words of the Lord are pure words: as silver tried in a furnace of earth, purified seven times.

Psalm 12:6

One morning with a friend I walked out of the city of Geneva to where the waters of the lake flow with swift rush into the Rhone, and we were both greatly interested in the strange sight which has impressed so many travelers. There are two rivers whose waters come together here, the Rhone and the Arve, the Arve flowing into the Rhone. The waters of the Rhone are beautifully clear and sparkling. The waters of the Arve come through a clayey soil and are muddy, gray, and dull.

I went to the guidebook and maps to find out something about this river that kept on its way undefiled by its neighbor for so long. Its source is in a glacier that is between ten thousand and eleven thousand feet high, descending "from the gates of eternal night, at the foot of the pillar of the sun." It is fed continually by the melting glacier which, in turn, is being kept up by the snows and cold. Rising at this great height, ever being renewed steadily by the glacier, the river comes rushing down the swift descent of the Swiss Alps through the lake of Geneva, and on. There is the secret of purity, side by side with its dirty neighbor.

Our lives must have their source high up in the mountains of God, fed by a ceaseless supply. Only so can there be the purity, and the momentum that will keep us pure, and keep us moving down in contact with men of the earth. Constant personal contact with Jesus is the ever new beginning of service.

S. D. Gordon

14

LOVE INSPIRED BY THE SPIRIT

Seeing ye have purified your souls in obeying the truth through the Spirit unto unfeigned love of the brethren, see that ye love one another with a pure heart fervently.

1 Peter 1:22

In its deepest sense love is the perquisite of Christianity. There is something like it, in germ, at least, outside the school of Christ; just as wild flowers recall the rich splendor of the hothouse. But in all such there are flaws, traces of selfishness and passion, which prevent their realizing God's fair ideal. Love, as the Bible uses the word, is the fruit of the spirit. It may be grafted on the natural stalk, but it is essentially His creation. To feel toward enemies what others feel toward friends; to descend as rain and sunbeams on the just as well as the unjust; to minister to those who are unprepossessing and repellent as others minister to the attractive and winsome; to be always the same, not subject to moods or fancies or whims; to suffer long; to take no account of evil; to rejoice with the truth; to bear, believe, hope, and endure all things, never to fail—this is love, and such love is the achievement of the Holy Spirit alone.

F. B. Meyer

February

15

Love Is Forever

Make love your aim. . . .   *1 Corinthians 14:1*, RSV

What a light must have shone on the apostle's face as he concluded this exquisite idyll, this perfect poem of love (1 Cor. 13). The change in tone and rhythm must have caused his amanuensis to look suddenly up into his master's face, and lo! it was as the face of an angel when he exalted, "The greatest of these is love" (1 Cor. 13:13). Why is love greatest?

Because it crowns the other two, and includes them.—Faith is the root; hope is the stem; love the perfect flower. You may have faith without hope, and hope without love; but you cannot have love apart from faith and hope.

Because it is most like God.—God's nature is not specially characterized by faith, because there is no uncertainty with His perfect knowledge; nor by hope, because there is no future to His eternal existence. But God is love; and to love is to resemble Him.

Because it will immeasurably outlast the other two.—Human knowledge, at best but the spellings of babes, will vanish in the perfect light of heaven. Eloquence will seem like the lispings of infancy. Prophecies will have no place, because the future will be revealed. Faith and hope will be lost in realization. *Only love is forever.*

F. B. Meyer

16

The Lord My Strength

I love you, O Lord, my strength. The Lord is my rock, my fortress and my deliverer; my God is my rock, in whom I take refuge. He is my shield and the horn of my salvation, my stronghold.

Psalm 18:1–2, NIV

February

He is "my strength" *to go up*. The psalmist says, "By my God have I leaped over a wall" (Ps. 18:29, KJV). The obstacles before me would be mountains of difficulty if He did not step in and supply strength for the climb. We live in the mountains of North Carolina. I have climbed many mountains. My wife and I almost daily took our children on mountain climbs when they were younger. We learned that we had to teach them to climb very small hills before they could manage a mountain. After we have come to Christ, God may start us out on a small hill before He asks us to climb a mountain. However, whatever our need, He has promised that His power is available. Without it we would be unable to make the trip—let alone climb the steep places of pain and stress.

The Lord is also "my strength" *to go down*. Going down is often more difficult than going up . . . To go down into the Valley of Humiliation (as Bunyan called it), or into "the valley of the shadow of death," would be impossible without Him. Indeed, my heart would grow faint with fear and I would be gasping for breath were it not for the wonderful companion by my side, the Lord Jesus Christ.

Here is another point we don't often consider: the Lord is "my strength" simply *to sit still*. "Be still, and know that I am God" (Ps. 46:10). "I wait for the Lord, my soul waits, and in his word I put my hope" (Ps. 130:5). Our natural desire is to be doing something; but there are times in our lives when it is wiser to wait and just be still.

"The Lord is my strength!" Our sufficiency is of God, as Paul says—or as the modern version puts it, "Not that we are competent to claim anything for ourselves, but our competency comes from God" (2 Cor. 3:5).

Billy Graham (TA)

17

UNEXPECTED BLESSINGS

The Lord is my shepherd, I shall not want; he makes me lie down in green pastures. . . .

Psalm 23:1–2, RSV

February

A pilgrim who lives on an estate is no longer a pilgrim. Tent-dwellers can't program green pastures. You can't set up a chain of them at comfortable intervals, like oases on a map. Finding them is the job of the shepherd, not of the sheep. When they come, they are serendipities, unexpected blessings. I think it is not accidental that the psalm says. "He *makes* me lie down in green pastures." Some translations put it, "He lets me . . . ," which misses the point, I think. Some green pastures I don't even recognize. Sometimes when my soul is being restored, I fret at the inactivity which itself seems like an interruption.

But in my pilgrimage, I have happily discovered that life is not ever and eternally an uphill climb. At selected times and places, God has stopped me at a plateau and I had time to admire the view, even note some progress. Then, in God's own time and in his own way, the journey continued.

If I could edit the psalm by adding one line to "He makes me lie down," it would be, "He makes me then to get up and go on." The greenest of pastures don't stay that way. They get overgrazed. Drought comes. They turn sere and brown.

We need green pastures as waystops. They provide refreshment and strength. They are God's special blessings at unexpected intervals of the road. But the road goes on, and we must go with it.

Stan Mooneyham

18

DEALING WITH DEATH

Yea, though I walk through the valley of . . . death, I will fear no evil: for thou art with me; thy rod and thy staff they comfort me.

Psalm 23:4

It is tragic that in our cultural conspiracy to obscure the reality and the finality of death we have missed the mysterious gift God has given to us. You know, the beautiful thing is that there is death, and I believe it can be good. Death is a true gift of God not to be avoided. God means for us all to pass through physical death; it's one of his

February

good gifts that we don't go on and on in this life. The late Saul Alinsky, a secular prophet in our time and leading organizer of the poor, once made this significant statement: "The single most important thing I ever learned was that I am going to die. For once you accept your own death, all of a sudden you are free. You no longer care except so far as your life can be used tactically to promote a cause you believe in." When we have accepted the inevitability of death, we can find a cause and say, "Lord, use me." Then life begins. Somehow the acceptance of death is the beginning of life. People who are afraid to die have usually not accepted either death or life.

Sometimes the theology of our time is written on the walls of public buildings, and occasionally you'll discover profound truth in some rather unlikely places. Recently I came across this sentence: "Death is nature's way of telling you to slow down."

Somehow the church of Jesus Christ needs to communicate this message: "Don't be afraid of death. Jesus is there. It's O.K." The important thing for each of us is to live life to the hilt. Eternal life begins now and death cannot interrupt its flow.

Bruce Larson

19

THE SCHOOL OF TRIAL

Examine me, O Lord, and prove me; try my reins and my heart.
Psalm 26:2

David knew what it meant to be tried and proven. And we modern Davids cannot expect to escape the school of trial.

Most of the grand truths of God have to be learned by trouble; they must be burned into us with the hot iron of affliction, otherwise we shall not truly receive them. No man is competent to judge in matters of the kingdom until first he has been tried, since there are many things to be learned in the depths which we can never know in the heights. He shall best meet the wants of God's people who has had those wants himself; he shall best comfort God's Israel who has needed comfort; and he shall best preach salvation who has felt his own need of it.

C. H. Spurgeon

20

GRACE IN THE MIDST OF GRIEF

For in the time of trouble he shall hide me in his pavilion: in the secret of his tabernacle shall he hide me; he shall set me up upon a rock.

Psalm 27:5

Choice discoveries of the wondrous love and grace of Jesus are most tenderly vouchsafed unto believers in the times of grief. Then it is that He lifts them up from His feet, where, like Mary, it is their delight to sit, and exalts them to the position of the favored John, pressing them to His breast and bidding them lean on His bosom.

The love of Christ in its sweetness, its fullness, its greatness, its faithfulness, passés all human comprehension.

Heaven on earth is abounding love to Jesus. This is the first and last of true delight—to love Him who is the first and the last. To love Jesus is another name for paradise.

C. H. Spurgeon

21

I WILL GUIDE THEE

Lead me in thy truth, and teach me; for thou art the God of my salvation; on thee do I wait all the day. . . . The meek will he guide in judgment; and the meek will he teach his way.

Psalm 25:5,9

> Benighted on a lone and dreary wild,
> Perplexed, exhausted, helpless, in despair,
> I cast me down, and thought to perish there.

February

When through the gloom a Face appeared and smiled;
And a sweet Voice said, "Courage! Rise, My Child!
And I will guide thee safely by the way."

As to night-watchers comes the morning ray,
So came that Voice to me; and on that Face
I seemed a loving tenderness to trace,
That soothed and cheered me as, forlorn, I lay;
I felt as feels the child whose throbbing grief
A mother's love assuages in its source;
And asking strength of Him who gave relief,
I straightway rose, and onward held my course.

W. L. Alexander

22

GOD'S BARREL IS BOTTOMLESS

Weeping may endure for a night, but joy cometh in the morning.
Psalm 30:5

David, the perceptive psalmist, seems to be echoing the message of his beloved Psalm 23 in the words of this psalm. It is a fact of life that the child of God must travel the valley of the shadow of death on his triumphant way to eternal life. But life will inevitably follow hard upon the heels of death, as surely as day succeeds night. Later in the psalm David expresses this truth in a different way; "Thou hast turned . . . my mourning into dancing; thou hast put off my sackcloth, and girded me with gladness" (v. 11).

This truth is taught elsewhere in the Scriptures as well. In 1 Kings 17:14, Elijah tells the widow of Zarephath: "The barrel of meal shall not waste, neither shall the cruse of oil fail. . . ." Outwardly, the situation for this poor widow looked pretty bleak. But the love of God shines through the circumstances, like sunlight filtering through a cloud, and suddenly it breaks forth into glorious beaming light to bathe the believer in its warmth. God's barrel is bottomless, never failing; the supply of His meal is measureless, never ending.

Christian, if you believe this, it will make a difference in your life.

February

It will add a dimension to your joy in spite of circumstances, an aura of serenity in a chaotic and restless world. The Source of that joy is both inside and outside the believer. The Spirit within causes the joy to flow out; the glory of God outside saturates the believer in His peace.

23

GOD'S WILL IS BEST

The Lord is my strength and shield; my heart trusted in him, and I am helped: therefore my heart greatly rejoiceth; and with my song will I praise him.

Psalm 28:7

"Remove this thorn, dear Lord," in vain I cried;
"Sufficient is My grace," my Lord replied.

"Not this, dear Lord," I prayed, "another way";
"Remember," spake my Lord, "I am thy Stay."

"My plans, dear Lord," I sighed, "they vanish, all";
"My plans are best," He said, "what'er befall."

Then to His will I bowed, and found it best;
Henceforth I walked with Him, my heart at rest.

Oswald J. Smith

24

THE BEAUTY OF HOLINESS

. . . worship the Lord in the beauty of holiness.   *Psalm 29:2*

An old but true adage says, "Beauty is as beauty does." If every Christian had a beautiful character, the cause of Christ would certainly advance with greater efficiency and impact. Too often, however, the Christian does not bear in his character the marks of true Christian beauty, as personified in the Lord Himself when He walked the

February

Galilean countryside. True Christian graces are collected along the path of consecrated Christian living. If the Christian is not learning something new each day to help him in the important task of living the Christ-life, then he is no longer progressing but stagnant. And in the stagnant pool, new life is virtually eliminated. So let us as Christians be open to the life-giving power of the risen Christ.

The great evangelist D. L. Moody put this truth in clear perspective when he wrote: "Our great problem is the problem of unlived truth. We try to communicate what we've never experienced in our life."

25

Guilt and Forgiveness

This poor man cried and the Lord heard him; and saved him out of all his troubles . . . The righteous cry and the Lord hears, and delivers them out of all their troubles. . . . Many are the afflictions of the righteous; but the Lord delivers him out of them all.

Psalm 34:6, 17, 19, NIV

In Psalm 34 there are these three great statements about our problems. The Christian life is not a way "out" but a way "through" life. The "out of" in these verses refers to deliverance not from but through difficulty. The English scholar Dr. Arthur Way phrased it, "Deliverance out of, not from the crisis of trial. So that the sense appears to be, 'bring me safely out of the conflict'" and, "not simply keep me from entering into it."

Another question: "I feel so guilty—how can I find relief?"

Guilt is a very debilitating feeling. It can destroy our attitude, our personal relationships, and our outreach. Sometimes we feel guilty because we've done things that are wrong for which we must accept the responsibility and also accept God's forgiveness . . . Forgiveness is an opportunity Christ extended to us on the cross. When we accept His forgiveness and are willing to forgive ourselves, then we find relief.

I have been told by doctors that a large percentage of the patients in psychiatric hospitals could be released if only they could be assured of the fact that they had been forgiven.

Billy Graham (HBBA)

26

THE FULFILLMENT OF MAN'S DESIRE

Delight thyself also in the Lord; and he shall give thee the desires of thine heart.

Psalm 37:4

God is love, an ever-flowing fountain, out of which streams the unceasing desire to make His creatures the partakers of all the holiness and the blessedness there is in Himself. This desire for the salvation of souls is in very deed God's perfect will, His highest glory.

This loving desire of God, to get His place in the heart of men, He imparts to all His children who are willing to yield themselves wholly to Him. It is in this that the likeness and image of God consist—to have a heart in which His love takes complete possession, and leads us to find spontaneously our highest joy in loving as He does.

It is thus that our text finds its fulfillment: "Delight thyself in the Lord" (and in His life of love) "and he will give thee the desires of thine heart." Count upon it that the intercession of love, rising up to heaven, will be met with the fulfillment of the desire of our heart. We may be sure that, as we delight in what God delights in, such prayer is inspired by God and will have its answer. And our prayer becomes unceasingly, "Thy desires, O my Father, are mine. Thy holy will of love is my will too."

Andrew Murray

27

TRUST IN GOD

Blessed is that man that maketh the Lord his trust.   *Psalm 40:4*

February

There are three keys which will let us into the innermost chambers of friendship with God—prayer, God's Word, and obedience. And with them goes a *key-ring* on which these keys must be strung. It is this: *implicit trust in God.* Trust is the native air of friendship. In its native air it grows strong and beautiful. Whatever disturbs an active, abiding trust in God must be driven out of doors, and kept out. Doubt chills the air below normal. Anxiety overheats the air. A calm looking up into God's face with an unquestioning faith in *Him* under every sort of circumstance—this is trust. Faith has three elements: knowledge, belief, and *trust.* Knowledge is acquaintance with certain facts. Belief is accepting these facts as true. Trust is risking something that is very precious. Trust is the lifeblood of faith.

S. D. Gordon

28

A Song to Sing

> . . . *enter his courts with praise. Give thanks to him and bless his name.*
> Psalm 100:4, TLB

My heart's so full of praise today it keeps trying to step ahead of me. It wants to go forth and sing a new song to the maker and giver of all good things.

Why is today so special? I don't honestly know. God is constantly replenishing my life and livelihood with a veritable overflowing cornucopia of blessings. Perhaps it's the weather or because a child smiled at me and tugged at my arm. Maybe it's the stray puppy that came straggling to our door nuzzling its way up to me.

Somehow something has drawn me from my routine self-adulation to the knowledge God is really good and I want to run to the highest mountaintop to shout my hosannas so the words can echo and reecho again and again in my heart. "God *loves* me! God loves *me!*" . . .

How great God is! How merciful! How good!

Phyllis C. Michael

February

29

THE BIBLE AND PRAYER

By day the Lord commands his steadfast love; and at night his song is with me, a prayer to the God of my life.

Psalm 42:8, RSV

A mind alive to new truth results in a heart ablaze with new excitement for the Lord. A consistent, daily study of the Scriptures is one of the most powerful ways the Lord talks to us. He focuses our need and then answers through the passages we study. When we come to the Bible with an open mind, sincerely asking for the Lord's truth to meet whatever we are facing, he speaks to us. Then we are ready for receptive prayer.

Prayer is listening to the Lord. When we are silent, patiently waiting, he talks to us. He floods our minds with insight and wisdom, guidance and discernment. So often people ask me, "What do you mean—the Lord talks to you?" There is only one answer: when I become quiet and really want to hear what he has to say about my life and ministry, he speaks. I do not hear voices. I don't need to. The thoughts he places within my mind are like spoken words, and yet, they are more powerful than an articulated sound.

Lloyd J. Ogilvie (AHA)

March

1

A Quiet Moment

The Lord will command his lovingkindness in the daytime, and in the night his song shall be with me.

Psalm 42:8

No matter how busy we are, how pressed for time, a moment spent in thinking about our oneness with a loving, sharing God erases the little worries and doubts that threaten to take over. Within us the unlimited power of God is there to support us just as any loving father will support a child. We have the opportunity to be all that we are intended to be. If God is in us, he does not come and go. He is with us constantly in sickness and in health, in sorrow and in joy. Through our union with him we are filled with courage and enthusiasm that supplies rather than saps energy as do fears and loneliness. Our thoughts focus on his order, not on the disorder of the world. Our oneness with him renews and strengthens. . . .

How great it is to awaken to a new day and affirm, "God, you watched over me while I slept. I know you will be with me throughout the busy day."

Harold Rogers

2

The Shaping of a Disciple

Why are you cast down, O my soul, and why are you disquieted within me? Hope in God; for I shall again praise him, my help and my God.
Psalm 42:11, RSV

When God wants to drill a man
   And thrill a man
   And skill a man,
When God wants to mold a man
   To play the noblest part;
When He yearns with all His heart
   To create so great and bold a man
That all the world shall be amazed,
   Watch His methods, watch His ways!
How He ruthlessly perfects
   Whom He royally elects!
How He hammers him and hurts him
   And with mighty blows converts him
Into trial shapes of day which
   Only God understands
While his tortured heart is crying
   And he lifts beseeching hands!
How He bends but never breaks
   When his good He undertakes;
How He uses whom He chooses
   And with every purpose fuses him
   By every act induces him
To try His splendour out
   God knows what He's about!

                        Author Unknown

3

DEALING WITH TROUBLES

God is our refuge and strength, a very present help in trouble.
                               Psalm 46:1

Don't run away from your troubles. Don't magnify them. Don't dwell on them, taking them to bed with you, spoiling your digestion by feeding upon them all day, and making everybody unhappy by throwing their shadow upon them. But with a resolute, courageous, and trustful spirit take them to God in prayer and then go forth to

March

meet and vanquish them, and you will find they are much less formidable than you feared.

An old farmer plowed around a rock in one of his fields for many years. He had grown actually morbid over it, for he had broken a cultivator and two plows besides losing a lot of valuable land in its vicinity. One day he made up his mind that he would dig it out and have done with it. Lo, when he put his crowbar under it he found it was less than a foot thick and that he could loosen it with a trifling effort and carry it away in his wagon. He smiled to think how all through the years it had haunted him.

One day we shall look back on our trials and our anxious cares and find how needless many of them were, so unreal and yet so distressing, that we can say like the old lady when she was reviewing her past life: "I've had so many trials, especially those that never came."

A. B. Simpson

> Who trusts in God, a strong abode
> In heaven and earth possesses;
> Who looks in love to Christ above,
> No fear his heart oppresses.

Joachim Madeburg

4

BE STILL

Be still, and know that I am God . . . God is our refuge and strength, a very present help in trouble.

Psalm 46:1, 10

> "Be still and know that I am God,"
> That I who made and gave thee life
> Will lead thy faltering steps aright;
> That I who see each sparrow's fall
> Will hear and heed thy earnest call.
> I am God.

"Be still and know that I am God,"
When aching burdens crush thy heart,
Then know I form thee for thy part
And purpose in the plan I hold.
Thou art the clay that I would mold.
Trust in God.

"Be still and know that I am God,"
Who made the atom's tiny span
And set it moving to my plan,
That I who guide the stars above
Will guide and keep thee in my love.
Be thou still.

Author Unknown

5

WAITING ON GOD

Truly my soul waiteth upon God: from him cometh my salvation.
Psalm 62:1

If salvation indeed comes from God, and is entirely His work, just as our creation was, it follows, as a matter of course, that our first and highest duty is to wait on Him to do that work as pleases Him. Waiting becomes then the only way to the experience of full salvation, the only way, truly, to know God as the God of our salvation. All the difficulties that are brought forward as keeping us back from full salvation, have their cause in this one thing: the defective knowledge and practice of waiting upon God. All that the church and its members need for the manifestation of the mighty power of God in the world, is the return to our true place, the place that belongs to us, both in creation and redemption, the place of absolute and unceasing dependence upon God.

"Truly my soul waiteth upon God; from him cometh my salvation." First we wait on God for salvation. Then we learn that salvation is only to bring us to God, and teach us to wait on Him. Then we find what is better still—that waiting on God is itself the highest

March

salvation. It is the ascribing to Him the glory of being All; it is the experiencing that He is All to us. May God teach us the blessedness of waiting on Him.

Andrew Murray

6

HIS SECRET PRESENCE

Cast me not away from thy presence; and take not thy holy spirit from me. Restore unto me the joy of thy salvation; and uphold me with thy free spirit.
Psalm 51:11–12

Because you thus have Christ by His Spirit, you cannot be orphans, for the Spirit of God is always with you. It is a delightful truth that the Spirit of God always dwells in believers—not sometimes, but always. He is not always active in believers, and He may be grieved until His sensible presence is altogether withdrawn, but His secret presence is always there. At no single moment is the Spirit of God wholly gone from a believer. The believer would die spiritually if this could happen, but that cannot be, for Jesus has said, "Because I live, ye shall live also." Even when the believer sins, the Holy Spirit does not utterly depart from him, but is still in him to make him smart for the sin into which he has fallen. The believer's prayers prove that the Holy Spirit is still within him. "Take not thy holy spirit from me," was the prayer of a saint who had fallen very foully, but in whom the Spirit of God still kept His residence, notwithstanding all the foulness of his guilt and sin.

C. H. Spurgeon

7

GOD COMFORTS

Thou hast kept count of my tossings; put thou my tears in thy bottle; Are they not in thy book?
Psalm 56:8, RSV

God counts the sorrows of His saints,
   Their groans affect His ears;
He hast a book for my complaints,
   A bottle for my tears.

When to His throne I raise my cry,
   The wicked fear and flee:
So swift is prayer to reach the sky;
   So near is God to me.

In Him, most holy, just and true,
   I have reposed my trust;
Nor will I fear what man can do,
   The offspring of the dust.

Author Unknown

8

SINGING IN THE SHADOWS

My soul is feasted as with marrow and fat, and my mouth praises thee with joyful lips, when I think of thee upon my bed, and meditate on thee in the watches of the night; for thou hast been my help, and in the shadow of thy wings I sing for joy.

Psalm 63:5–7, RSV

We all have one of three things in common: we have known the night of suffering, are in the night right now, or are deeply troubled about someone who is. And we have something else in common—the question as to why God allows it. In the dark night of suffering, we readily chime in with Job's counselor, Elihu, as he rolls back the curtain on the nakedness of human anguish, "Where is God my maker who gives songs in the night?"

Only one who has endured the long night and has heard the Lord's song in the midst of suffering has any right to answer. But the answer does come to us from Psalm 42, a succor to sufferers through the ages. And there, along with Luther, Kierkegaard, Bonhoeffer, and nameless millions of God's people, we discover a way to deal with suffering by listening for the Lord's song of hope in the night of pain, persecution, grief, or discouragement. Out of the depths, the psalmist shouts the assurance, "The Lord will command his lovingkindness in the daytime; and his song will be with me in the night" (Ps. 42:8).

Lloyd J. Ogilvie (AHA)

9

THE WEAPON OF THE WORD

He only is my rock and my salvation, He is my defense.   Psalm 62:2

Here are two symbols of what God is to His children. Anyone who has walked among the giant rocks of Colorado cannot help but be struck with the aptness of this symbol for strength. A rock may serve as a bulwark against an enemy in front, as a shelter from an enemy above, and as a platform against an enemy beneath. In the same sense, God is a bulwark, a shelter, and a platform or high place. But more than that, God is a defense, a "weapon," and I use the word carefully. God may be taken into the battle both as a means of offense and defense. If I can use the Word of God, the Scriptures themselves, as a weapon, I will be a far more effective Christian than if I try to use weaker weapons!

The great English prime minister, William E. Gladstone, said of the Bible's influence on men, "I have known ninety-five great men of the world in my time and of these eighty-seven were followers of the Bible."

10

MEDITATION MAKES THE WAY PLAIN

When I remember thee upon my bed, and meditate on thee in the night watches.

Psalm 63:6

I am told that it was the habit of Charles H. Spurgeon to recognize the presence of God by uplifting his heart to Him once each quarter of an hour. My informant told me that often, in the midst of his gladdest hours, he noticed him suddenly turn his thoughts, and the thoughts of those who a moment before had been laughing at his wit, into the presence of the Lord.

This habit of meditating on passages of God's Word is also a helpful way of inducing that devoutness of spirit which realizes the Lord's presence. The Bible is like a garden where the Lord God walked. There will be times when the sense of His presence will be more impressive than others. St. Bernard said of Him, "He entered not by the eyes, for His presence was not marked by color; nor by the ears, for there was no sound; nor by the breath, for He mingled not with the air; nor by the touch, for He was untouchable. How, then, did I know He was present? Because of His quickening power.

"As soon as He entered, He awoke my slumbering soul. He moved and pierced my heart, which before was strange and stony, hard and sick. He began to open the prison-house, to make the crooked straight, and the rough way smooth, so that my soul could bless the Lord."

F. B. Meyer

11

THE JOYFUL SOUND

Blessed is the people that know the joyful sound: they shall walk, O Lord, in the light of thy countenance. In thy name shall they rejoice all the day.
Psalm 89:15–16

"Glad tidings of great joy" was what the angel called the gospel message. This is what is here spoken of as "the joyful sound." That blessedness consists in God's people walking in the light of God and rejoicing in His name all the day. Undisturbed fellowship, never-ending joy is their portion. Even in the Old Testament such was at times the experience of the saints. But there was no continuance; the Old Testament could not secure that. Only the New Testament can and does.

In every well-ordered family one finds the father delighting in his children and the children rejoicing in their father's presence. And this

March

mark of a happy home on earth is what the heavenly Father has promised and delights to work in His people; *walking in the light of His countenance and rejoicing in His name all the day*. It has been promised, it has been made possible in Christ through the Holy Spirit filling the heart with the love of God. It is the heritage of all who are seeking to love God with all their heart and strength.

Andrew Murray

12

SEARCH THE SCRIPTURES

The Lord gave the word. . . .   *Psalm 68:11*

The Bible is not a thing to be worshiped. A savage might bow down to a telescope, but an astronomer knows better. The way to know a telescope is to use it. It is not to be looked at, but looked through. To bind a Bible beautifully, to lift it reverently, to speak of it with admiration, to guard it with all care, is not at all to the point. Look through it. Find God with it. See what God was to the men of the Bible and then let Him be the same to you. See the proofs of His power and prove that power for yourself, in yourself. Search the Scriptures for the testimony of Jesus and honor the Scriptures by being an honor to the One they reveal.

M. D. Babcock

Some unknown wise man has said it succinctly: "The Bible does not need to be rewritten—just reread."

13

ABIDING—WHAT DOES IT MEAN?

He that dwelleth in the secret place of the most High shall abide under the shadow of the Almighty.

Psalm 91:1

To abide in the Will of God is to abide in absolute safety. David said to Abiathar, "Abide thou with me; fear not: for he that seeketh my life seeketh thy life: but with me thou shalt be in safeguard" (1 Sam. 22:23). So speaks God to the humblest believer. Is not this the true interpretation of that Ninety-first Psalm, that to all commentators seems such a mystery? Is not that Secret Place of the Most High, where one abides under the very shadow of the Almighty, covered with His feathers and hiding trustfully under His wings— simply the Will of God! There abiding, in vain, does the Fowler spread his snares for our feet, or the adversary hurl at us his darts of death. Into that sacred chamber of the Divine Presence neither the pestilence that walks in darkness nor the destruction that wastes at noonday can find entrance. Here we tread upon the young lion and adder and trample under foot even the Dragon.

Fellowship with God is the all-sufficient antidote to anxiety—the cure of care. Anxious thoughts are not only useless, but worse, for they burden us with the anticipation of troubles that never come, while they avert or avoid no real and inevitable troubles, and only double them by anticipation.

A. T. Pierson

The beginning of anxiety is the end of faith, and the beginning of true faith is the end of anxiety.

George Mueller

14

VICTOR, NOT VICTIM

Say among the nations that the Lord reigneth from the tree.
Psalm 96:10, Latin version

In the realm of grace, Christ reigns from His Cross. On the tree He was Victor, not Victim. The dying Savior was the triumphant Lord, and His sovereignty can be found in His last utterances, for seven times His parched lips opened amidst the awful conflict of the Cross.

March

It is not without reason that the number chosen is *seven*, signifying completeness, and thus expressive of His supremacy or sovereignty in the realm of grace.

The progress of the seven cries is Christlike in that they begin with His enemies and end with Himself. All through His life it was others first, self last. There is therefore no preacher like the dying Christ; no pulpit like the Cross, no congregation like those around the Cross; no sermon like those seven powerful words.

Herbert Lockyer

15

GUIDED BY GOD

And he led them forth by the right way, that they might go to a city of habitation.

Psalm 107:7

All our movements should be under the direction of God. In very olden times God guided His people by a pillar of fire and cloud, which lifted and moved when they were to move, showing them the way, and which rested and settled down when they were to halt. In these days of so much fuller revelation there is no need for any such visible token of guidance, yet the guidance is no less real and no less unmistakable.

It was an angel that brought to Joseph the bidding to flee into Egypt. Angels do not now appear to our eyes; but who will say that they do not whisper in our ears many a suggestion which we suppose to come from our own hearts? At least we know that in some way God will always tell us what to do; and if only we have ears to hear we shall never fail of guidance. We should always wait for God's bidding before taking any step. Especially in times of danger, when we are moving under His guidance, should we wait and not move until He brings us word.

It ought to give us great comfort and a wonderful sense of safety to know that God is caring for us so faithfully. Our whole duty is to be ready always to obey. Whenever the voice comes bidding us arise and depart, there is some reason for it, and we should not hesitate to obey. Wherever we are sent we should quietly stay till again God sends to call us away. The place of duty is always the place of safety, and we should never move until God brings us word.

J. R. Miller

16

THE GOODNESS OF GOD

Forget not all his benefits. Psalm 103:2

It is a delightful and profitable occupation to mark the hand of God in the lives of ancient saints, and to observe His goodness in delivering them, His mercy in pardoning them, and His faithfulness in keeping His covenant with them. But would it not be even more interesting and profitable for us to notice the hand of God in our own lives? Ought we not to look upon our own history as being at least as full of God, as full of His goodness and of His truth, as much a proof of His faithfulness and veracity, as the lives of any of the saints who have gone before? We do our Lord an injustice when we suppose that He wrought all His mighty acts, and showed Himself strong for those in the early time, but does not perform wonders or lay bare His arm for the saints who are now upon the earth.

C. H. Spurgeon

17

"IT'S A BEAUTIFUL DAY"

Enter into his gates with thanksgiving, and into his courts with praise: be thankful unto him, and bless his name.

Psalm 100:4

Rather than letting times of frustration cause us to say an unkind word or plunge us into a hasty action that will turn the day into shambles, let's use these moments to become quiet and turn our thoughts to God. We can release our cares to him constantly with thanksgiving that he will take them and draw us even closer to him.

Recently I watched a blind man waiting for a traffic signal to change. He stood quietly, leaning on his white cane. His head was cocked a bit so that his ears could better catch the sounds of traffic that he might be able to judge when its direction changed. Two persons who had their sight stepped off the curb. One leaped back to avoid being struck by a car hurrying to beat the change. The other darted in and out and finally made it across the street. The blind man quietly waited. I looked at his face. It was composed, trusting.

When the signal changed I said, "Now we can go."

He replied, "Thank you. It's a beautiful day, isn't it?"

I prayed, "Lord, forgive me. He never sees a sunset or a sunrise, yet he can say, 'It's a beautiful day.'"

Now when I am tempted to become impatient, I picture him standing quietly and I say to myself, "It's a beautiful day."

Harold Rogers

18

The Touch of Trouble

Then they cried to the Lord in their trouble, and he delivered them from their distress.

Psalm 107:19, RSV

The psalmist has found the quickest argument before his God. There is nothing that so quickly makes the bell ring in heaven as the touch of a troubled hand. When a man is full of the interests of life, of prosperity, and self-content; when the voices of applause resound on every side; when his house is full of children, and his barn of sheaves, his prayer halts, and God seems far away. But let trouble come—let the waters, swollen by many confluent streams, begin to rise within his soul, so that lover and friend are far away, and he be overwhelmed with terror, then God bends His ear and heart.

O child of sorrow, do not assume that you are cast away! It is true that your Lord cried from His cross, "Why hast thou forsaken me?"

But even He, though laden with the sins of the world, the Father held near His heart. And He has not left you, neither can He.

Try and think of trouble as storing your heart with seeds of joy; as acting upon you as the fire upon the primeval earth, scattering jewels through its crust; or as the glaciers that brought the rich soil into the valleys; or as the husbandman who buries the seeds of spring in the autumn fields. A veiled angel, nothing else!

F. B. Meyer

19

THE FIXED HEART

O God, my heart is fixed.   *Psalm 108:1*

What is a "fixed" heart? Not merely a heart full of confidence or faith but a heart whose faith is centered upon God. It is not faith that is the secret of the fixedness (or stability) of the heart, but the rock Christ Jesus, on whom faith rests its confidence.

There is only one center that is absolutely immovable and unchangeable. And that is God. The strength or stability of the believer is not based on the tenacity of his grasp, so much as the firmness of the Rock on which he rests. We must not look at our faith, but at Him on whom our faith depends. As we reach this condition of rest, all our fear vanishes.

20

THE ANCHORAGE OF THE SOUL

He maketh the storm a calm, so that the waves thereof are still.
Psalm 107:29

In all lives there are periods of tumult and storm. We are whirled about by angry billows, and it seems as though we shall never reach the harbor of peace and rest. Some give themselves up to such experiences as a fact which they cannot avoid, or attempt to drown their

March

fears and dull their senses to suffering and danger. But faith cleaves its way through the murky mists and driving cloud-wrack, and establishes a sure connection with the throne of the Eternal Father. This is what the New Testament calls the anchorage of the soul, and however severe the storm that sweeps over the earth, the soul that shelters there is safe. "Then they cried unto the Lord in their trouble, and he delivered them out of their distresses."

At this moment you may be passing through a storm of outward trouble. Wave after wave beats upon you, as one calamity is followed by another, until it seems as though the little barque of your life must be overwhelmed. Look up to God and cry to Him. He sees you, and will not allow you to be engulfed.

F. B. Meyer

21

AFTER

Happy is he that hath the God of Jacob for his help, whose hope is in the Lord his God.

Psalm 146:5

After the winter, so cold and so drear,
Comes now the springtime with gladness and cheer;
After the shadows have all passed away,
Sunshine will follow in God's perfect day.

After the sorrow, the grief and the loss,
After the anguish and shame of the cross;
After the darkness, the conflict and strife
Comes now the joy of victorious life.

After the heart has been robbed of its love,
God in great goodness His mercy will prove;
After the loneliness, after the night
Teardrops will vanish and faith turn to sight.

After the flowers have all withered and died
Hope will yet linger whatever betide,

Life cannot perish, God's Word is still true,
What He has promised He surely will do.

Oswald J. Smith

22

TRIUMPHANT IN TRIAL

Precious in the sight of the Lord is the death of his saints.
Psalm 116:15, NIV

The death of the righteous is no accident. Do you think that the God whose watchful vigil notes the sparrow's fall and who knows the number of hairs on our heads would turn His back on one of His children in the hour of peril? With Him there are no accidents, no tragedies, and no catastrophies as far as His children are concerned.

Paul, who lived most of his Christian life on the brink of death, expressed triumphant certainty about life. He testified, "To me to live is Christ, and to die is gain" (Phil. 1:21). His strong, unshakeable faith took trouble, persecution, pain, thwarted plans, and broken dreams in stride.

He never bristled in questioning cynicism and asked, "Why, Lord?" He knew beyond the shadow of a doubt that his life was being fashioned into the image and likeness of his Savior; and despite the discomfort, he never flinched in the process.

Billy Graham (TA)

23

THE PROMISE BOOK

Thy word have I hid in mine heart, that I might not sin against thee.
Psalm 119:11

The Bible reminds us of a dictaphone. God has spoken into it, and as we read its pages, they transfer His living words to us. There are many things in the Bible, which, at first, we may not be able to understand, because, as the heaven is higher than the earth, so are God's thoughts higher than ours. Mr. Spurgeon used to say that when he ate fish, he did not attempt to swallow the bones, but put them aside on his plate! So when there is something beyond your understanding, put it aside, and go on to enjoy that which is easy of spiritual meditation.

The Bible contains many thousands of promises. It is God's book of signed checks. When you have found a promise which meets your need, do not ask God to keep His promise, as though He were unwilling to do so, and needed to be pressed and importuned. Present it humbly in the name of the Lord Jesus! Be sure that, so far as you know, you are fulfilling any conditions that may be attached; then look up into the face of your heavenly Father, and tell Him that you are depending on Him to do as He has said. It is for Him to choose the time and manner of His answer; but wait quietly, be patient, and you will find that not a moment too soon, and not a moment too late, God's response will be given. "My soul, wait thou only upon God; for my expectation is from him" (Ps. 62:5); "Blessed is she that believed: for there shall be a performance of those things that were told her from the Lord" (Luke 1:45).

Whether for the body, the soul, or spirit, there is no guide like Holy Scripture, but never read it without first looking up to its Author and Inspirer, asking that He will illuminate the page and make you wise unto salvation.

F. B. Meyer

24

Answered Prayers

I love the Lord, because he hath heard my voice and my supplications. Because he hath inclined his ear unto me, therefore will I call upon him as long as I live.

Psalm 116:1–2

Most of us who would rise to testify to unanswered prayer would likely have to say that most of our prayers that have gone unanswered have been prayers for things. But is there one of us who has prayed unsuccessfully for the enlargement of patience, self-control, courage, poise, self-understanding? Wherever the Holy Spirit has taken possession of men, ordinary people have become capable of extraordinary achievement. I have listened to polished and well-educated ministers whose words were delivered flawlessly but whose message carried no conviction. And I have listened to others who stumbled through a poorly prepared sermon whose words carried the weight of the eternal because they were delivered in the enlarging and capacitating power of the Holy Spirit. We haven't begun to explore the possibilities here. Every once in awhile in the marketplace, in the bank, in the apartment building, in the church, one meets an individual who is living out this quality of life. What impresses us about them is that their deeds stick, their words carry, their influence counts and their life convinces.

Ernest T. Campbell

25

THE BIBLE

O how I love thy law! It is my meditation all the day . . . Thy word is a lamp unto my feet, and light unto my path.

Psalm 119:97, 105

The Book of books, holy, sublime and true,
    Spirit-inspired in every thought and word,
    Revealing God, and Christ as Savior-Lord,
Teacher of all that men should be and do;
A heavenly light within earth's midnight gloom,
    A quickening life amidst death's dread decay,
    A steadfast hand, pointing the upward way,
A voice of triumph o'er the grave and tomb:

Here is a peace which sets the spirit free,
    Here is a love which casts out every fear,
    Here is a hope which gives the life good cheer
And here are visions of the world to be;
Here then I rest—and thus I ever may,
E'en when this earth and heaven have passed away!

Henry W. Frost

March

26

THE FAR LOOK

I lift up my eyes to the hills. . . .　　　　　　　　*Psalm 121:1* NIV

Some years ago the late Lord Northcliffe of England, editor and owner of *The London Times*, was threatened with complete blindness. His eyes were examined by specialists, but nothing essentially wrong with them could be found. The specialists concluded that he needed the "far look." He had been using his eyes too much for reading fine print and for close observation. He was advised to take days in the country away from the printed pages where he could look on the vast horizons of God's creation. The simple remedy corrected the great man's eye trouble. Many of God's dear children are in serious danger of becoming spiritually blind by the continued viewing of the near— the problems close at hand, a narrow span of interests, resulting in a sort of spiritual astigmatism.

Oliver G. Wilson

Meister Eckhardt, the German mystic, described spiritual insight thus: "When God lights the soul with wisdom, it floods the faculties and that man knows more than ever could be taught him."

27

GLADNESS FROM GOD

The Lord hath done great things for us.　　　　　　　*Psalm 126:3*

These words were the testimony given by the Jews after their return from Babylon to Jerusalem. Their experience appeared at first to be almost too good to be true; they felt "like them that dream." But as soon as they fully realized their perfect freedom their mouths became "filled with laughter" and their "tongue with singing."

In this situation they realized to some extent the truth of Bildad's statement in Job 8:20–21: "God will not cast away a perfect man, neither will he help the evil-doers: till he fill thy mouth with laughing, and thy lips with rejoicing." They were thus filled, and their praise and thanksgiving astonished the nations around them, causing them to exclaim: "The Lord hath done great things for them."

To this the Jews replied: "The Lord hath done great things for us; whereof we are glad." Oh, how sad they had recently been! They had hung their harps upon the willows and "wept" as they "remembered Zion." But now, through coming back to Zion and to God, their tears had dried, and they were glad. The Lord had done "great things" for them.

But have I not cause for gladness too? Has He not done great things for me? He has brought me out of bondage into liberty, out of slavery to the Evil One, into the "arms of Jesus." Yes, indeed, the Lord has done great things for me, whereof I, too, am glad!

John Roberts

28

In His Image

They that make them are like unto them . . . .　　　*Psalm 135:18*

That men become like their ideals is commonplace; and that the heathen resemble their deities is notorious. Men first impute to their deities their own vices, as the Greeks and Romans to the gods and goddesses of their Pantheon; and then endeavor to honor them by imitation.

But, in another sense, this is gloriously true of our relation to the Lord Jesus. If we make Him our ideal, and trust Him with all our hearts, His beauty shall dawn upon our face, and we shall be changed into His image, from glory to glory. We know that when He shall be revealed finally, we shall be like Him, for we shall see Him as He is; and, in a measure, this process of transformation is taking place in those who see Him by the eye of faith, and are becoming like Him.

F. B. Meyer

March

29

PRACTICING GOD'S PRESENCE

The Lord delights in the way of the man whose steps he has made firm;
though he stumble, he will not fall, for the Lord upholds him with his hand.
Psalm 37:23, 24, NIV

The God of the Bible, the God whom you and I know in Jesus
Christ, is no distant, disinterested figure whose attention is fixed on
cosmic concerns. The God of the Bible, the God unveiled fully in
Jesus, is a God of love who has committed himself to an intimate,
constant personal relationship with us human beings. He is a God who
is present with us now, and will always be present. He is a God whom
we need only look for to discover—only acknowledge to experience.
It is because God truly is present with us that you and I can find trust
by practicing his presence.

God needs only to be acknowledged to be experienced. Just as
David makes the Lord central in these verses from Psalm 37, so you
and I can make the reality of God central in our awareness . . . the
knowledge that God is with us gives us the courage to go on. The
remembrance that God is beside us brings flashes of joy even in
sorrow.

Larry Richards

30

A SENSE OF HIS PRESENCE

For there is not a word in my tongue, but, lo, O Lord, thou knowest it
altogether.
Psalm 139:4; see Hebrews 4:13

If there is not a word in your tongue, not a syllable you speak, but
he "knowest it altogether," how exact should you be in "setting a
watch before your mouth, and in keeping the door of your lips"! How

wary does it behoove you to be in all your conversation; being fore-warned by your Judge, that "by your words you shall be justified, or by your words you shall be condemned"! How cautious, lest "any corrupt communication," any uncharitable, yea, or unprofitable dis-course, should "proceed out of your mouth"; instead of "that which is good to the use of edifying, and meet to minister grace to the hear-ers"! . . .

To attain (this end), spare no pains to preserve always a deep, a continual, a lively, and a joyful sense of his gracious presence. Never forget his comprehensive word to the great father of the faithful: "I am the Almighty (rather, the All-sufficient) God; walk before me, and be thou perfect!" Cheerfully expect that he, before whom you stand, will ever guide you with his eye, will support you by his guardian hand, will keep you from all evil, and, "when you have suffered a while, will make you perfect, will stablish, strengthen, and settle you," and then "preserve you unblameable unto the coming of our Lord Jesus Christ!"

John Wesley

31

THE PATH TO PEACE

Blessed are the peacemakers: for they shall be called the children of God.
Matthew 5:9

We live in an atmosphere of antagonism, and an environment of enmity. Yet amid such adversity Christ calls us to produce peace.

This peace is love quietly, strongly, persistently meeting every onslaught against it with good will. It is that inner attitude of tranquil-lity and tolerance in the face of angry attacks. It is the willingness to accept the assaults of others even at the price of personal humiliation. It implies that even though my enemies and detractors may be at war with me I can be at peace with them.

This principle of producing peace was of course best exemplified in the life of our Lord. For though He did nothing but good amongst men, His jealous opponents were determined to destroy Him. When

March

they had done their very worst and He hung in burning shame and agony upon the cross, a tough Roman centurion looked upon His bruised and broken body to exclaim: "Surely, this man was the son of God!"

For though Christ had been reviled, He did not revile in return. Though He had been falsely accused, He did not react in flaming anger. Instead, He was silent before His assailants, asking only in quiet tones, "Why do you do this to me?" Of course they really did not know. Steeped in their own sin and selfishness, it was impossible for them to see the enormity of their evil. It is always thus with men at war with others. So from the depths of His Spirit, Christ cried out, "Father, forgive them, for they know not what they do!"

We must do the same.

There can be no other path to peace.

W. Phillip Keller (SS)

April

1

THE SUFFERING SAVIOR

It is finished!   *John 19:30,* NIV

Shortly after Jesus had uttered these words, His head fell limp upon His chest. A Roman soldier came and thrust a spear into His side and out came blood and water. Physicians say that a mixture of blood and water indicates that He died of a broken heart. Christ suffered to the uttermost. He poured out the last ounce of His blood to redeem us; He did not spare Himself. His suffering on the cross was complete.

Here was the Son of God dying on a cross which was made for the vilest of sinners. His was the act of substitution raised to the highest degree. Jesus Christ was the Lamb of God who had come to take away the sin of the world by His voluntary suffering and death. Here was the blood of God poured out in selfless love for a dying, hopeless, doomed world. By His suffering and death on the cross He had removed the last barrier between God and man.

Billy Graham (TA)

2

OUR SIN AND HIS LOVE

But we see Jesus, who was made a little lower than the angels for the suffering of death, crowned with glory and honor; that he by the grace of God should taste death for every man.

Hebrews 2:9

The suffering of Jesus is distinctive in itself; quite apart from any other suffering. It was purely voluntary: the coming down here as He

April

did, the lowly life He led, the suffering of spirit through His life, and the great climax—the Cross. It was all done of His own free accord for us. He took our place and took what belonged to us. This reveals the real love and meaning of Jesus' suffering.

The Cross spells out two stories: one in black, ugly pot-black, the story of sin. Sin carpentered the cross, and wove the thorns, and drove the nails: *our sins*. And a story, too, in red, bright-flowing red, the story of love, *His love*, that yielded to Cross and nails and shame for us. And only the passion of His love burning within will make us hate sin, as only His blood can wash it out.

S. D. Gordon

3

THE CROSS OF CHRIST

Looking unto Jesus the author and finisher of <u>our</u> faith; who for the joy that was set before him endured the cross, despising the shame, and is set down at the right hand of . . . God.

Hebrews 12:2

There are two well-known pictures each with the same title, "The Shadow of the Cross." One by Holman Hunt represents the interior of a carpenter's shop, with Joseph and the Boy Jesus at work. Mary also is present. The Boy Jesus pauses in His work, and as He stretches Himself the shadow of the Cross is formed on the wall. The other picture is a popular engraving which depicts the Infant Jesus running with outstretched arms to His mother, the shadow of the Cross being cast by His form as He runs. Both pictures are fanciful in form, but their underlying idea is assuredly true. If we read the Gospels just as they stand, it is clear that the death of Jesus Christ was really in view from the outset of His earthly appearance.

W. H. Griffith-Thomas

Till He hung on it, the Cross was the symbol of slavery and vulgar wickedness; but He converted it into the symbol of heroism, self-sacrifice and salvation. It was only a wretched framework of coarse and blood-clotted beams, which it was a shame to touch; but since then the world has gloried in it; it has been carved in every form of beauty and every substance of price; it has been emblazoned on the flags of nations and engraved on the scepters and diadems of Kings. The Cross was planted on Golgotha a dry, dead tree; but lo! it has blossomed like Aaron's rod; it has struck its roots deep down to the heart of the world, and sent it branches upwards, till today it fills the earth, and the nations rest beneath its shadow and eat of its pleasant fruits.

James Stalker

4

THE TOWERING CROSS

For the message of the cross is foolishness to those who are perishing, but to us who are being saved it is the power of God.
1 Corinthians 1:18, NIV

The significance of the cross has been captured by some of our great hymn writers. On a hill overlooking the harbor of Macao, China, Portuguese settlers once built a massive cathedral. But a typhoon proved stronger than the work of man's hands. Some centuries ago the building fell in ruins except for the front wall. High on the top of that wall, challenging the elements down through the years, stands a great bronze cross.

When Sir John Bowring saw it in 1825 he was moved to write those words now so familiar to many:

> In the cross of Christ I glory,
> Towering o'er the wrecks of time:
> All the light of sacred story
> Gathers round its head sublime.

As Easter draws near each year we consider anew the significance of Jesus' death upon the cross. Choirs and congregations across the world sing,

April

When I survey the wondrous cross,
On which the Prince of Glory died,
My richest gain I count but loss,
And pour contempt on all my pride.

Isaac Watts

Billy Graham (TA)

5

THE GRAVE IN THE GARDEN

Come, see the place where the Lord lay.   Matthew 28:6

The garden grave of Jesus offers a parable of grace. If the One who was buried in such a lovely spot is accepted as Savior, He quickly changes our grave of sin and wilderness of despair into a garden of fragrant flowers. When we come to His grace, and allow Him to bury our sin and self deep within it, we find the grave to be a garden. If as the kernel of wheat, we fall into the ground and die, we then bring forth fruits and flowers both beauteous and bountiful. We also have the pledge and pattern of resurrection here. If the grave represents death, the garden stands for victory over death. The One who was buried in a grave has a wonderful way of transforming graves into gardens.

Herbert Lockyer

6

LIVING BY FAITH

But that no man is justified by the law in the sight of God, it is evident: for, The just shall live by faith.

Galatians 3:11

To live by faith is to believe that . . . God's purposes for men will ultimately prevail . . . against Auschwitz and Hiroshima, against Belfast and Bangladesh, against Vietnam and South Africa, against assassinations in Memphis and Dallas and Los Angeles—yes, and against the petty hatreds and antagonisms of your heart and mine—God sets the resurrection of His Christ and invites our trust. As one who trusted, Nicolas Berdyaev could say: "It is not possible for my faith to be shaken by man, however low he may sink; for this faith is grounded not on what man thinks about man, but on what God thinks about him."

In the light of the Easter triumph we keep busy with our father's business here on earth. As Paul said, "We are afflicted in every way, but not crushed; perplexed, but not driven to despair; persecuted, but not forsaken; struck down, but not destroyed" (2 Cor. 4:8-9, RSV).

Ernest T. Campbell

7

THE POWER OF GOD

. . . the immeasurable greatness of his power in us who believe, according to the working of his great might . . . .

Ephesians 1:19, RSV

Think of the power of a plant, pushing out of a little seed to struggle up through darkness and very heavy dirt, alone and unaided, and to push its way up into the world, even if it has to crack cement sidewalks to do it.

Think of the power of a small bundle of sticks of dynamite—just a small bundle—suddenly transformed into so much power that it can blast apart a whole mountain side and pave the way for super highways.

Think of the power of a rocket, no higher than a several-story building, which can be made to shove so hard against the side of the earth that it can crash through all the pull of gravity and soar out into the universe's unknown space.

Now think of the power of *God*, to take a broken, dead body in a

April

dusty little tomb in the Middle East some two thousand years ago, breathe back into it the eternal life of his own Son; roll stones away; lift it from a spot near Bethany, up through this atmosphere and all known heavens, through hosts of spiritual enemies and even out of time to his own right hand, the place of authority and blessing and power forever and forever! *This* is the power given to you, if you are a believer!

Raymond C. Ortlund

8

THE LOWLY SAVIOR

He that descended is the same also that ascended up far above all heavens, that he might fill all things.

Ephesians 4:10

How low did He descend? He bowed from the heavens, and came down, and darkness was under His feet. Down to hunger and thirst, to agony and bloody sweat, to the Cross and Passion; down to death and burial even in a borrowed tomb; down to the shadow-world of Hades, to the spirits in prison, and if there be any lower, there too!

But He ascended from these low depths, with the keys of Death and Hades at His girdle. He ascended on high, leading captivity captive; and as He passed upward, He annexed each province as He went. This same Jesus who descended is now ascended, with no change in His nature, that He may fill all hearts with grace and love.

Is there one person who reads this page, in loneliness, poverty, sickness, sorrow, and pain, who can fail to get this comfort? Read the Gospels again as the Diary and Day-Book of the living Savior! He who descended is the same also who ascended; and He ascended that He might fill the lowest depths of human need. Though ascended to the right hand of the Majesty on high, He is the same loving, tender Savior as when the children flocked around His knees, and His tears brimmed over at the grave of His friend.

F. B. Meyer

9

Walking in His Will

And walk in love, as Christ loved us and gave himself up for us, a fragrant offering and sacrifice to God. Husbands, love your wives, as Christ loved the church and gave himself up for her.

Ephesians 5:2, 25, RSV

So that we might never be in doubt about what is God's perfect will, the Messiah both stated and exemplified its essence. Two salient statements become our foundation of building a life on God's perfect will. "For I came down from heaven, not to do My own will, but the will of Him who sent Me . . . And this is the will of Him who sent Me, that everyone who sees the Son and believes in Him may have everlasting life; and I will raise him up at the last day" (John 6:38, 40, NKJV). Add to that the Master's clear description of eternal life and you are on the holy ground of God's perfect will.

Jesus' prayer on the night he was betrayed, just before the crucifixion, allows us to look into the heart of God's purpose. "And this is eternal life, that they may know You, the only true God, and Jesus Christ whom You have sent" (John 17:3, NKJV). After praying that, Jesus went to the cross to make his prayer a reality. Calvary is the ultimate exposure of the permissive will of God and the accomplishment of his perfect will. What God allowed in the anguish of Golgotha was for what he intended: a new creation of people who would have as their passion to know and do his will.

Lloyd J. Ogilvie (AHA)

10

Lessons from the Lily

Why take ye thought for raiment? Consider the lilies . . . .

Matthew 6:28

April

Without any toiling or spinning on their own part, God clothes the flowers in loveliness far surpassing any adornment which the most skillful human arts can provide. Flowers bloom but a day and fade. We are better than flowers. If our Father lavishes so much beauty on perishing plants, is there any danger that He will not provide raiment for His own?

We ought to study the beautiful things in nature and learn lessons from them. Here it is a lesson of contentment we are to learn. Who ever heard a lily complaining about its circumstances? It accepts life's conditions.

The lily grows from within. So ought we to grow, having within us the divine life, to be developed in our character and spirit. The lily is an emblem of beauty; our spiritual life should unfold likewise in all lovely ways. It is a picture of perfect peace. Who ever saw wrinkles of anxiety in a lily's face? God wants us to grow into peace. The lily is fragrant; so should our lives be. The lily sometimes grows in the black bog, but it remains unspotted. Thus should we live in this world, keeping ourselves unspotted amid its evil. These are a few of the lessons from the lily.

J. R. Miller

11

Clear Shining after Rain

And he shall be as the light of the morning, when the sun riseth, even a morning without clouds; as the tender grass springing out of the earth by clear shining after rain.

2 Samuel 23:4

The way of Christ as King, according to David's description, is like "clear shining after rain," whereby the tender grass is made to spring out of the earth. So have we often seen it. After a heavy shower of rain, or after a continued rainy season, when the sun shines, there is a delightful clearness and freshness in the air that we seldom perceive at other times. Perhaps the brightest weather is just when the rain has ceased, when the wind has driven away the clouds, and the sun peers forth from his chambers to gladden the earth with smiles.

And thus is it with the Christian's exercised heart. Sorrow does not last forever. After the pelting rain of adversity comes ever and anon the clear shining. Tried believer, consider this. After all your afflictions there remains a rest for the people of God. There is a clear shining coming to your soul when all this rain is past. When your time of rebuke is over and gone, it shall be to you as the earth when the tempest has sobbed itself to sleep, when the clouds have rent themselves to rags, and when the sun peers forth once more as a bridegroom in his glorious array. To the end, sorrow cooperates with the bliss that follows it, like rain and sunshine, to bring forth the tender blade. The tribulation and the consolation work together for our good.

C. H. Spurgeon

12

THE BOOK

Thy word have I hid in mine heart, that I might not sin against thee . . .
I will delight myself in thy statutes: I will not forget thy word.
Psalm 119:11,16

The books men write are but a fragrance blown
From transient blossoms crushed by human hands;
But high above them all, splendid and alone,
Staunch as a tree, there is a Book that stands

Unmoved by storms, unchallenged by decay;
The winds of criticism would profane
Its sacred pages, but the Truth, the Way,
The Life are in it—and they beat in vain.

O traveler from this to yonder world,
Pause in the shade of God's magnificent,
Eternal Word—that tree whose roots are curled
About our human need. When strength is spent,

April

Stretch out beneath some great, far-reaching limb
Of promise, and find rest and peace in Him.

Helen Frazee-Bower

13

ANGER AHEAD

A soft answer turns away wrath, but harsh words cause quarrels.
                                                      Proverbs 15:1, TLB

Thomas Jefferson once said, "When angry, count ten before you speak; if very angry, count a hundred." I think we all agree that nothing is accomplished by anger that a smile can't accomplish better. That's what an old proverb says. But this is so hard to remember when someone deliberately sets out to plague us.

I saw a badly mutilated sign along the roadside not long ago which read ANGER AHEAD. Originally, I think the sign must have read, DANGER—CURVE AHEAD. This activated my thinking process. Anger? Danger ahead? Yes, I guess anger is a dangerous curve ahead—a turning point in which there is considerable danger of losing all one might have gained by keeping one's temper throttle in control.

I have four words that take less time than counting to ten but, for me at least, they seem to be more effective. When I feel a temper tantrum coming on, I ask myself, "What will I gain?" The answer just has to be, "Nothing!" Nothing worthwhile is ever gained when your cool is lost!

Phyllis C. Michael

14

TWILIGHT OF THE DAWN

Now Peter was sitting outside in the courtyard.   *Matthew 26:69,* RSV

The good news of Easter is that Peter left too soon! The world was not coming to a stop—it was coming to a start! God reversed the sentence that man had imposed on Jesus. " . . . On the third day he shall rise again" (Matthew 20:19). Those who had come to Joseph's garden prepared to mourn left rejoicing. They had come walking, but they left running. "He is not here. He is risen as he said" (Matthew 28:6).

Death had done its worst, and its worst was not enough. God had now pronounced his divine "Amen" on all that Jesus came to do and say and be. The kingdom of God had a future after all. The twilight through which Peter had passed was not the twilight of the night, but the twilight of the dawn . . . .

The Resurrection affirms God's intention to establish his kingdom here on earth. God's aim is not to evacuate the faithful but to work through men and women who share the Galilean vision to bring the kingdoms of this world beneath the rule of God. "But after I am raised again, I will go on before you into Galilee" (Matthew 26:32, NEB). He still has business on this earth.

Ernest T. Campbell

15

ANTIDOTE FOR DOUBT

For the Lord gives wisdom; from his mouth come knowledge and understanding; he stores up sound wisdom for the upright; he is a shield to those who walk in integrity . . . .

Proverbs 2:6–7, RSV

The cure for doubts about God is the wisdom of God. Doubt is a sure sign that we need deeper experience of who God is, how he works in our lives, and what he is ready to teach us. Wisdom is God's intelligence entrusted to us, providing supernatural knowledge, discernment, and insight. It is more than human sagacity or I.Q. The gift of wisdom maximizes all levels of intelligence. If doubt in life's trials leads us to complexities beyond our capacities, we are encouraged by James to ask for wisdom.

"If any of you lacks wisdom, let him ask of God." The Greek word for "lacks" is *leipetai* from *leipō*, meaning to be destitute or fall short.

April

Actually it comes from an ancient banking term meaning to have a shortage of resources. Doubt alerts us to the realization of a spiritual overdraft, an insufficiency to face life's questions, concerns, and difficulties—as well as unresolved intellectual problems. The word for ask, *aiteō*, is in the present active imperative, implying that we should "keep on asking." The word for wisdom is *sophias*, which is practical and applicable knowledge. It is important to distinguish that it is not just knowledge, *gnōseōs*, but wisdom, knowledge which is gained in actual relationships and situations. It is the quality of understanding which makes a person astute in discerning God's nature and seeing his handiwork in our lives and in the world.

Lloyd J. Ogilvie (AHA)

16

COMMITMENT

Commit your work to the Lord, and your plans will be established.
Proverbs 16:3, RSV

No athlete sets a new record without constant practice and preparation. There are no great, long-term marriages which have not required the commitment of both husband and wife. Marriage requires the hard work of mutual adjustment, forgiveness, and effort to discern and do what love requires. The significant accomplishments in scientific research are the result of endless hours of committed investigation. It takes testing and repeated failures to discover a hidden truth or power. Battles are won, movements begun and sustained, programs for human welfare launched and accomplished because of the commitment of an individual or group who believe that what needs to be done can be done.

I am convinced that the Lord offers each of us a challenge which we must be committed to do. Often it changes as we and the circumstances around us change. What is it for you—right now? What seemingly impossible task is before you? If you are sure it has been given to you to do, have you committed yourself to do it by the talents you

April

already have and the spiritual power the Lord will give you? It will be accomplished. Don't give up! The final stages of success are always preceded by disappointment and discouragement. Press on—victory is near. Our task is to be faithful to the vision the Lord has committed to us—the final result is up to him.

Lloyd J. Ogilvie (AHA)

17

The Medicine of a Merry Heart

A merry heart maketh a cheerful countenance.   *Proverbs 15:13*

We can promote a cheerful heart by dwelling on the bright things of our lot; by counting up the mercies which are left, rather than dwelling on what we have lost. When the heart is full of the light and love of God, can it be other than cheerful? How can this be obtained except by a living union with Jesus Christ?

Acid dropped on steel and allowed to remain will soon corrode it. And if we allow worries, anxieties, care-worn questioning to brood in our hearts, they will soon break up our peace, as swarms of tiny gnats will make a paradise uninhabitable. There is one thing that we can do. We must hand them over to Jesus just as they occur.

God seeks to mold us by circumstances, and you must believe that God has put you down just where you are because your present position is the very best place in the universe to make you what He wants you to become.

F. B. Meyer

18

Heavenly Home Life

For as he thinketh in his heart, so is he: Eat and drink, saith he to thee; but his heart is not with thee.

Proverbs 23:7

April

The real test of a man's life is his home life. It is not in what his lips say, nor in what his church profession may be, but in what he is, and in what he is in the one place where his life comes out most plainly, the home. If there be a seamy side, it will surely stick out here. If there be a sweet masterful keeping of the seams out of existence, so far as the eyes can see, it will be felt here. Character is not revealed best by public service or by church activities, nor by righting public evils, invaluable as all of this is. The real man may be found only at home. You don't know a man's character until you know his home life.

A Scottish missionary, home on furlough from her work in India, told this story. She had been teaching a group of children one day, telling them the story of Jesus, bringing out, bit by bit, incidents showing His character. As she was talking, one child, listening intently, grew excited, and then more excited. At last she was unable to restrain herself, and blurted out eagerly: "I know him; He lives near us."

Was there ever such praise of a human? Have any of us ever been taken or mistaken for Jesus? When the home folks begin to wonder in their secret hearts if it can possibly be that Jesus is back, living in you, in disguise, the sweetest victory of His grace will be told.

S. D. Gordon

19

No Longer Alone

Whoso putteth his trust in the Lord shall be safe.　　　*Proverbs 29:25*

An eminent pastor said to a man facing bitter disappointment, "Just when you think God has forgotten, he shows up."

We get quiet. We turn to him even momentarily, not to a God who is far off, but to his presence inside us. Jesus said, "The kingdom of God is within you" (Luke 17:21). The kingdom of God—the rule of God, the love of God, the power and wisdom of God—is right in the midst of us, in the center of our being. It is wherever he rules the hearts and minds of people. There are two sets of laws: the laws of natural man and the laws of God's kingdom which supersede the laws of man. While we do not ignore the laws of man, we depend more on the laws of God.

In that brief interval of quietness when by mental effort we transport ourselves from the moment of confusion to peace and calmness, we can say as did the apostle Paul, "Now unto him that is able to do exceeding abundantly above all that we ask or think" (Eph. 3:20). In that instant we are no longer alone.

Harold Rogers

20

DRAWING NEAR TO HEAR

To draw near to listen is better than to offer the sacrifice of fools. . . .
Ecclesiastes 5:1, RSV

This is certainly half of our business, when we kneel to pray. It is a drawing nigh to hear. One has truly said that the closet is not so much an oratory, in the narrow sense of making requests, as an observatory, from which we get new views of God, and new revelations of Him.

We are all inclined to be rash with our mouths. We run hurriedly into the presence of God, leave our card as on a morning call, and then plunge into the eager rush of life. We have spoken to Him, but we have not paused, not stayed to hear what He would say in reply. We have suggested many things to Him, but have not sought for His comments, or reactions, in return. We do not take time to fix the heart's gaze on the unseen and eternal, or to abstract our mind from the voices of the world, so as to hear the still small voice that speaks in silence and solitude.

> Only the waters which in perfect stillness lie
> Give back an undistorted image of the sky.

F. B. Meyer

April

21

WE ARE HIS

I am my beloved's, and my beloved is mine.　　　*Song of Solomon 6:3*

In the earlier stages of Christian life, we think most of what we have in Christ; afterwards we love to dwell on His possession of us. We are His estate, for Him to cultivate and rear successive crops for His praise and glory. We are His jewels, to obtain which He renounced all, and on which He will expend infinite care, cutting our facets, and polishing us to shine brightly in His light. We are His house in which He can dwell, opening out unexpected apartments and passages. We are members of His body, through which He will fulfill His holy purpose. We are His bride, to win whom He came from afar. We are owned, possessed, inhabited, loved, with a peculiar personal affection. As Keble says: "Thou art thy Savior's darling: doubt no more."

F. B. Meyer

22

THE LORD IS MY SONG

Behold, God is my salvation; I will trust, and not be afraid: for the Lord Jehovah is my strength and my song; he also is become my salvation.
Isaiah 12:2

Note, the word is not "The Lord gives me strength," but "The Lord *is* my strength"! How strong is a believer? I say it with reverence, he is as strong as God—"The Lord is my strength." God, the infinite Jehovah, in the infinity of His nature, is our strength.

The next is, "The Lord is my song," that is to say, the Lord is the giver of our songs; He breathes the music into the hearts of His people; He is the creator of their joy. The Lord is also the subject of their songs: they sing of Him and of all that He does on their behalf.

The Lord is, moreover, the object of their song; they sing unto the Lord. Their praise is meant for Him alone. They do not make melody for human ears, but unto the Lord. "The Lord is my song." Then I ought always to sing: and if I sing my loudest, I can never reach the height of this great argument, nor come to the end of it. This song never changes. If I live by faith my song is always the same, for "The Lord is my song." Our song unto God is God Himself. He alone can express our most intense joy. O God, You are my exceeding joy. Father, Son, and Holy Ghost, You are my hymn of everlasting delight.

C. H. Spurgeon

23

TRUSTING OUR FATHER

Surely God is my salvation; I will trust and not be afraid. The Lord, the Lord, is my strength and my song; he has become my salvation.

Isaiah 12:2, NIV

When we become Christians we can say "Our Father," for those who receive Christ have the right to become children of God (John 1:12). So then we can look to God as our Father. We are to put our trust in Him and come to know Him in the close, intimate companionship of father and child. We can have a personal sense of His love for us and His interest in us, for He is concerned about us as a father is concerned for his children.

As Peter Marshall once put it, "God will not permit any troubles to come upon us, unless he has a specific plan by which great blessing can come out of the difficulty."

It is through the suffering, the tests and trials of life, that we can draw near God. A. B. Simpson once heard a man say something that he never forgot. "When God tests you, it is a good time for you to test Him by putting His promises to the proof, and claiming from Him just as much as your trials have rendered necessary."

There are two ways of getting out of a trial. One is to simply try to

April

get rid of the trial, and be thankful when it is over. The other is to recognize the trial as a challenge from God to claim a larger blessing than we have ever had.

Billy Graham (TA)

24

PERFECT PEACE

You will keep in perfect peace him whose mind is steadfast, because he trusts in you. Trust in the Lord forever, for the Lord is the Rock eternal.
Isaiah 26:3–4, NIV

Trouble will not hurt us unless it does what many of us too often allow it to do—harden us, making us sour, bitter, and skeptical. The trouble we bear trustfully brings to us a fresh vision of God, and, as a result, we discover a new outlook on life.

If we make our sorrow and trouble an occasion for learning more of God's love and of His power to aid and bless, then it will teach us to have a firmer confidence in His providence; and as a result of this, the brightness of His love will fill our lives.

Trust with a childlike dependence on God, and no trouble can destroy you. Even in that last dark hour of death, when your flesh and your heart fail, you will be able to depend on peace upon Him who "is the strength of my heart and my portion forever" (Ps. 73:26).

Billy Graham (TA)

25

GUIDED BY THE QUIET VOICE OF GOD

And thine ears shall hear a word behind thee, saying, This is the way, walk ye in it, when ye turn to the right hand, and when ye turn to the left.
Isaiah 30:21

There is a tender awe in knowing that there is Someone at your side guiding every step, restraining here, leading on there. He knows the way better than the oldest Swiss guide knows the mountain trail. He has love's concern that all shall go well with you. There is a great peace for us in that, and with it a tender awe to think who He is, and that He is close by your side. When you come to the splitting of the road into two, with a third path forking off from the others, there is peace in just holding steady and very quiet while you put out your hand and say, "Jesus, Master, guide here." And then to hear a Voice so soft that only in great quiet is it heard, softer than faintest breath on your cheek, or slightest touch on your arm, telling the way in fewest words or syllables—that makes the peace unspeakable.

S. D. Gordon

He does not lead me year by year
Nor even day by day.
But step by step my path unfolds;
My Lord directs my way.

Barbara C. Ryberg

26

COURAGE

Strengthen ye the weak hands, and confirm the feeble knees. Say to them that are of a fearful heart, Be strong, fear not; behold, your God will come with vengeance, even God with a recompence; he will come and save you.
Isaiah 35:3-4

Be strong!
We are not here to play, to dream, to drift.
We have hard work to do, and loads to lift.
Shun not the struggle—face it, 'tis God's gift.

Be strong!
Say not the days are evil. Who's to blame?
And fold the hand and acquiesce—oh, shame!
Stand up, speak out, and bravely, in God's name.

Be strong!

April

It matters not how deep entrenched the wrong,
How hard the battle goes, the day how long;
Faint not—fight on! Tomorrow comes the song.

Maltbie D. Babcock

27

WATER AND FIRE

When you pass through the waters I will be with you. . . .
Isaiah 43:2, RSV

Our challenges as Christians—as children of the all-powerful and ever-loving God—when tempted to stoop low under what we believe to be a burden of disappointments, is to claim the words of the prophet when he said, "Should you pass through the sea, I will be with you; or through the rivers, they will not swallow you up. Should you walk through fire, you will not be scorched and the flames will not burn you" (Isa. 43:2, JB).

With that confidence we can then begin to understand even just a little bit of what Frederick Faber meant when he said, "There are no disappointments to those whose wills are buried in the will of God."

When Roy and I were married, we both agreed that we would like a large family of children. We dreamed long life for each of them as they gave themselves to the Lord. By God's grace we have tried to set a good example for our children . . . the intent of our hearts has been to obey God's Word as best we understood it. We dreamed of raising all of our children—our natural ones and our adopted ones—never once considering the possibility of loss by death. We adopted children that we felt had a special need, and we had the joy of seeing them flower for a time before death took two of them by accident and our baby by illness. At each of those moments we could have bowed our heads and shouted, "Why?" But instead we chose to trust God even in our moments of anger and deep hurt. We've had to learn to pray, "Not my will but thine be done."

For the Christian, disappointments are opportunities to learn more of Christ and of his will for our lives. And it is in our disappointments that we learn to live out the words, "And we know that in all things God works for the good of those who love him . . . " (Rom. 8:28, NIV).

Dale Evans Rogers (GHT)

28

THE REFINER'S FIRE

Behold, I have refined thee, but not with silver; I have chosen thee in the furnace of affliction.

Isaiah 48:10

Silver is tried by fire, and the heart by pain, "We went through fire." But in the fire you will not be burned; only your dross shall be removed. "I will . . . purge away thy dross" (Isa. 1:25). The smell of burning shall not pass upon you, for the form of the Son of God shall be at your side.

The main end of our life is not to *do*, but to *become*. For this we are being molded and disciplined each hour. You cannot understand why year after year the stern ordeal is perpetuated; you think the time is wasted; you are doing nothing. Yes, but you are situated in the set of circumstances that gives you the best opportunity for disclosing, and therefore acquiring, the qualities in which your character is naturally deficient. And the Refiner *sits* patiently beside the crucible, intent on the process, tempering the heat, and eager that the dross should pass off, and his own face becomes perfectly reflected in the surface.

F. B. Meyer

29

A ROCK I CAN TRUST

On mine arm shall they trust.   Isaiah 51:5

In seasons of severe trial, the Christian has nothing on earth that he can trust, and is therefore compelled to cast himself on his God alone.

April

When his vessel is on its beam-ends, and no human deliverance can avail, he must simply and entirely trust himself to the providence and care of God. Happy storm that wrecks a man on such a rock as this! O blessed hurricane that drives the soul to God and God alone!

There is no getting to our God sometimes because of the multitude of our friends; but when a man is so poor, so friendless, so helpless that he has nowhere else to turn, he flies into his Father's arms and is blessedly clasped therein. When he is burdened with troubles so pressing and so peculiar, that he cannot tell them to any but his God, he may be thankful for them; for he will learn more of his Lord then than at any other time. Oh, tempest-tossed believer, it is a happy trouble that drives you to the Father.

C. H. Spurgeon

30

GOD'S CHOSEN CHILD

Fear not, for I have redeemed you; I have called you by name, you are mine.

Isaiah 43:1, RSV

What a breathtaking promise: *I have redeemed you; I have called you by name, you are mine!* The Lord assures us that we are his, and the word of the Lord here gives us positive assurance that we are never alone. There is just no room for feelings of loneliness. But at the same time we have no assurance from the Lord that he will keep us from having hard times or will provide answers before our moment of real need.

We *can* be certain, though, that as we stand on the raw edge of our need, God will meet us—even as he met the needs of the people of Israel when he performed a miracle and opened up a path for them *through* the sea and saved them from what appeared to be sure doom.

I recall so well in 1948, after I had committed my life to Jesus Christ, there were times when I felt a crushing sense of loneliness among my peers in show business. They thought I had gone "off the deep end" in my Christian experience and lifestyle. One day an ac-

April

tress friend asked, "Evans, what is the matter with you? You are not the same. . . . "

And I wasn't the same. Instead of "Evans" being on the throne of my life, Jesus was. This meant that I was no longer interested in some of the worldly activities that had filled my life before. Let me tell you, I felt very alone and lonely even in the midst of the people and the busyness in my professional life. . . . Those were desperate days for me, but again and again I received comfort and peace from such promises as found in Hebrews 13:5, "God himself has said: *I will not fail you or desert you . . .* " (JB).

Dale Evans Rogers (GHT)

May

1

Beauty for Ashes

The Spirit of the Lord God is upon me . . . to give unto them beauty for ashes, the oil of joy for mourning, the garment of praise for the spirit of heaviness . . . .

Isaiah 61:1, 3

All of us live amid a dying world. Death dominates the planet—not just physical death, but also the death of hopes, dreams, ambitions, love, family, friends, and a hundred other human aspirations.

Yet in spite of all this decadence and despair life can be beautiful. We can bring comfort, cheer, and consolation to our contemporaries. We can be those who weep with those who smile through their tears.

We can draw near to help people pick up the pieces and make a fresh start. We can bring beauty for ashes. We can share the Spirit of God's joy to replace the spirit of a heavy heart.

W. Phillip Keller (SS)

2

Enduring Kindness

For the mountains shall depart, and the hills be removed; but my kindness shall not depart from thee, neither shall the covenant of my peace be removed, saith the Lord. . . .

Isaiah 54:10

In today's unstable world, we see all around us evidences of the truth of Isaiah's prophecy. Mountains and hills are indeed fragile in the face of earthquakes and man-made upheavals. What happened to

Hiroshima at the end of World War II could happen to an entire country or continent with the sophisticated weapons of war that exist today. But our God is like the Rock of Gibraltar which cannot be moved. If God could fail, then all creation could be obliterated. His children can know that God will never leave them nor forsake them, for His love is without end and His "kindness shall not depart from thee."

There is a phrase in the Psalms that emphasizes this truth for me even better than does the prophet Isaiah. In Psalm 72:17 Solomon says, "His name shall endure for ever." The words, "endure for ever," occur more than ten times in the Psalms alone—always in relation to the Lord, His name, His righteousness, His praise, His truth, and His judgments. In other books of the Bible, His mercy and His word are described as enduring forever. The One who endures forever is our God, our Lord, our Savior! We may know with a certainty set down indelibly in God's record book that eternity is ours in His company! Along with all these other attributes, we know that His kindness will be ours forever!

3

A TIME FOR TRUST

He who trusts in me shall possess the land and inherit my Holy Mountain.
Isaiah 57:13, TLB

Every act of trust increases my capacity for God. Every time I trust Him I have more room for Him. He dwells within me in ever richer fullness, occupying room after room in my life. That is a glorious assurance, and one that is filled with infinite comfort. Let me repeat it again, for it is the very music of the soul; little acts of trust make more room for God. In my trifles I can prepare for emergencies. Along a commonplace road I can get ready for the hill. In the green pastures and by the still waters I can prepare myself for the valley of the shadow. For when I reach the hill, the shadow, the emergency, I shall be God-possessed: He will dwell in me. And where He dwells

May

He controls. If He lives in my life He will direct my powers. It will not be I that speaks, but my Father who speaks in me. He will govern my speech. He will empower my will. He will enlighten my mind. He will energize and vitalize my entire life.

J. H. Jowett

I have held many things in my hands, and I have lost them all; but whatever I have placed in God's hands, that I still possess.

Martin Luther

4

GOD'S LOVE

As one whom his mother comforteth, so will I comfort you.

Isaiah 66:13

In Isaiah 12 the prophet says, "O Lord . . . thou comfortedst me," and in this passage we are able to see the tender way in which God comforts those who are His. "As one whom his mother comforteth, so will I comfort you." The psalmist has assured us that "like as a father pitieth his children, so the Lord pitieth them that fear him" (Ps. 103:13). Our Lord has, therefore, taken the place of both father and mother. Even more than this, Isaiah says: "Can a woman forget her little child, and not have love for her own son?" (Isa. 49:15, TLB). This lack of love is just about impossible to comprehend, yet it might be so in one case out of a thousand. God's love, however, goes far beyond and far deeper than that even of a mother. Therefore He declares: "I will never forget thee."

He also tells us that we shall be His in that day when He makes up His jewels. "I will spare them, as a man spareth his own son that serveth him" (Mal. 3:17). And then we have the words of Jesus: "If ye then, being evil, know how to give good gifts unto your children, how much more shall your Father which is in heaven give good things to them that ask him?" (Matt. 7:11)

Can we wonder, then, at God saying to the prophet, "Comfort ye my people," when we see how He in turn is more to them than a father and mother combined? What a comfort it is to learn from this passage what our God is to us, and how He owns, remembers, pities, comforts, and undertakes, as an almighty parent, to provide for all our needs.

5

OBEDIENCE

Obey my voice . . . and I will be your God.　　　　　*Jeremiah 11:4*

Let us listen to what the Lord Jesus says about obedience (John 14:21–23). "He that keepeth my commandments, he it is that loveth me; and he that loveth me shall be loved by my Father, and I will love him, and we will make our abode with him." And in John 15:10, "If ye keep my commandments, ye shall abide in my love." These words are an inexhaustible treasure. Faith can firmly *trust Christ to enable us to live such a life of love and of obedience.*

No father can train his children unless they are obedient. No teacher can teach a child who continues to disobey him. No general can lead his soldiers to victory without prompt obedience. Pray God to imprint this lesson on your heart: *the life of faith is a life of obedience.* As Christ lived in obedience to the Father, so we, too, need obedience for a life in the love of God.

Andrew Murray

6

LIFE IS A JOURNEY

Be not afraid . . . for I am with thee to deliver thee, saith the Lord.
Jeremiah 1:8

Life is a journey. It is a trip through a strange land where you have never been before, and you never know a moment ahead where you are going next. Strange languages, strange scenes, strange dilemmas; new tangles, new experiences, and some old ones with new faces, so that you do not know them. It is just as chock-full of pleasure and enjoyment as it can be, if you could only make some provision for the drudgery and hard things that seem to crowd in so thick and fast sometimes, as to make people forget the gladness of it.

Now I have something to tell you that seems too utterly good to be believed, and yet keeps getting better all the way along. It is this: the Master has planned that your life journey shall be a personally conducted one on this ideal plan. He has arranged with His best friend, who is an experienced traveler, to go with you and devote Himself wholly to your interests.

S. D. Gordon

No distant Lord have I, loving afar to be;
Made flesh for me—He cannot rest, until He rests in me.
Brother in joy or pain; Bone of my bone was He,
Now with me closer still—He dwells Himself in me.

I need not journey far this distant Friend to see;
Companionship is always mine, He makes His home with me.
I envy not the twelve; nearer to me is He,
The life He once lived here on earth, He lives again in me.

Maltbie Babcock

7

THE PERSONALITY OF THE PROMISER

And I will deliver thee out of the hand of the wicked, and I will redeem thee out of the hand of the terrible.

Jeremiah 15:21

Note the glorious personality of the promise—I will, I will. The Lord Jehovah Himself interposes to deliver and redeem His people. He pledges Himself personally to rescue them. His own arm shall do it, that He may have the glory. Neither our strength nor our weakness is taken into the account, but the lone I, like the sun in the heavens, shines out resplendent in all-sufficiency. Why then do we calculate our forces, and consult with flesh and blood to our grievous wounding? Peace, unbelieving thoughts, be still, and know that the Lord reigns.

Seeing that we have such a God to trust, let us rest upon Him with all our weight; let us resolutely drive out all unbelief, and endeavor to get rid of doubts and fears, which so much mar our comfort; since there is no excuse for fear where God is the foundation of our trust. A loving parent would be sorely grieved if his child could not trust him; and how ungenerous, how unkind is our conduct when we put so little confidence in our heavenly Father, who has never failed us, and who never will! We have been in many trials, but we have never yet been cast where we could not find in our God all that we needed.

C. H. Spurgeon

8

THE DIVINE PLAN

Blessed is the man that trusteth in the Lord, and whose hope the Lord is. For he shall be as a tree planted by the waters, and that spreadeth out her roots by the river, and shall not see when heat cometh, but her leaf shall be green.

Jeremiah 17:7–8

Faith in God never depends on faith in something or someone else. We have faith in him first and then we arrive at faith in his power. If God is in control, there is no need to feel insecure. Things may happen which suggest insecurity, but this does not mean there will be insecurity. It probably means that a personal plan has been blocked, perhaps only temporarily. There is a divine plan. A person sees only with human eyes, but the divine plan is for all of life.

A loving Father will never plunge us into rough water and abandon us. He is there, loving, protecting, strengthening, regardless of the outcome.

Harold Rogers

May

9

THE OMNIPRESENCE OF GOD

. . . Do not I fill heaven and earth? saith the Lord.   *Jeremiah 23:24*

How strongly and beautifully do these words express the omnipresence of God! And can there be, in the whole compass of nature, a more sublime subject? . . . What deep instruction may it convey to all the children of men; and more directly to the children of God! . . .

Indeed, this subject is far too vast to be comprehended by the narrow limits of human understanding. We can only say: The great God, the eternal, the almighty Spirit, is as unbounded in his presence as in his duration and power. In condescension, indeed, to our weak understanding, he is said to dwell in heaven; but, strictly speaking, the heaven of heavens cannot contain him; he is in every part of his dominion. The universal God dwells in universal space.

John Wesley

10

TRUST IN THE DARK

He hath set me in dark places . . .   *Lamentations 3:6*

When we reach heaven, we may discover that the richest and deepest and most profitable experiences we had in this world were those which were gained in the very roads from which we shrank back with dread. The bitter cups we tried to push away contained the medicines we most needed. The hardest lessons that we learn are those which teach us the most and best fit us for service here and glory hereafter. It is the easiest thing in the world to obey God when He commands us to do what we like, and to trust Him when the path is all sunshine. The real victory of faith is to trust God in the dark and through the dark.

To all who wonder why a loving God has subjected them so often to the furnace, my only answer is, *God owns you and me*, and He has a right to do with us just as He pleases. If He wants to keep His silver over a hot flame until He can see His own countenance reflected in the metal, then He has a right to do so. It is the Lord, it is my loving Teacher, it is my heavenly Father; let Him do what seems to Him good. He will not lay on one stroke in cruelty, or a single one that cannot give me grace to bear. Life's school days and nights will soon be over. Pruning-time will soon be ended. The crucibles will not be needed in heaven.

Theodore L. Cuyler

11

PRACTICE WISDOM

Daniel gained insight in every kind of vision and dream.
Daniel 1:17, MLB

In its final essence, "insight" or practical wisdom is certainly God-given and divinely inspired. That is why Christians, of all people, should excel in the intellectual realm. This was Daniel's secret of excellence, the will to learn which sustained him throughout his life and kept him in the forefront of his fellows—politically, physically, and spiritually.

George Bernard Shaw defined wisdom thus: "Men are wise in proportion not to their experience but to their *capacity* for experience. It is not what I experience that determines my insightfulness, but what I learn from that experience." God alone can give us that insight.

12

SEEING THE MIRACLES AGAIN!

Those who are wise will shine like the brightness of the heavens, who lead many to righteousness, like the stars forever and ever.
Daniel 12:3, NIV

May

A man born without arms learned to dress and feed himself with his feet. His "handwriting" was beautiful, accomplished with a pencil held in his teeth. He earned a living and lived normally in almost every way.

"Nothing is a handicap," he said, "until you begin to think of it as a handicap."

That is precisely the handicap most of us live with: we *think* we are handicapped. We see the world as a wilderness and not as a paradise. We behold the mud instead of the stars. Or, in religious terms, we experience the absence of God instead of his presence . . . *There is never a moment when he could be more present.*

The problem is with us. We lose the ability to discern his presence. We forget how to pray. The paradise reverts to wilderness.

How to see again! That is what we want. How to live every day as though the world were paradise and not wilderness, as though all of life were filled with the miracles of God!

That is what we desire more than anything else—to see the miracles again!

John Killinger

13

The Lord Is Good

The Lord is good, a strong hold in the day of trouble; he knows those who take refuge in him.

Nahum 1:7, RSV

The phrase, "The Lord is good," often appears in Scripture, being found in some of the most unlikely places throughout the Old Testament. Here in this prophecy of the fall of a great city, the writer cannot overlook this essential quality of the great Jehovah God. Even in the midst of chaos, "The Lord is good." In our own troubled day, it is comforting to be able to rely on One who never changes, who "is the same yesterday, today and forever"! If we place our trust in Him, we can do no better, we can find no firmer stronghold, no stronger foundation. Who else can we trust in the world around us?

Someone has wisely said, "Even as you cannot outrun God when you dodge His will, it is equally impossible to outrun His care when you are in His will."

14

THE PERVASIVE POWER OF PEACE

Blessed are the peacemakers, for they shall be called sons of God.
Matthew 5:9, NKJV

Peace is a key word of Jesus' life and ministry. He came to establish it, his message explained it, his death purchased it, and his resurrected presence enables it. The messianic predictions were that he would be the Prince of Peace (Isaiah 9:6). The angels who announced his birth sang, "On earth, peace, good will toward men!" (Luke 2:14). His persistent word of absolution to sinners was, "Go in peace!" Just before he was crucified, the Lord's last will and testament was, "Peace I leave with you, My peace I give to you; not as the world gives do I give to you. Let not your heart be troubled, neither let it be afraid" (John 14:27). When the Lord returned after the resurrection, his first word to the disciples was "Shalom." Peace. The life of Jesus was saturated with his mission to bring the peace of God and to initiate the healing relationships of peace with God.

Lloyd J. Ogilvie (CGB)

15

GOD OUR STRONGHOLD

The Lord is good, a strong hold in the day of trouble; and he knoweth them that trust in him.

Nahum 1:7

What should it mean to me that I am known of God? The Living Bible puts it well: "The Lord is good. When trouble comes, He is the place to go! And He knows everyone that trusts in Him!" To be known of God means, for one thing, that He is my shelter and protection. In John 10:14, Jesus said: "I am the good Shepherd and know my sheep. . . . " This puts it vividly for me: In one sense of God's knowledge of me, I am one of His sheep.

But there is a negative side to His knowledge as well. All things are known to Him—and He knows us as we are. What about the one who has no knowledge of God, the one who has no room for God in his life? By implication, this verse (both the Old Testament expression and the New Testament truth) teaches that those who deny His existence, those who live as though He does not exist, are in turn not known of Him in the sense of having received His shelter and protection. In a way, when we Christians live our lives anxiously, uptight about those things that happen to us, or seem threatening to happen, we are denying God His rightful place of prominence in our lives. What blessings we miss by thus ignoring the place of safety and shelter He wants to give us!

16

The Sun of Righteousness

Unto you that fear my name shall the Sun of righteousness arise with healing in his wings. . . .

Malachi 4:2

Christ, to the Christian growing older, seems to be what the sun is to the developing day, which it lightens from the morning till the evening. When the sun is in the zenith in the broad noonday, men do their various works by his light; but they do not so often look up to him. It is the sunlight that they glory in, flooding a thousand tasks with clearness, making a million things beautiful. But as the world rolls into the evening, it is the sun itself at sunset that men gather to look at and admire and love.

Phillips Brooks

In a wheel there is one portion that never turns around, that doesn't move. That is the axle. So, in God's Providence there is an axle which never moves. Christian, here is a sweet thought for you. Your situation is ever changing: sometimes you're up, and sometimes you're down. Yet there is an unmoving point in your life. What is that axle? It is the axle of God's everlasting love toward his covenant people. The exterior of the wheel is changing; but the center stands forever fixed. Other things may move; but God's love never moves; it is the axle of the wheel, and will endure.

Author Unknown

17

THE WORD OF GOD

Man shall not live by bread alone, but by every word that proceedeth out of the mouth of God.

Matthew 4:4

The illustration that our Lord uses, in which the Word of God is compared to our daily bread, is most instructive.

Bread is indispensable to life. We all understand this. However strong a person may be, if he takes no nourishment, he will grow weaker and life will become extinct. Even so with the Word of God. It contains a heavenly principle and works powerfully in them that believe.

Bread must be eaten. I may know all about bread. I may have bread, and may give it to others. I may have bread in my house and on my table in great abundance, but that will not help me; if through illness I am unable to eat it, I will die. And so a mere knowledge of God's Word and even the preaching of it to others will not avail me. It is not enough to think about it. I must feed on God's Word and take it into my heart and life. In love and obedience I must appropriate the words of God and let them take full possession of my heart. Then they will indeed be words of life.

Bread must be eaten daily. And the same is true of God's Word. The psalmist says: "Blessed is the man whose delight is in the law of the Lord; and *in his law doth he meditate day and night.*" "O how I love thy law; it is my meditation *all the day*." To secure a strong and powerful spiritual life, God's Word every day is indispensable.

Andrew Murray

18

SHINING AT HOME

The people who sat in darkness have seen a great light and for those who sat in the region and shadow of death light has dawned.

Matthew 4:16, RSV

Manned lighthouses are rapidly becoming a rarity in this modern day, but if you have ever seen a lighthouse in action you will have noticed how the area immediately surrounding the base of the lighthouse was left dark and dismal. This should not be the case for the Christian, but too often, it is at home that our Christian witness suffers. The solution is found in a closer touch with the Lord through His Word and prayer.

Andrew Bonar summed up what it means to live the Christian life at home when he wrote: "A holy Christian life is made up of a number of small things: little words, not eloquent sermons; little deeds, not miracles of battle or one great, heroic deed of martyrdom; the little constant sunbeam, not the lightning; the avoidance of little evils, little inconsistencies, little weaknesses, little follies and indiscretions, and little indulgences of the flesh make up the beauty of a holy life."

19

FILLED WITH HIS PRESENCE

Blessed are they (who) hunger and thirst after righteousness: for they shall be filled.

Matthew 5:6

He actually comes into my spirit by His Spirit to reside. He is the living Christ who, very much alive, arises to become the dominant person in my experience. He fills my life.

This "filling" by God's Spirit of which Jesus spoke and about which much has been said in the New Testament appears to confuse many. It really need not be so if we understand in simple terms what is meant.

To be filled with the presence of God is to enjoy His company and companionship in all of life. It is to know Him as our life mate, exactly as in a beautiful marriage. Two people never really "know" each other until they become fully open and available to each other. It is only when each has invited the other to come into his or her life and fully share all their experience that their days are "filled" with the other's presence and person.

This is why Jesus referred to Himself as the groom, and His church (you and me) as His bride. He comes into our lives to fill them continuously with His own person, His own presence, His own influence.

W. Phillip Keller (SS)

20

A MEASURE OF MERCY

Blessed are the merciful: for they shall obtain mercy.   Matthew 5:7

In my own life I am acutely aware that I am a roughhewn man. Because of my rather tough, rough up-bringing in a frontier environment, I simply do not possess the polish of the "man about town." There are characteristics in my make-up which may seem harsh and unyielding. But, despite this, my life has been deeply touched by the mercy of those who took the time to try and understand me—who cared enough to forgive so many faults and who in mercy made me their friend.

Often these were people to whom I had shown no special kindness. Their bestowal of mercy on me was something totally unexpected and undeserved. Because of this, it has been a double delight. More than that, it has been an enormous inspiration that lifted and challenged me to respond in a measure beyond my wildest dreams.

Mercy does just that to people. It excites and stimulates their hope. It reassures them that life can be beautiful. It convinces them that there is good reason to carry on and push for better things if others care that much.

This all implies that if someone has extended mercy to me, surely I, in turn, can and must extend mercy to others.

But, to really find the true source of inner inspiration for this sort of conduct, the Christian simply must look beyond his fellow man. He must look away to the mercy of God our Father. Nothing else in all the world will so humble us. Nothing else will so move our stony spirits to extend mercy. Nothing else will so powerfully induce us to do the proper thing in extending genuine mercy to our contemporaries.

W. Phillip Keller (SS)

21

EYES OF THE HEART

Blessed are the pure in heart, for they shall see God.

Matthew 5:8, NKJV

A woman exclaimed wistfully, "How I wish my husband could see me. The real me! He looks at me but somehow he looks right past me. I try to tell him about me but he doesn't *see* what I'm saying." The tragedy is that her husband is a Christian, but has never had Christ's healing touch on the scales over his heart-eyes. His wife and his friends all long for him to be healed. He is missing the wonder of intimacy in which the essential *I* meets the real *you*.

A personal word. I had been a Christian and a pastor for several years before I had an experience which healed my heart-eyes. It was when I discovered the promise of the indwelling Christ that I began to see. A new discernment came as a result. I began to see beneath the surface of people and events. The indwelling Lord refracted my spiritual vision and gave me x-ray intuition. I saw the meaning of the Scriptures as never before. An understanding of how to communicate Christ's strength for people's struggles was imputed as a gift. Sensitivity in situations multiplied my analytical capacity. Most of all, I began to "see" my family and friends. I could say with Elizabeth Barrett Browning: "Earth's crammed with heaven, and every common bush afire with God." The secret was in saying yes to the Lord's offer to live in me and be my heart-eyes. Christ Himself is the eye of the heart.

Lloyd J. Ogilvie (CGB)

22

SERVANTS IN SOCIETY

Blessed are those who have been persecuted for the sake of righteousness, for theirs is the kingdom of heaven. Blessed are you when men cast insults at you, and persecute you, and say all kinds of evil against you falsely, on account of Me. Rejoice, and be glad, for your reward in heaven is great, for so they persecuted the prophets who were before you.

Matthew 5:10–12, NASB

No, He never promised us a rose garden. He came up front with us and admitted that the arena of this world is not a friend of grace to help us on to God. Nevertheless, strange as it may seem, He went on to tell that handful of Palestinian peasants (and all godly servants in every generation) that their influence would be nothing short of remarkable. They would be "the salt of the earth" and they would be "the light of the world." And so shall we! So far-reaching would be the influence of servants in society, their presence would be as significant as salt on food and as light on darkness. Neither is loud or externally impressive, but both are essential. Without our influence this old world would soon begin to realize our absence. Even though it may not admit it, society needs both salt and light.

Charles R. Swindoll (IYS)

May

23

A STUDY OF SALT

You are the salt of the earth. . . .   *Matthew 5:13,* NKJV

When Jesus called the disciples the salt of the earth, he was first of all giving them an affirming image of value, vitality, and viability. All three are implied, as a study of salt at that time reveals. Salt was used to pack fish, as the fishermen among the disciples knew. All the disciples knew that salt was very valuable. In fact, the word for salary comes from the wages of a "sack of salt" paid to Roman soldiers: sal—salt; salarus—salary. Salt was also used beneath the tiles of an oven. But the main use of the precious commodity was to season and preserve food. Jesus' implied message is that our influence is to pervade, permeate, purify, and preserve. We are to be combatants against blandness and dullness. It is quite a revolution of images to think of ourselves as the zest and flavor of the world. But like salt, our influence is to be inadvertent. We are to bring out the essential qualities of others. No one can at the same time draw attention to himself and make others great.

Lloyd J. Ogilvie (CGB)

24

PERSONAL PRAYER

When thou prayest, enter into thy closet, and when thou hast shut thy door, pray to thy Father which is in secret.

Matthew 6:6

This shutting of the door is significant in several ways. It shuts the world out. It secures us against interruption. It ought to shut out worldly thoughts and cares and distractions, as well as worldly presences. Wandering in prayer is usually one of our sorest troubles. Then it shuts us in, and this also is important and significant. It shuts us in alone with God. No eye but His sees us as we bow in the secrecy. No ear but His hears us as we pour out our heart's feelings and desires. Thus we are helped to realize that with God alone have we to do, that He alone can help us. As we are shut up alone with God, so also are we shut up to God. There is precious comfort in the assurance that when we thus pray we are not talking into the air. There is an ear to hear, though we can see no presence, and it is the ear of our Father. This assures us of loving regard in heaven, also of prompt and gracious answer.

J. R. Miller

25

PRAYER CHANGES ME

For if you forgive men for their transgressions, your heavenly Father will also forgive you. But if you do not forgive men, then your Father will not forgive your transgressions.

Matthew 6:14–15, NASB

Before God will forgive us, we must be certain that our conscience is clear. A familiar verse from the Psalms frequently pops into my mind when I begin to pray: "If I regard wickedness in my heart, The Lord will not hear" (Ps. 66:18). If I want cleansing, I must be certain things are right between myself and others.

Prayer includes praise and thanksgiving, intercession and petition, and confession. In prayer we focus fully on our God. We capture renewed zeal to continue, a wider view of life, increased determination to endure. As we strengthen our grip on prayer, it is amazing how it alters our whole perspective.

The late Dr. Donald Barnhouse, greatly admired American pastor and author of the last generation, once came to the pulpit and made a statement that stunned his congregation: *"Prayer changes nothing!"* You could've heard a pin drop in that packed Sunday worship service in Philadelphia. His comment, of course, was designed to make Christians realize that God is sovereignly in charge of everything. Our times are literally in His hands. No puny human being by uttering a few words in prayer takes charge of events and changes them. God does the shaping, the changing, it is He who is in control. Barnhouse was correct . . . except in one minor detail. Prayer changes *me*. When you and I pray, *we* change, and that is one of the major reasons prayer is such a therapy that counteracts anxiety.

Charles R. Swindoll (SYG)

26

THE SIN OF ANXIETY

Do not be anxious about your life . . .   Matthew 6:25, RSV

Thousands of years ago the philosopher Seneca observed, "The mind that is anxious about the future is miserable." The only adequate solution to this anxiety is found in this admonition of Jesus recorded in Matthew 6. As soon as we have shifted our anxiety, along with our sins, to the waiting shoulder of our Savior, we have taken the path of perfect peace and quiet contentment, for our future is assured in His hands.

Peace of mind is the object most universally sought in the world today, by people of all ages. Many, after exhausting themselves in fruitless search, have ended life in a mental institution or by suicide.

Ian McLaren asks, "What does your anxiety do? It does not empty tomorrow, brother, of its sorrow: but ah! it empties today of its strength. It does not make you escape the evil: it makes you unfit to cope with it if it comes."

27

TEMPTATION

And lead us not into temptation, but deliver us from evil: For thine is the kingdom, and the power, and the glory, for ever. Amen.

Matthew 6:13

This petition is a prayer that we may never be called needlessly to meet temptation. Sometimes God wants us to be tried, because we can grow strong only through victory. We have a word of Scripture which says: "Blessed is the man that endureth temptation; for when he is tried, he shall receive the crown of life." Yet we ought never ourselves to seek any way of life in which we shall have to be exposed to the peril of conflict with sin. Temptation is too terrible an experience, fraught with too much danger, to be sought by us, or ever encountered save when God leads us in the path on which it lies. We must never rush unbidden or unsent into any spiritual danger. When God sends us into danger, we are under His protection; when we go where He does not send us, we go unsheltered.

John Burroughs, the naturalist, says that when a hawk is attacked by crows or kingbirds, he does not make a counterattack, but soars higher and higher in ever widening circles until his tormentors leave him alone.

J. R. Miller

28

SURPRISED BY JOY

Therefore I tell you, do not be anxious about your life. . . . But seek ye first his kingdom and his righteousness, and all things shall be yours as well.
Matthew 6:25,33, RSV

Have you ever seen an anxious person who also exuded a spirit of joy? Yet both Paul and Jesus admonished the early Christians to be joyful. I don't read that either teacher taught that Christians are to evidence a fearful or anxious spirit. One of the shades of meaning in the word "blessed" which prefaces each of the Beatitudes is this very concept: "Be joyful" (see the Amplified Bible).

Over and over again the New Testament tells us that the hallmark of the Christian life is to be a joyous spirit. How can we be joyful if our souls are riddled with anxiety and worry? This is the idea Jesus was seeking to convey here. Along with freeing us from the penalty of our sin at Calvary, Jesus also gave us the key to the marvelous freedom of the joyful spirit. This joy or happiness does not come to us because we make it the object of our pursuit. Rather, it is the byproduct of the Christian life. As C. S. Lewis so aptly put it, we are "surprised by joy" when we yield control of our lives to the Master. Joy doesn't come from desperate seeking—it comes as a result of self-surrender.

Stuart Briscoe

29

TRUE TRUST

Therefore I tell you, do not be anxious about your life, what you shall eat or what you shall drink, nor about your body, what you shall put on. Is not life more than food, and the body more than clothing?
Matthew 6:25, RSV

Again and again throughout His Word, our Lord exhorts us to avoid anxious care. Clearly, care, even though occasioned by real problems, is, if carried to excess, a sin in the sight of God. Again and again throughout Scripture God tells His children to cast all their cares upon Him.

The very essence of anxious care is a presumption on the creature's part that he is wiser than his Creator. Anxious care is in reality trusting ourselves to do what we cannot trust our Lord to do.

In reality, we try to think of those things which we fancy God has forgotten. We stagger about beneath a load which we have been unwilling to turn over to our Heavenly Load-bearer. This presumption on our part is plain disobedience to His commands and lack of belief in His Word.

More than this, however, anxious care often leads into acts of sin—forsaking God as Counselor and relying instead upon human wisdom. It is as if one were to go to a broken pump for water instead of going directly to the spring which provided the water for the pump.

On the other hand, if we cast our burden upon Him, cast each burden as it comes along upon Him, in simple faith, and if we are "careful for nothing" because He takes care of us, it will keep us in close communion with Him and strengthen us to meet every temptation. It was truly a wise man who said, "Thou wilt keep him in perfect peace whose mind is stayed (resting) on thee: because he trusteth in thee" (Isa. 26:3).

30

A SOURCE OF STRENGTH

Jesus said, Do not be anxious about tomorrow, for tomorrow will be anxious for itself. Let the day's own trouble be sufficient for the day.

Matthew 6:34, RSV

Perhaps more than anything this great teaching of Jesus is saying that we have a source of inner strength from God that can see us through present difficult times, but not to worry about the future, that when the time comes He will supply the needed strength.

In His great prayer the Master said, "Give us this day our daily bread" (Matt. 6:11). Never once did he tell us to pray for tomorrow's needs.

As we think of these promises and stand firm upon them, we should remember that our Lord does not say He will deliver us from effort, uncertainty, the strain of our jobs, or family and individual problems. He does promise a source of strength to help our human capabilities meet life head-on and victoriously regardless of what it may throw at us.

Harold Rogers

31

ONE DAY AT A TIME

Take therefore no thought for the morrow: for the morrow shall take thought for the things of itself. Sufficient unto the day is the evil thereof.

Matthew 6:34

This reason our Lord gives against anxiety for the future is that we have nothing to do with the future. God gives us life by days, little

May

single days. Each day has its own duties, its own needs, its own trials and temptations, its own griefs and sorrows. God always gives us strength enough for the day as He gives it, with all that He puts into it. But if we insist on dragging back tomorrow's cares and piling them on top of today's, the strength will not be enough for the load. God will not add strength just to humor our whims of anxiety and distrust. . . .

No one was ever crushed by the burdens of one day. We can always get along with our heaviest load till the sun goes down; well, that is all we ever have to do. Tomorrow? Oh, you may have no tomorrow; you may be in heaven. If you are here God will be here too, and you will receive new strength sufficient for the new day.

> One day at a time—but a single day,
>   Whatever its load, whatever its length;
> And there's a bit of precious Scripture to say
>   That according to each shall be our strength.

J. R. Miller

June

1

FOLLOWING JESUS

. . . A scribe came up and said to him, "Teacher, I will follow you wherever you go." And Jesus said to him, "Foxes have holes, and birds . . . have nests; but the Son of man has nowhere to lay his head."

Matthew 8:19, 20, RSV

The homelessness of Jesus is the source of his power over men! ". . . He hath no place to lay his head" (Matt. 8:20). Not in your ideology or mine. Not in your theology or mine. Not in your church or mine. "He hath no place to lay his head." He is not in the inn of black theology or white supremacy, either one. He is not in the inn of laissez-faire capitalism or the socialist state. He is not in the inn of the American dream or Soviet Russia's latest ten-year plan. He is outside all of these. And this is our salvation and our hope.

God did not come in Jesus Christ to ratify our judgments, to confirm our values, to help us fulfill our wishes. Rather, he came as one outside to bring the light of God to bear on all our strivings.

Ernest T. Campbell

2

THE STORMS OF LIFE

And, behold, there arose a great tempest in the sea, insomuch that the ship was covered with the waves: but he was asleep.

Matthew 8:24

Storms may arise even when we are in the plain line of duty. We should not be discouraged by the difficulty or trouble that comes, and conclude that we are in the wrong path. Christ's presence with His

June

disciples does not keep the storms away. There are no promises in the Bible that Christian people shall not meet trials. Religion builds no high walls about us to break the force of the winds. Troubles come to the Christian just as surely as to the worldly man. There are the storms of temptation; these sweep down with sudden and terrific power from the cold mountains of this world. Then there are storms of sickness, of disappointment and adversity, of sorrow, that make the waves and billows to roll over the soul.

On the Sea of Galilee travelers say that a boat will be gliding along smoothly over a glassy surface, unbroken by a ripple, when suddenly, without a moment's warning, a tempest will sweep down, and almost instantly the boat will be tossed in the angry waves. Thus many of life's storms come. Temptations come when we are not looking for them. So disasters come. We are at peace in a happy home. At an hour when we think not, without warning, the darling child we love so much lies dead in our arms. The friend we trusted, and who we thought could never fail us, proves false. The hopes cherished for years wither in our hands in a night, like flowers when the frost comes. The storms of life are nearly all sudden surprises. They do not hang out danger-signals days before to warn us. The only way to be ready for them is to be always ready.

J. R. Miller

3

THE TOUCH OF HIS HAND

Then he (Jesus) touched their eyes, saying, "According to your faith be it done to you."

Matthew 9:29, RSV

> In the still air the music lies unheard;
>   In the rough marble, beauty hides unseen:
> To wake the music and the beauty, needs
>   The master's touch, the sculptor's chisel keen.
>
> Great Master, touch us with Your skillful hand;
>   Let not the music that is in us die!

June

Great Sculptor, hew and polish us; nor let,
   Hidden and lost, Your form within us lie!

Spare not the stroke! Do with us as You will
   Let there be naught unfinished, broken, marred;
Complete Your purpose that we may become
   Your perfect image, O our God and Lord!

Horatius Bonar

4

HEALING IN A TOUCH

Then he touched their eyes and said, "According to your faith will it be done to you"; and their sight was restored.

Matthew 9:29–30, NIV

Where there is hurting—and that is everywhere—there is need for touching.

The wife of an associate of mine was visiting a nursing home with a group of carol singers. On the "disturbed" floor, she paused to take the hand of an elderly woman and hold it while she talked gently about Christmas, about the woman's neat appearance, about anything and everything. The woman could not talk, but with effort she slowly lifted to her lips the hand that held hers.

"She bit you!" the group leader said in dismay.

"No," my friend's wife replied, tears in her eyes. "She kissed me."

There *is* healing in a touch. Healing on both sides. Please don't keep your hands off.

Stan Mooneyham

5

THE SURRENDERED LIFE

You received without paying, give without pay.   Matthew 10:8, RSV

June

As Christians, we are commanded and challenged to give *ourselves*. And this must be a continuing process just as our growth in Christ is a continuing and constant forward movement. While still at Wheaton College, Jim Elliot wrote, "One does not surrender a life in an instant. That which is lifelong can only be surrendered in a lifetime." What a depth of spiritual wisdom for one who had just attained legal voting age. Many Christians *never* learn this lesson. As my life grows spiritually, my surrender of it to Christ must grow deeper and greater. And as I grow spiritually, my surrendered life becomes that much more valuable in God's program for His Church.

Sir Harry Lauder's only son was killed in World War I. Said he to a friend: "When a man comes to a thing like this, there are just three ways out of it—there is drink; there is despair; and there is God. By His grace, the last is for me!"

6 ────────────────

What to Do with Doubts

Now when John heard in prison about the deeds of the Christ, he sent word by his disciples and said to him, "Are you he who is to come, or shall we look for another?"

Matthew 11:2–3, rsv

Could this be the same John the Baptist who confidently presented Jesus as "the Lamb of God which taketh away the sin of the world"? John's prison experience must have caused him to doubt, but he expressed his doubt to the right Person—the Lord Jesus. And Jesus has a simple, unassailable answer, in essence, "What I am doing shows who I am." Every one of my doubts, and it is normal for me to doubt, is answered in the Person of Christ. My faith, if it is anchored in the Rock, may be shaken but it can never be uprooted! Remember John when you face doubts, and take your doubts to the same One!

English statesman and philosopher Francis Bacon, said on this subject: "If we begin with certainties, we shall end in doubt; but if we begin with doubts, and are patient in them, we shall end in certainties."

June

7

RESTING

Come unto me, all ye that labor and are heavy laden, and I will give you rest. Take my yoke upon you, and learn of me; for I am meek and lowly in heart: and ye shall find rest unto your souls. For my yoke is easy, and my burden is light.

Matthew 11:28–30

Once my hands were always trying,
Trying hard to do my best;
Now my heart is sweetly trusting,
And my soul is all at rest.

Once my brain was always planning,
And my heart, with cares oppressed;
Now I trust the Lord to lead me,
And my life is all at rest.

Once my life was full of effort,
Now 'tis full of joy and zest;
Since I took His yoke upon me,
Jesus gives to me His rest.

A. B. Simpson

8

KEEPING THE SABBATH

For the Son of man is lord even of the sabbath. Matthew 12:8, RSV

The Lord made this clear-cut statement to the strict Pharisees. They kept the sabbath, it is true, but not out of a spirit of love. These legalistic fault-finders had questioned the Lord and His disciples for their "unlawful" sabbath activities. Jesus' answer showed them that they had put the cart before the horse. If you do not live for the Lord because you love Him, your good and lawful life means nothing for eternity and little for today. But if you are motivated by love, even

June

your mistakes will be covered and your failures forgiven. If you love the Lord with your whole heart, you may confidently expect Him to show you how best to live on His special day.

The great evangelist of the last century, Dwight L. Moody, pointed to the importance of the sabbath when he said, "You show me a nation that has given up the Sabbath and I will show you a nation of decay."

9

FATHER'S PRAYER

The effectual fervent prayer of a righteous man availeth much.

James 5:16

When Father prays he doesn't use
  The words the preacher does;
There's different things for different days,
  But mostly it's for us.

When Father prays the house is still,
  His voice is slow and deep,
We shut our eyes, the clock ticks loud,
  So quiet we must keep.

He prays that we may be good boys,
  And later on good men;
And then we squirm, and think we won't
  Have any quarrels again.

You'd never think, to look at Dad,
  He once had tempers, too.
I guess if Father needs to pray,
  We youngsters surely do.

Sometimes the prayer gets very long
  And hard to understand,
And then I wiggle up quite close,
  And let him hold my hand.

I can't remember all of it,
  I'm little yet, you see;

June

But one thing I cannot forget,
My father prays for me.

Author Unknown

10

THE CARPENTER'S SON

Is not this the carpenter's son?   *Matthew 13:55*

All the wisdom of the world is mere child's play, yes, folly, compared with the knowledge of Christ. For what is more wonderful than to know and acknowledge the great, unspeakable mystery that the Son of God, the express Image of the Eternal Father, has taken our nature on Him and become in fashion as a man?

At Nazareth He must have helped His father build houses, for Joseph was a carpenter. Therefore Christ was called "the carpenter's son"; yes, Himself "the carpenter."

What will the people of Nazareth think of the Last Day, when they shall see Christ sitting in Divine Majesty, and may say to Him, "Lord, didst Thou not help build my house? How then camest Thou to this high glory?"

This, however, is the needful thing, that we Christians should with all diligence learn and know that the Son of God did so deeply humble Himself, was born so poor and in such a low estate, all on account of our sins; and that for our sakes He hid His majesty so long.

Martin Luther

11

THE ROCK OF AGES

And the king was sorry; but because of his oaths . . . he sent and had John beheaded in the prison.

Matthew 14:9–10, RSV

June

As we look at this tragic moment in history, we wonder why Jesus did not use His God-given power to release John the Baptist from prison. Instead, He sent John's disciples back to the prisoner with encouraging words about His own ministry, words which must have strengthened the Baptist's faith even in his last moments before his death at the hands of Herod. It is often difficult for us, with our finite understanding, to fathom the workings of an infinite God. John's death must have thrown his disciples into confusion, but it was the means God used to lead them into a saving knowledge of the Lord.

Our view of God must be something like the sailor in this story: A storm threw him upon a rock where he clung in fear for his life until the tide went down. Later a friend asked him, "Jim, didn't you shake with fear when you were hanging onto that rock?"

"Yes, but the rock didn't," was the significant reply. In our father God, Christ is the Rock of Ages.

12

PRAYING IN SUCCESS

And when he had dismissed the crowds, he went up on the mountain by himself to pray. When evening came, he was there alone.

Matthew 14:23, RSV

Philip Melanchthon, the devoted protégé of Martin Luther, put it this way: "Trouble and perplexity drive me to prayer, and prayer drives away perplexity and trouble."

It seems natural for us as Christians to pray *up* to success, but to cease praying *in* success. This wasn't true with Jesus. After one of His most striking miracles, that of feeding the five thousand, He felt an even greater need for prayer. As Jesus needed strength-giving time alone with His Father, we, too, need spiritual sustenance to help us live the victorious, overcoming life in the face of towering temptations and expanding evil. Also remember that in success the temptation to pride grows greater and greater. Humble dependence upon God in prayer, then, will put self in its proper place.

June

13

Out of the Cloud

A bright cloud overshadowed them.   *Matthew 17:5*

The cloud was a symbol of the Divine presence. One of the writers says the disciples were afraid as they saw the cloud come down over the Master and the heavenly visitants. God still comes to us often in thick clouds, and we are afraid, too. But the cloud meant no harm to the disciples. No cloud means any harm to a disciple when God is in the cloud; and always, if we only listen, we may hear words of love.

> Sorrow touched by love grows bright
> With more than rapture's ray;
> And darkness shows us worlds of light
> We never saw by day.

There are times when God's ways with us seem very hard, and we think disaster is coming to every fair prospect in our life. In all such hours we should remember that He who rules over all is the Son of God, our Friend and Savior; and our trust in Him should never doubt nor fear. What so staggered the disciples then we now see to have been the most glorious and loving wisdom. So in our sorest trials there are the truest wisdom and the richest love. Hereafter we shall know. It was out of the cloud that this voice came. Out of the clouds that hang over us come often the tenderest voices of divine love, the most precious disclosures of divine grace.

J. R. Miller

14

Successful Marriage

Do whatever God has told you.   *Genesis 31:16,* TEV

June

How blessed is the man whose wife says to him, "Do whatever God has told you," as was the case with Jacob here. Every Christian should be concerned that the one with whom he has taken or will take the marriage vow is one who is wholly committed to God's will. There is no alliance so troubling and discouraging as that of the consecrated Christian with the carnal unbeliever—yet, all too often, in this day of rapid courtships and hasty marriages people find themselves regretting at leisure a marriage they have formed in haste. This all-important step should never be taken thoughtlessly or hastily. Rather, the choice of a life's companion should be subjected to the scrutiny of God's Word and will, not an action taken hurriedly.

Someone has said, "A successful marriage requires falling in love many times, always with the same person."

15

Faith That Moves Mountains

For truly, I say to you, if you have faith as a grain of mustard seed, you will say to this mountain, "Move from here to there," and it will move; and nothing will be impossible to you.

Matthew 17:20, RSV

Just as Jesus' disciples seem to have been "playing around" as far as their depth of faith was concerned, you and I are often likewise guilty of "playing in the sand pile" when we should be "moving the mountain." We often hear of tremendous victories in the lives of other Christians, but we forget that there has been genuine work involved in achieving that victory. Jesus warned His disciples, "this kind does not go out except by prayer and fasting" (Matthew 17:21, MLB).

The kind of faith that moves mountains is a serious, realistic relationship to the God from whom this faith comes. Subject your faith to close examination to see if it measures up. As someone has said, "Faith does not demand miracles but it often accomplishes them." Another wise man put it this way: "Faith is not believing that God *can*, but that God *will!*"

HUMILITY DEFINED

Whoever humbles himself like this child, he is the greatest in the kingdom of heaven.

Matthew 18:4, RSV

Andrew Murray describes humility thus: "Humility is perfect quietness of heart. It is to expect nothing, to wonder at nothing that is done to me, to feel nothing done against me. It is to be at rest when nobody praises me, and when I am blamed or despised. It is to have a blessed home in the Lord, where I can go in and shut the door, and kneel to my Father in secret, and be at peace as in a deep sea of calmness, when all around is trouble."

Humility is an often overlooked virtue of the Christian life. Please notice, however, that it comes as an act of the *will* of the Christian. Humility is not a gift of God, as salvation is. I must humble myself by a conscious act of my will. All of us are susceptible to pride, regardless of our age. Because we are susceptible, we must be always on the alert for the subtle progress of pride in our lives. While God does not hand humility to us "on a silver platter," He does give us grace to discover it if we will yield ourselves to Him. Remember, too, that humility does not connote spinelessness or cowardice. Humility is merely living in the consciousness of our own unworthiness in the light of His righteousness—living a life *pleasing* to Him because it is *yielded* to Him.

17

THE OMNIPOTENCE OF CHRIST

All power is given unto me in heaven and in earth.   Matthew 28:18

Just think of what the disciples had learned to know of the power of Christ Jesus here on earth. And yet that was but a little thing as compared with the greater works that He was now to do in and through them. He has the power to work even in the feeblest of His servants with the strength of the almighty God. He has power even to use their apparent impotence to carry out His purposes. He has the power over every enemy and every human heart, over every difficulty and danger.

But let us remember that this power is never meant to be experienced as if it were our own. It is only as Jesus Christ as a living person dwells and works with His divine energy in our own heart and life that there can be a power in our preaching as a personal testimony. It was when Christ had said to Paul, "My strength is made perfect in weakness," that he could say what he had never learned to say before. "When I am weak, then am I strong." It is the disciple of Christ who understands aright that all the power has been entrusted to Him, to be received from Him hour by hour, who will feel the need and experience the power of that precious word: "Lo, I am with you always," the Almighty One.

Andrew Murray

18

SPIRITUAL RICHES

Jesus said . . . "It will be hard for a rich man to enter the kingdom of heaven."

Matthew 19:23, RSV

Edmund Burke said: "If we command our wealth, we shall be rich and free. If our wealth commands us, we are poor indeed."

What is the nature of true riches? The rich person whose *only* wealth is counted in *material* things is certainly poorer than the poor person who counts wealth only in spiritual things. "Money talks"— but not in eternity. The younger we are when we learn this lesson, the greater will be our spiritual enrichment. There is nothing evil about material things—the evil lies in our attitude toward these *things*. If we place primary importance upon the things of God, we need not worry about our material possessions standing in the way of our spiritual destination.

June

19

RICHES IN CHRIST

I am the God of Abraham, and the God of Isaac, and the God of Jacob?
God is not the God of the dead, but of the living.

Matthew 22:32

In this text Christ powerfully reminds His listeners of the resurrection of the dead; for if there were no hope of the resurrection of the dead, nor of another and better world after this short and miserable life, why does God offer to be our God, to give us all that is necessary and healthful for us, and in the end to deliver us out of all trouble, both temporal and spiritual? To what purpose is it that we heed His Word and believe in Him? What does it serve us that we sigh and cry to Him in our anguish and need, that we wait with patience for His comfort and salvation, for His grace and benefits which He shows us in Christ? Why do we praise and thank Him for the same? Why are we daily in danger, and suffer ourselves to be persecuted and slain for the sake of Christ's Word, which we teach and hold for our greatest treasure?

Because through His Word the everlasting and merciful God talks and deals with us concerning our future life, where we shall be when we depart from this life, and He gives unto us His Son, our Savior, who delivers us from sin and death, and has purchased for us everlasting righteousness, life, and salvation. Therefore we are sure that we do not die like the beasts that have no understanding; but that all who die in Christ shall through Him be raised again to everlasting life.

Martin Luther

20

PRAYER AND PEACE

And he arose.   *Mark 4:39*

June

Our Savior hears the prayers of His children. The roar of the storm He did not hear in His sound sleep; but the moment there was a cry from His disciples for help He instantly awoke. What a revelation of heart have we here! He is never asleep to His people when they call upon Him. Amid the wildest tumults of this world He ever hears the faintest cry of prayer. Nor is He ever too weary to listen to His children in distress.

We have another illustration of this same quickness to hear prayer in the hours of our Lord's sufferings on the Cross. His life was fast ebbing away. His own agony was intense beyond description. Around Him surged a storm of human passion. Curses fell upon His ear. But amid all this tempest of hate He was silent. To all these bitter insults and keen reproaches He answered not a word. Then amid the derisions and jeers of the multitude there broke a voice of prayer. It came from one of the crosses beside Him. It was the penitential cry of a soul—"Lord, remember me." And in all the tumult of the hour He heard this feeble supplication. In His own agony He gave instant answer. Doubt not that this Jesus always hears prayer. His love is ever on the watch, ready to catch the faintest note of human distress.

J. R. Miller

21

WE'VE BEEN ADOPTED!

This is my beloved Son: hear him.　　　　　　　　*Mark 9:7*

If the Father says, "This is my Son," observe the graciousness of our adoption! With such a Son the Lord had no need of children. He did not make us His children because He needed sons, but because we needed a father. The infinite heart of the Father was well filled by the love of the Only-begotten. There was enough in Jesus to satisfy the love of the divine Father, and yet He would not rest till He had made Him "the firstborn among many brethren." Herein we ought to admire exceedingly the grace of God. "Behold what manner of love the Father hath bestowed upon us that we should be called the sons of God." When a man is childless, and desires an heir, it may be that he adopts a child to fill the vacancy which exists in his house; but the heavenly Father had no such want, for He says, "This is my beloved Son." Our adoption is, therefore, not for His gain, but for ours: it is a matter of divine charity, arising out of the spontaneous love of God. Thanks be unto the Father evermore!

C. H. Spurgeon

22

Living Sacrifices

And if thy hand offend thee, cut it off: it is better for thee to enter into life maimed, than having two hands to go into hell, into the fire that never shall be quenched.

Mark 9:43

Our Lord had just come from the Mount of Transfiguration. The great scheme of the world's redemption was clear to His mind and heart, and His sacrificial death in Jerusalem called to Him. No lamb ever went to the altar more willingly than He; and with that fire of love burning in His heart He calls on all who love Him to present themselves living sacrifices, even though in the process they should be exposed to salt, with its searching sting, and fire, its consuming flame.

Of course, it is best to retain the precious members of our body in perfect purity and righteousness. They are not only natural, but most important assets to the working force of a successful life. No one has a right to perform this amputation unless it is the only alternative to death or uselessness. A skilled mechanic repairing a machine inadvertently caught his fingers in the machine, and found his arm being drawn between mighty rollers. Not a moment was to be lost; he caught up a hatchet lying near, and with a blow severed his arm at the elbow. He was just in time to save his life. Such hours come to us all. It may be a friendship not compatible with the high ideals of family life, or a habit, sapping our nervous energy, or a form of amusement. Whatever hinders us in our best moments must, if we cannot master it and compel it to keep within bounds, be yielded to the knife.

F. B. Meyer

June

23

A REBIRTH OF WONDER

Whosoever shall not receive the kingdom of God as a little child, he shall not enter therein.

Mark 10:15

What we need is a second childhood, a rebirth of wonder. We need to open out on the word made flesh. Perhaps on this storm-ridden day we should go home and read the Nativity stories in a new translation, or lie on the floor and listen to the sweep of Handel's *Messiah,* or open ourselves to the Nativity in art or drama until the color and dynamic of God's coming gets through. . . .

"The theological student, fresh out of theological school, asked the little man, 'And what is your ultimate concern?' The little man, having also read Tillich, replied with a sigh, 'That the Ultimate be concerned about me.'"

The Ultimate is, and this is the wonder and glory of it all.

Ernest T. Campbell

24

DISCIPLING AND DISCIPLES

And Jesus, looking upon him, loved him, and said to him, "You lack one thing; go, sell what you have, and give to the poor, and you will have treasure in heaven; and come, follow me." At that saying his countenance fell, and he went away sorrowful; for he had great possessions.

Mark 10:21–22, RSV

I have seen more character in the faces of some men in breech-cloths than I have seen in the faces of some church elders. In those sun-browned, wind-burned faces I have seen the same yearnings, the waiting friendliness, even the ready humor as that in the faces of my own compatriots. It has occurred to me that one of the troubles with a lot of our so-called "discipling" is that we don't take time to look into faces. We think we are the only ones with anything worth sharing, and that we can do it by rote or by writ.

In the story of the rich young ruler, there is an interesting progression. We are told in Mark 10, "Jesus beholding him loved him, and said unto him. . . . " The order is not insignificant. First, Jesus beheld him, then loved him, then spoke to him.

Often we get it backwards, figuring that saying is the place to start. Sometimes we follow our words with loving and occasionally with "beholding," but I fear that much of what passes for witnessing operates sight unseen, touch untouched, and feelings unfelt.

As if it all took place in a vacuum.

Sad.

That is why I think one who has been a Christian six months or sixty years had better think twice and pray often before sitting someone down willy-nilly for discipling.

For a discipler is someone who not only teaches. But who listens. And looks. And loves.

Stan Mooneyham

25

Accomplish the Impossible

And Jesus looking upon them saith, "With men it is impossible, but not with God: for with God all things are possible."

Mark 10:27

Doing the impossible! A songwriter put it this way: "God specializes in things thought impossible." He made it rhyme with rivers that were "uncrossable," but God's power extends far beyond crossing rivers without bridges or boats. And He has always been in the business of doing the impossible. Jeremiah said of Him, "Ah Lord God! behold, thou hast made the heaven and the earth by thy great power and stretched out arm, and there is nothing too hard for thee" (32:17).

God's power over the impossible was expressed by Jesus in other contexts as well. In this passage of Mark, He was referring to the impossibility of the rich man being saved. In Matthew 17:20, He is talking about the all-conquering strength of faith when He says: "If you have faith as a grain of mustard seed, you will say to this mountain, 'Move hence to yonder place, and it will move; and nothing will be impossible to you'" (RSV). In reference to His own blasting of the barren fig tree, Jesus said, "Truly I say to you, if you have faith and never doubt, you will not only do what has been done to the fig tree, but even if you say to this mountain, 'Be taken up and cast into the sea,' it will be done. And whatever you ask in prayer, you will receive, if you have faith" (Matt. 21:21, RSV).

These verses reveal that the tremendous power resident in God is available to the one who believes in Him. His Spirit takes up residence in the believer, and through that all-powerful Spirit the believer himself can accomplish the impossible.

26

FORGIVENESS IS A TWO-WAY STREET

When you stand praying, forgive, if ye have aught against any: that your Father also which is in heaven may forgive you your trespasses.
Mark 11:25

Forgiveness is a two-way street. If we ask it for ourselves, then we must accord it to others, regardless of the circumstances. We pray, "Forgive us as we forgive. . . ." This phrase was embodied in the model prayer so that we would not only pray it but meditate on it every day. From first to last, forgiveness was high on the Master's priority list. Even on the cross he taught it. Still it is one of the most difficult lessons we have to learn.

Wherever there are people, there are differences, personality conflicts, resentment, and even bitterness. We are prone to argue that we are justified in feeling as we do, but with the coming of our Lord the law of an eye for an eye was abolished and in its place was forgiveness. Vengeance is no longer ours. It is a responsibility we leave to God. To forgive is to forget, to start anew. Difficult, yes, but not impossible with his help and example. This is the only way to over-come evil and estrangement. It is the way of the cross.

Harold Rogers

27

THE WAY OF PEACE

. . . to guide our feet into the way of peace.   Luke 1:79

A great many people think that the Christian life is hard and unpleasant, that it is a rough and steep road; but truly it is a way of pleasantness and peace. The only really happy people in this world are those who are following Christ along the way of redemption. They have their share of troubles, disappointments, sorrows; but all the time in the midst of these they have a secret peace of which the world knows nothing. There are paths in the low valleys, among the great mountains, which are sweet pictures of the Christian's way of peace. High up among the peaks and crags the storms sweep in wild fury, but on these valley-paths no breath of tempest ever blows. Flowers bloom and springs of water gurgle along the wayside, and trees cast their grateful shadow, and bird-songs fill the air. Such is Christ's "way of peace" in this world.

J. R. Miller

28

MERCY

Through the tender mercy of our God; whereby the dayspring from on high hath visited us.

Luke 1:78

What would we ever have done if God had not been merciful? There could never have been a soul saved in this world. There is a story of a man who dreams that he is out in an open field in a fierce

June

driving storm. He is wildly seeking a refuge. He sees one gate over which "Holiness" is written. There seems to be shelter inside, and he knocks. The door is opened by one in white garments; but none save the holy can be admitted, and he is not holy. So he hurries on to seek shelter elsewhere. He sees another gate, and tries that; but "Trust" is inscribed above it, and he is not fit to enter. He hastens to a third, which is the palace of Justice; but armed sentinels keep the door and only the righteous can be received. At last, when he is almost in despair, he sees a light shining some distance away, and hastens toward it. The door stands wide open, and beautiful angels meet him with welcomes of joy. It is the house of Mercy, and he is taken in and finds refuge from the storm, and is hospitably entertained.

Not one of us can ever find a refuge at any door save the door of Mercy. But here the vilest sinner can find eternal shelter; and not mere cold shelter only, for God's mercy is "tender." We flee for refuge, and find it. Strong walls shut out all pursuing enemies, and cover us from all storms. Then, as we begin to rejoice in our assurance, we learn that we are inside a sweet home, and not merely a secure shelter. Our refuge is in the very heart of God; and no mother's bosom was ever so warm a nest for her own child as is the divine mercy for all who find refuge in it.

J. R. Miller

29

GOD'S HANDS ARE BIGGER

Give, and it will be given to you. A good measure, pressed down, shaken together and running over, will be poured into your lap. For with the measure you use, it will be measured to you.

Luke 6:38, NIV

As a boy I grew up in the South. My idea of the ocean was so small that the first time I saw the Atlantic I couldn't comprehend that any little lake could be so big! The vastness of the ocean cannot be understood until it is seen. This is the same with God's love. It passes knowledge. Until you actually experience it, no one can describe its wonders to you.

A good illustration of this is a story my wife told me about a man in China who was selling cherries. Along came a little boy who loved cherries; and when he saw the fruit, his eyes filled with longing. But he had no money with which to buy cherries.

The kindly seller asked the boy, "Do you want some cherries?" And the little boy said that he did.

The seller said, "Hold out your hands." But the little boy didn't hold out his hands. The seller said again, "Hold out your hands," but again the little boy would not. The kind seller reached down, took the child's hands, filled them with two handfuls of cherries.

Later, the boy's grandmother heard of the incident and asked, "Why didn't you hold out your hands when he asked you to?" And the little boy answered, "His hands are bigger than mine!"

God's hands, also, are bigger than ours!

Billy Graham (TA)

30

ALONE WITH GOD

And it came to pass, as he was alone praying. . . .   Luke 9:18
He departed again into a mountain himself alone.   John 6:15

Man needs God. God made him for Himself, to find his life and happiness in God alone.

Man needs to be alone with God. His fall consisted in his being brought, through the lust of the flesh and the world, under the power of things visible and temporal. His restoration is meant to bring him back to the Father's house, the Father's love and fellowship. *Salvation means being brought to love and to delight in the presence of God.*

Man needs to be alone with God. Without this, God cannot have the opportunity to shine into his heart, to transform his nature by His

June

divine working, to take possession and to fill him with the fullness of God.

Man needs to be alone with God, to yield himself to the presence and the power of His holiness, of His life, and of His love. Christ on earth needed it; He could not live the life of a Son here in the flesh without at times separating Himself entirely from His surroundings and being alone with God. How much more must this be indispensable to us!

Andrew Murray

July

1

THE SECRET IS SURRENDER

Instead, seek his kingdom, and these things shall be yours as well.
Luke 12:31, RSV

In the concerns which cause stress, we desperately need a gospel which is passionately our own. When the stress of worry wilts our confidence, we have a blessed opportunity to turn it into *eustress.* Surrender is the key. The yield point in the stress comes when we are refortified by the knowledge that nothing can separate us from the Lord and that he will use everything. Relinquishment of a concern is the point when we receive our actual infusion of the Lord's power. Mahalia Jackson found that secret in the stress of mounting concerns: "God can make you anything you want to be, but you have to put everything in his hands."

My experience goes even further. God can make you all that *he's planned* for you to be when you trust everything to his loving care. To take all that we are and have and hand it over to God may not be easy, but when it is done, the world has one less candidate for misery. Luther said, "I have held many things in my hands, and I have lost them all, but whatever I have placed in God's hands, that I still possess." The stress of our worries finally opens our hearts to hear the Lord's command: "Seek first the kingdom of God."

Lloyd J. Ogilvie (AHA)

2

PRAYER BRINGS POWER

. . . his disciples said unto him, Lord, teach us to pray, as John also taught his disciples.
Luke 11:1

July

Without doubt these disciples were praying men. He had already talked to them a great deal about prayer. But as they noticed how large a place prayer had in His life, and what some of the marvelous results were, the fact came home to them with great force that there must be some fascination, some power, some secret in prayer, of which they were ignorant. This Man was a master in the fine art of prayer. They really did not know how to pray, they thought.

How their request must have delighted Him! At last they were being aroused concerning the great secret of power. May it be that this simple recital of His habit of prayer may move everyone of us to get alone with Him and make the same earnest request. For the first step in learning to pray is to pray. "Lord, teach me to pray." And who can teach like Him? Prayer brings power. Prayer is power. The time of prayer is the time of power. The place of prayer is the place of power. Prayer is tightening the connections with the divine dynamo so that the power may flow freely without loss or interruption.

S. D. Gordon

I know not by what methods rare,
But this I know, God answers prayer;
I know that He has given His word,
Which tells me prayer is always heard,
And will be answered, soon or late;
And so I pray, and calmly wait.

Author Unknown

3

ASKING FOR THE HOLY SPIRIT

If ye then, being evil, know how to give good gifts unto your children: how much more shall your heavenly Father give the Holy Spirit to them that ask him?

Luke 11:13

Christ had just said (v. 9), "Ask, and it shall be given you. . . ." God's giving is inseparably connected with our asking. He applies this especially to the Holy Spirit. As surely as a father on earth gives bread to his child, so God gives the Holy Spirit to them that ask Him. The whole ministration of the Spirit is ruled by the one great law: *God must give, we must ask.* When the Holy Spirit was poured out at Pentecost with a flow that never ceases, it was in answer to prayer. The inflow into the believer's heart, and His outflow in the rivers of living water, ever still depend upon the law: Ask, and it shall be given.

The story of the birth of the church in the outpouring of the Holy Spirit, and of the first freshness of its heavenly life in the power of that Spirit, will teach us how *prayer on earth,* whether as cause or effect, *is the true measure of the presence of the Spirit of heaven.* As little as the power of the Spirit could be given without Christ sitting on the throne, *could it descend without the disciples on the footstool of the throne.* For all the ages the law is laid down here at the birth of the church, that whatever else may be found on earth, the power of the Spirit must be prayed down from heaven. The measure of believing, continued prayer will be the measure of the Spirit's working in the church. Direct, determined, definite prayer is what we need.

Andrew Murray

4

KNOCKED DOWN, BUT NOT OUT!

We are persecuted, but we never have to stand it alone; we may be knocked down but we are never knocked out! Every day we experience something of the death of Jesus, so that we may also know the power of the life of Jesus in these bodies of ours.

2 *Corinthians 4:9–10, J.B. Phillips*

There is an interesting parallel here with the sport of boxing: a boxer is not out even though he may have been knocked down. Neither is a child of God "out," even though he may have been knocked down. On this day commemorating the Declaration of Independence, it is profitable to think of the *attitude* of our courageous forefathers.

In the game of life, a defeated attitude leads to defeat. On the other

July

hand, a positive outlook leads to victory. Think back to the passage of the children of Israel through the Red Sea. Seemingly they had been "knocked down" and there was no way to escape—until they looked up and received God's direction to go through the Red Sea. You and I as Christians must reach this point of yieldedness to God's direction before God can lead us according to His purpose and plan.

As the poet Henry Van Dyke puts it:

> Lord, the newness of this day
> Calls me to an untried way:
> Let me gladly take the road,
> Give me strength to bear my load,
> Thou my guide and helper be—
> I will travel through with Thee.

5

THE DISPENSATION OF THE SPIRIT

How much more shall your heavenly Father give the Holy Spirit to them that ask him?

Luke 11:13

The writer of a little book on prayer tells us he has learned through his own experience the secret of a better prayer life, and would gladly pass on that which has helped him. As he was meditating on prayer, the great thought came with power, that we are now living in the dispensation of the Spirit. He says: "I feel deeply that in this time of the working of the Holy Spirit, all we may do in God's service is of little value unless it is inspired by the power of the Holy Spirit. This brought me to the well-known, precious, and inexhaustible text, 'How much more shall your heavenly Father give the Holy Spirit to them that ask him?' "

As I thought on this truth, I felt anew that the main thing for each of us is to receive, afresh from the Father, the Holy Spirit for our daily needs and daily life. Without this we cannot please God, nor can we be of any real help to our fellowmen. This brought the further thought that our prayers, if they are to raise our lives to fulfill God's purpose, must have their origin in God Himself, the highest source of power.

146

July

Water cannot rise higher than its source. And so it happens that if the Holy Spirit prays through us, as human channels or conduits, our prayers will be answered by the divine working in ourselves and in others. "I believe more and more," says the writer, "that the Christian life of each one of us depends chiefly on the quality of our prayers and not on the quantity."

Andrew Murray

6

Whose Slave Am I?

(Jesus said): "A man's life does not consist in the abundance of his possessions."

Luke 12:15, NIV

The things which own us don't have to be just cars, houses, and lands. Ideas, convictions, and prejudices can possess our minds and attitudes. These are the worst kind of tyrants, I've discovered. They make us judgmental, quarrelsome, schismatic. They drive us to all kinds of spiritual excesses under the disguise of "truth." Often they are simply human biases, yet they demand uncritical loyalty even at the sacrifice of relationships.

When that happens, we no longer hold our convictions; they hold us. And they—at least, mine—tenaciously resist being tested against other, possibly higher, priorities. Though we may possess such ideas in abundance, they do not necessarily contribute to abundant living. Instead, our ideas restrict us, imprison us and subtract from our liberty as sons and daughters of God.

Giving another person space in which to grow—and make mistakes while growing—requires greater trust than the more possessive of us are willing to give. Our unbending bias simply will not allow it. Yet there can be no spiritual reality for us or them without the risk.

Jesus was right. Life is more than meat and drink, houses and land, convictions and prejudices. It is also peace and contentment, love and trust, skipping and dancing.

Stan Mooneyham

July

7

His Forever

For where your treasure is, there will your heart be also.   Luke 12:34

Our Savior told of a man who, in plowing his field, heard his plowshare chink against buried treasure, and the man hastened to sell all that he had to buy the field. In speaking thus, He pictured Himself as well as us. He found us before we found Him. The treasure is His people, to purchase whom He gave up all that He had, even to His throne (Matt. 13:44). "But you are a chosen race, a royal priesthood, a holy nation, God's own people, that you may declare the wonderful deeds of him who called you out of darkness into his marvelous light" (1 Pet. 2:9 RSV).

Where his treasure is, there is a man's heart. If it is in ships on the treacherous sea, he tosses restlessly on his bed, concerned for its safety. If it is in fabrics, he guards against moths; if it is in metal, against rust and thieves. Is Christ less careful with His own? Does He not guard with equal care against all that would deteriorate our value in His esteem? Need we fear the thief? Will not our Lord keep us that the evil one shall not touch us (Matt. 6:19–20)?

God's treasure is His forever. "They shall be mine, says the Lord of hosts, my special possession . . ." (Mal. 3:17, RSV). He will hold His own, as men cling to a treasure.

F. B. Meyer

8

Excuses

Jesus replied: "A certain man was preparing a great banquet and invited many guests. At the time of the banquet he sent his servant to tell those who had been invited, 'Come, for everything is now ready.' But they all alike began to make excuses. . . ."

Luke 14:16–17, NIV

I will go, when _____. I will give, after _____. I will obey, but first _____.

The excuses sound like those of an anxious cluster of otherwise patriotic American citizens called for jury duty! The point of Jesus' story was that when we put God on hold while we do what we think is more needful, he may not be there when we finally get back to him. He just may have hung up and called somebody else, which is exactly what the supper host did.

"Later" is one of our most used words. In Spanish, it is the concept of "mañana"—tomorrow, any tomorrow, but certainly not today. Then I will see what I can do.

In the Old Testament we hear much about offerings of first fruits. God's portion came right off the top. Nowadays we are more likely to be known by and for our last fruits. Today's churches may be hesitant to talk about first fruits, but Uncle Sam is not. He is very tough about his claim upon first fruits, which he calls the "withholding tax." He's pretty sure that's the only way he will ever get what he requires. God, too, I think.

Near the hold button on the hotline to heaven, these classic words would be appropriate:

> If not I, who?
> If not here, where?
> If not now, when?

Stan Mooneyham

9

SALT FOR SOCIETY

Salt is good: but if the salt have lost his savor, wherewith shall it be seasoned?

Luke 14:34

It is a sad comment on society that it needs salt. You do not think of salting life, but death, to keep it from rotting. This, then, was Christ's verdict on the society of His time. It had enjoyed the benefit of all the Greek intellectualism and Roman government could effect, and yet was like a carcass on the point of putrefaction. But is not this the state of all society, from which religion is banished, or where it has become a system of rites and dogmas? Go into any large factory or financial institution, or a tavern, where men feel able to talk freely, and there is too often the smell of the barnyard in the stories that pass around, and the jokes that pass from lip to lip.

Here is something that each of us can do. Perhaps we cannot speak: we cannot shed a far-reaching ray of light to warn from the black rocks, and guide to harbor: we seem shut away from the scenes of important Christian activity, but we can be good salt, checking the evil which would otherwise infect the air of our world, and breed disease in young and healthy lives.

F. B. Meyer

10

THE JUSTIFIED PRODIGAL

But when he came to himself he said, " . . . I will arise and go to my father, and I will say to him, 'Father, I have sinned . . . I am no longer worthy to be called your son, treat me as one of your hired servants.' " . . . . But while he was yet at a distance, his father saw him and embraced him and kissed him.

Luke 15:17–20, RSV

The Prodigal Son returns expecting to be rejected. Instead he is accepted by his father, who stands in the story as a paradigm of God. God loves us. We can hear that a thousand times on a quiet Sunday morning to little effect. But when that point comes where we suffer the unspeakable pain of rejection, let the words come back, let the truth come home—God loves us! He accepts us as we are. Our striving is only to accept his acceptance of us.

The most neglected and misunderstood teaching of the Christian faith is the doctrine of justification by faith. The term itself is heavy and the explanations usually given to interpret it heavier still. What justification by faith essentially means is this: that our acceptance with God is not the goal but the starting point of the Christian life. Our acceptance with God is not a thing to be hoped for, or worked for, or striven for. It is what God has already done for us in Christ. Faith is our acceptance, in humility and gratitude, of God's acceptance of us.

Ernest T. Campbell

11

THE SENSE OF GOD'S PRESENCE

And from his fullness have we all received grace upon grace.
John 1:16, RSV

God does not show favoritism among His children. There is no God-given grace provided to one of our fellow Christians that is not available to us as well. Have we made the mistake of thinking that God could not bring forth another Luther, Calvin, Spurgeon, or Graham in this day? God has already done His part—it only remains for someone to say with Moody, "By God's grace, I will be that man."

Real dedication to the cause of Christ was exemplified in the life of George Frederic Handel. When Handel composed the *Messiah*, for twenty-three days he completely withdrew from the world. So wrapped up was he in his music that the food brought to him was often left untouched. Describing his feeling when the "Hallelujah Chorus" burst on his mind, Handel said, "I did think I did see all Heaven before me and the great God Himself."

Do I have that great sense of God's presence?

12

ON PRIDE OF POSSESSIONS

(John the Baptist said:) He who comes from above is above all; he who is of earth belongs to the earth, and of the earth he speaks; he who comes from heaven is above all.
John 3:31, RSV

When a man of huge possessions was boasting to his friend of the largeness of his estate, Socrates desired him to bring a map of the

July

earth, and to point out Attica therein. When this was done (although not very easily, as it was a small country), he next desired Alcibiades to point out his own estate therein. When he could not do this, it was easy to observe how trifling the possessions were in which he so prided himself, in comparison to the whole earth.

How applicable is this to the present case! Does anyone value himself on his earthly possessions? Alas, what is the whole globe of earth to the infinity of space? A mere speck of creation. And what is the life of man, yes, the duration of the earth itself, but a speck of time, if it be compared to the length of eternity? Think of this: Let it sink into your thought, till you have some conception, however imperfect, of that

> Boundless, fathomless abyss,
> Without a bottom or a shore.

John Wesley

13 ————————————

TRUE WORSHIP

But the hour cometh, and now is, when the true worshipers shall worship the Father in spirit and in truth: for the Father seeketh such to worship him.
John 4:23

How shall we secure the favor of this great God? How, but by worshiping him in spirit and in truth; by uniformly imitating him we worship, in all his imitable perfections, without which the most accurate systems of opinions, all external modes of religion, are idle cobwebs of the brain, dull farce, and empty show? Now, God is love: Love God, then, and you are a true worshiper. Love mankind, and God is your God, your Father, and your Friend. But see that you deceive not your own soul; for this is not a point of small importance. And by this you may know: If you love God, then you are happy in God; if you love God, riches, honors, and the pleasures of sense are no more to you than bubbles on the water: You look on dress and equipage, as the tassles of a fool's cap; diversions, as the bells on a fool's coat. If you love God, God is in all your thoughts, and your

152

whole life is a sacrifice to him. And if you love mankind, it is your one design, desire, and endeavor, to spread virtue and happiness all around you, to lessen the present sorrows, and increase the joys, of every child of man; and, if it be possible, to bring them with you to the rivers of pleasure that are at God's right hand forever more.

John Wesley

14

THE NATURE OF TRUE WORSHIP

God is spirit and those who worship him must worship in spirit and in truth.
John 4:24, RSV

What does it mean to "worship in spirit"? Should I interpret this verse to mean it is unnecessary to worship in the company of others? Does this verse mean that I do not need church attendance to worship completely? It is true, the child of God may worship anywhere. Worship is an attitude of heart, not a place. But, just as I must depend on others for physical food, I must also depend on others for a well-rounded spiritual diet. There are times when I can worship in solitude, perhaps surrounded by nature's beauty. But I will miss much of the blessing of communion with God if I never share this blessing with fellow Christians.

Dr. D. James Kennedy has an insightful comment on this whole idea: "Most people think of the church as a drama, with the minister as the chief actor, God as the prompter, and the laity as the critic. What is actually the case is that the congregation is the chief actor, the minister is the prompter, and God is the critic!"

15

LEANING TOO LATE

When he heard that Jesus was come out of Judea into Galilee, he went unto him, and besought him that he would come down, and heal his son: for he was at the point of death.

John 4:47

July

The trouble in his home sent this man to Christ. Perhaps he never would have gone at all if it had not been for his son's illness. Many of those who went to Christ in the olden days were driven by their distress of heart. They tried everything else first, and then at the last moment they hurried to Jesus. The same is true in these days. Many persons who have never prayed before have gotten down upon their knees by the bedside of their sick and dying children and cried to God on their behalf. Many persons have first been sent to God by their own troubles. It was not until the prodigal was in sore want, and every other resource had been exhausted, that he said he would arise and go to his father. Many sinners never think of Christ until they are in despair under the scene of guilt. Not until they see the storm of wrath gathering do they seek the shelter of the Cross. But what a comfort it is that even going so late to the Savior He does not reject or cast away those who come!

J. R. Miller

16

Our Daily Bread

Jesus then took the loaves, and when he had given thanks, he distributed them to those who were seated; so also the fish, as much as they wanted.
John 6:11, RSV

The Lord who came to save His people was sensitive to His people's hunger. In the presence of the supreme need the smaller need was not forgotten. He knows the body as well as the soul. He ministers to the transient as well as the eternal. That is ever the characteristic of true kingliness; it has a kingly way of doing the smaller things. I can measure my own progress toward spiritual maturity by the importance I place on spiritual principles. "He that is faithful in that which is least, the same also is great."

The Lord is not oppressed by the multitude of His guests. "He himself knew what he would do." We need not jostle one another for His bounty. We shall not crowd one another out. "There is bread enough and to spare."

Even in the material realm this is true, and everybody would have his daily bread if the will of the Lord were done. There is no stinginess in the divine Host! It is the greed of the guests which mars the satisfaction of the feast.

Finally, notice how carefully the Lord of glory gathered up the fragments (v. 12). Our infinitely wealthy Lord does not throw things away. He does not waste bread. Can He afford to lose a soul? "He goes out after that which is lost until He finds it!"

J. H. Jowett

17

THE GROUND OF OUR CONFIDENCE

No man is able to pluck them out of my Father's hand.   John 10:29

The safety of God's children does not rest on their own attainments, or even their own fidelity and decision, but on the power of God. However great may be the strength of our enemies, or however subtle their efforts to overcome the believer, it is our comfort to know that no man can pluck them out of the Father's hand. It implies that we are being held by God Himself.

"Hold me up, and I shall be safe" (Ps. 119:117). "I will uphold thee with the right hand of my righteousness" (Isa. 41:10). Here is the secret of our comfort: not what we are or hope to become, but what God is.

"I know whom I have believed, and am persuaded that he is able to keep that which I have committed unto him against that day" (2 Tim. 1:12). The ability of our God is the ground of our confidence. Greater is He who is with us than all those who can be against us.

"I am persuaded," said the apostle, "that neither death, nor life, nor angels, nor principalities, nor powers, nor things present, nor things to come, nor height, nor depth, nor any other creature, shall be able to separate us from the love of God, which is in Christ Jesus our Lord" (Rom. 8:38–39).

Evan H. Hopkins

July

18

INVITATION TO FREEDOM

If the Son therefore shall make you free, ye shall be free indeed.
John 8:36

Jesus' invitation to freedom is not based on rules and regulations, but on relationships—with God and with other men. Paul reminds us that if we are led by the Spirit we are not under the law. The Spirit is the source of life. "The harvest of the Spirit is love, joy, peace, patience, kindness, goodness, fidelity, gentleness, and self-control. There is no law dealing with such things as these" (Galatians 5:22–23). Relationship, not rules and regulations, is the key.

The truth is that we experience freedom when "God's thing" becomes "our thing" and when "our thing" is seen in the context of the whole family of man. While Christ's invitation is a declaration of independence from behavior-centered, belief-centered, performance-oriented religion—in which human controls and arbitrary legalism make us slaves—it is also a declaration of interdependence. It is not a freedom to indulge my appetites and desires or to give license to my "lower nature," but to become "servants to one another in love."

Maxie Dunnam

19

QUALITY LIVING

Your father Abraham rejoiced . . . to see my day; he saw it and was glad.
John 8:56, RSV

Abraham had a marvelous spiritual vision. Before he died he saw more than 1800 years into the future—without the aid of astronomical instruments. I wonder about my spiritual vision. Is my contact with God close enough and vital enough—or am I dwelling "afar off"? Genesis 25:8 says of Abraham, " at a ripe old age, after a long and full life, Abraham expired." That epitaph should be written over the life of every Christian. The length of life is not the important thing—it is the quality of it that counts! And quality grows out of a right relationship to God. In the knight's pledge from the "Idylls of the King" Tennyson calls for quality living: "Live pure, speak truth, right the wrong, follow the king; else wherefore born?"

This is a tremendous motto for the Christian. He must live a pure life, which means a holy one; he certainly must speak the truth and do what he can to right conditions that are wrong. Above all, he must follow the King, the Lord Jesus Christ, the author and finisher of our faith. That's quality living.

20

OUR GREAT SHEPHERD

He calleth his own sheep by name, and leadeth them out.   John 10:3

These words suggest three precious thoughts: First, there is divine *possession*. We who believe in Him belong to the Good Shepherd. We are His own sheep. He has set His mark upon us. He distinguishes His own in a way that they can never be confounded in His sight with those that are of the world.

Then, second, there is divine *knowledge*. He says, "I. . . know my sheep" (v. 14). He has intimate acquaintance with them, so that He can call each sheep by name.

Third, there is divine *guidance*. "He leadeth them out." He goes before them. Each day he leads them into fresh pastures; into new paths of service, into untrodden fields of patient following. If the Shepherd knows His sheep, it is that the sheep may know their Shepherd. "I know my sheep, and am known of mine." This mutual knowledge implies sympathy, love, community of nature (1 John 4:7; Gal. 4:9; 1 Cor. 8:3; John 17:3, 25).

Christ first took our nature that we might afterwards receive His. He who laid down His life for us, now gives His life to us.

                                                    Evan H. Hopkins

July

21

PASTURES OF PLENTY

By me if any man enter in, he shall . . . find pasture.   *John 10:9*

In our common life in this world, if we are faithfully following Christ, we are continually in fields of rich pasture. Christ never leads us into any places in which there is nothing to feed us. Even in the hot plains of trial and sorrow there is food. We sometimes think there is only barrenness in our toilsome life, filled with temptations, cares and sacrifices; but the Good Shepherd is ever with us, and there is always pasture.

Thus the whole world is a rich field when Jesus leads His flock. If any Christians are not well fed, it is because they will not feed. The trouble must be that they do not hunger for spiritual food. The saddest thing in this world is not a passionate cry for bread, but a soul that has no hunger. Many souls die in the midst of the provision made by the Good Shepherd, not for want of food, but for want of appetite.

J. R. Miller

In the Christian life many of the places we may be led into will appear to us as dark, dangerous, and somewhat disagreeable. But it simply must be remembered that He is there with us in it. He is very much at work in the situation. It is His energy, effort, and strength expended on my behalf that even in this deep, dark place are bound to produce a benefit for me.

W. Phillip Keller

22

THE GOOD SHEPHERD

I am the good shepherd; I know my sheep and my sheep know me—just as the Father knows me and I know the Father—and I lay down my life for the sheep.

John 10:14–15, NIV

Note four things about Jesus the Good Shepherd. He *owns* the sheep: they belong to Him. He *guards* the sheep: He never abandons them when danger is near. He *knows* the sheep, knows them each by name and leads them out (v. 3). And *He lays down His life* for the sheep, such is the measure of His love.

How thankful we should be, weak, wandering, and foolish as we are, that we have such a shepherd. Let's learn to keep close to Him, to listen to His voice, and follow Him. This is especially important in times of spiritual peril. Jesus tells us not to be misled by the voice of strangers (v. 5), and there are many strange voices being heard in the religious world of our day. Don't be deceived by false teachers. Jesus is the Good Shepherd: trust Him. And Jesus is the door of salvation: enter by that door and you will find the full and abundant life He came to bring (vv. 7–10).

Billy Graham (TA)

23

Hearing with the Heart

My sheep hear my voice and I know them and they follow me and I give them eternal life. . . .

John 10:27–28, rsv

How does one test one's growth in the Lord? This verse gives the answer—by one's ability to *hear* the Lord's voice. This, in essence, is spiritual discernment. Never before in the history of the world and the church has spiritual discernment been more greatly needed! A further test of growth in grace is found in the next phrase, "And they follow me." Discernment must be followed by obedience and each successive experience in following sharpens the spiritual ears of the disciple. Conversely, disobedience and refusal to follow tends to dull the spiritual ear. It is significant that the last phrase, "And I give them eternal life," follows in the wake of listening obedience.

A great English preacher, Frederick William Robertson, thus linked obedience and eternity: "It has been well remarked, it is not said that after keeping God's commandments, but in keeping them there is great reward. God has linked these two things together, and no man can separate them—obedience and peace."

O that every child of God might have a listening and obedient heart!

24

God's Timing

On his arrival, Jesus found that Lazarus had already been in the tomb four days.

John 11:17, NIV (read verses 17–44)

Divine delays do not indicate abandonment. It must have felt that way to Mary and Martha, and looked that way to the disciples, who theorized that Jesus was putting his personal safety ahead of the needs of his friend Lazarus. But Jesus had his own purpose in waiting. Not only was the raising from death a greater evidence of God's glorious power, it created a greater joy and wonder in the hearts of Jesus' loved ones.

There are times when we can only appreciate the Lord, and only appreciate the good things that he gives us, when our blessings stand in contrast with suffering.

God's timing, even when the waiting is long and painful, never suggests abandonment but always promises a greater joy to follow.

Larry Richards

25

Life on the Line

Peter said unto him, Lord, why cannot I follow thee now? I will lay down my life for thy sake.

John 13:37

Peter was well aware that some disaster was about to break in on his Master's life. He could not but realize that the One whom he loved

July

with passionate devotion was passing into the shadow of a great eclipse; and the fear that they were likely to be permanently separated was unendurable. In the ardor of that hour he so minimized the thought of death, and all that it might involve, that he went out to court its dangers. Better to die once and now, he thought, if the Master is to die, than live long years apart from Him.

We have all felt that way! If only we could be freed once and for all from the clinging pain we must endure, or that thorn in the flesh, that gnawing, stinging problem from which there seems to be no deliverance. A sudden departure would be so much easier than the long waiting which now confronts us. It is far easier to rush into the battle, where the excitement and fever may be trusted to make us oblivious to pain, than to wait through long, icy nights on sentry duty. But this may be God's call for us.

F. B. Meyer

26

BALM FOR TROUBLED HEARTS

Let not your heart be troubled. *John 14:1*

It was a time of the deepest grief and the sorest sorrow for the disciples when Jesus said, "Let not your heart be troubled." Not only were they to lose their best Friend, but they were to lose Him in the saddest way—by death in the shame of the cross. Nor was that all of their sorrow. They had hoped He was the Messiah; now that hope was gone. They were in utter desolation—in a starless midnight. Surely there *could* be no comfort for such grief as theirs, they thought that night, as with breaking hearts they sat there in the darkness.

Yet right into the midst of this despairing grief came the words, "Let not your heart be troubled." Let us never say, therefore, that there is any, even the bitterest grief, for which there is no possible comfort. No matter how dark the night is, Christ can put stars into our sky, and bring a glorious morning after the darkness. There *is* comfort for Christ's disciples in the most hopeless grief. We have but to look forward a few days to see the sorrow of these men turned to

161

blessed joy. So it always is. However we may grieve, there is never any reason why we should lose our peace.

J. R. Miller

27

I Don't Know about Heaven

And when I go and prepare a place for you, I will come again and will take you to myself; that where I am there you may be also.

John 14:3, RSV

Not many specifics. An earlier verse speaks of "many mansions" in the Father's house, but whether of marble or stucco or aluminum siding, I do not know. Or care.

We also don't know how we shall spend out time (talk about a "terrestrial" concept!) in heaven, what we shall look like, how we shall get around, how we shall relate to others including our loved ones, what we shall wear. Such things Jesus does not tell in nearly the detail that some of his present-day spokesmen presume to offer. On earth, he did tell his followers not to be concerned about what they should eat and drink and put on, and the advice would seem to be at least as applicable to heaven. What satisfied me is the assurance "that where I am there you may·be also." If he is there, that's good enough for me. If I'm with him, what better place to be, even if I cannot begin to define "place" or have a floor plan in advance?

Stan Mooneyham

28

Knowing God

He that hath seen me hath seen the Father.

John 14:9

God may be truly and experientially known through the Lord Jesus Christ Who is none other than the eternal Word become flesh, the very Deity incarnate in our humanity, the "Lamb slain from the foundation of the world," the only but all-sufficient Redeemer, Reconciler and Restorer of men to God. In Him alone, in Him directly and heart-satisfyingly, we may know the Creator-Spirit of the universe and hold fellowship with Him as our heavenly Father. Our Lord Jesus said, "I am the way, the truth and the life: no man cometh unto the Father but by Me." Later He added, "This is life eternal, that they may know thee the only true God and Jesus Christ, whom thou has sent."

J. Sidlow Baxter

The face of Christ does not indeed show us everything, but it shows us the one thing we need to know—the character of God. God is the God who sent Jesus.

P. Carnegie Simpson

29

PRAYER IN THE NAME OF CHRIST

Whatsoever ye shall ask in my name, that will I do, that the Father may be glorified in the Son.

John 14:13

How wonderful the link between our prayers and Christ's glorifying the Father in heaven. Much prayer on earth brings Him much glory in heaven. Little prayer means, as for as we are concerned, little glory to the Father. What an incentive to much prayer, to unceasing intercession. Our prayer is indispensable to the glorifying of the Father.

So deep was the desire of Christ in the last night that His desciples should learn to believe in the power of His name, and to avail themselves of His promise of a sure and abundant answer, that we find the promise repeated seven times over. He know how slow men are to believe in the wonderful promise of answer to prayer in His name. He longs to rouse a large and confident faith, and to free our prayer from every shadow of a doubt, and to teach us to look upon intercession as the most certain and most blessed way of bringing glory to God, joy to our own souls, and blessing to the perishing world around us.

Andrew Murray

30

PRAYING IN JESUS' NAME

If ye shall ask any thing in my name, I will do it.　　　*John 14:14*

We need do but one thing: tell God about our condition, about our faith, our solicitude, and our worldly and prayer-weary heart; and then pray in the name of Jesus.

We can come before God and say to Him, "I do not have a right to pray because I do not have a truly prayerful heart. Much less do I have any right to receive what I ask for. Everything which Thou seest in my heart, O Lord, is of such a nature that it must close Thy heart to me and all my supplications. But hear me, not for my sake, nor for the sake of my prayer, and not even because of my distress, for it is a result of my own sinfulness. But hear me for Jesus' sake."

We have learned that to pray in the name of Jesus is the real element of prayer in our prayers.

It is the helpless soul's helpless look unto a gracious Friend.

O. Hallesby

Prayer is releasing the energies of God. For prayer is asking God to do what we cannot do.

Charles Trumbull

31

SMOOTH STONES

Peace I leave with you; my peace I give to you; not as the world gives do I give to you. Let not your hearts be troubled, neither let them be afraid.
John 14:28, RSV

July

When someone says "Pebble Beach," I think of the classic golf tournament held there every year. But I've learned more about the area and there's a vital spiritual lesson to be learned from it.

At Pebble Beach, the waves dash with a ceaseless roar and thunder among the stones on the shore. The pounding waves toss and grind the stones together and throw them against the jagged cliffs. Day after day and night after night the wearing down of the stones continues without a pause. People come from all over the world to gather the beautiful polished stones to use as ornaments on mantles.

Close to Pebble Beach lies a towering cliff which breaks the force of the dashing waves. In this quiet cove, sheltered by the cliff, an abundance of stones has accumulated. Because they have been sheltered from the turmoil and beating of the waves, they remain rough and angular and devoid of beauty.

Life may buffet us with billows of sorrow and trouble but these only serve to polish and refine us. They give us the opportunity to prove the genuineness of the Savior's comforting, healing words, "Lo, I am with you always, to the close of the age" (Matt. 28:20, RSV).

August

1

ALIVE IN JOY

Because I live you will live also.   *John 14:19*, RSV

You can't beat that, can you! To be alive in joy is to accept the living Christ into our lives, to receive his forgiveness, to give ourselves to his lordship—receiving joy for our sadness, hope for our despair, courage for our anxiety, sympathy for our sorrow, meaning for our boredom, love for our hostility, forgiveness for our guilt, life for our death. "I came that you might have life and have it abundantly" (John 10:10).

There is no living but *now* living. The eminent editor Norman Cousins said, "The editorial page is an exercise in present tense." Christian living is an exercise in present tense—packing all the resources and experiences of the past and all the hope and possibilities for the future into living now.

Maxie Dunnan

2

A BRAVE AND VIGOROUS PEACE

Peace I leave with you, my peace I give unto you: not as the world giveth, give I unto you.

John 14:27

If we are really Christ's, then back into the very bosom of the Father where Christ is hidden, there will He carry us. We too shall look out and be as calm and as independent as He is. The needs of men will touch us just as keenly as they touch Him, but the sneers and gibes of men shall pass us by as they pass by Him and leave no mark on His unruffled life and spirit.

166

August

For us, just as for Him, this will not mean a cold and selfish separation from our brothers. We will be infinitely closer to their real life when we separate ourselves from their outside strifes and superficial pride, and know and love them truly by knowing and loving them in the Lord.

This is the power and progress of true Christianity. It leads us into, it abounds in peace. It is a brave, vigorous peace, full of life, full of interest and work. It is a peace that means thoroughness, that refuses to waste its force and time in little superficial tumults which come to nothing, while there is so much real work to be done, so much real help to be given, and such a real life to be lived with God. That peace, His peace, may Jesus give to us all.

Phillips Brooks

3

ABIDING IN CHRIST

Abide in me, and I in you. John 15:4

Dear child of God, you have often meditated on this blessed passage. But do you not feel how much there is still to learn if you are to have Christ's almighty power working in you as He would wish you to have? The great need is to take time in waiting on the Lord Jesus in the power of His Spirit until the two great truths get complete mastery of your being: As Christ is in God—this is the testimony from heaven; as the branch is in the vine—this is the testimony of all nature: the law of heaven and the law of earth combine in calling to us: "Abide in Christ." "He that abideth in me, bringeth forth much fruit." Fruit, more fruit, much fruit, is what Christ seeks, is what He works for, is what He will assuredly give to the soul who trusts Him.

To the feeblest of God's children Christ says: *Ye are in Me.* "Abide in me. Ye shall bear much fruit." To the strongest of His messengers He still has the word, there can be nothing higher: "Abide in me, and ye shall bear much fruit." To one and all the message comes: Daily, continuous, unbroken abiding in Christ Jesus, is the one condition of a life of power and of blessing. Take time and let the Holy Spirit so

August

renew in you the secret abiding in Him that you may understand His meaning: "These things have I spoken unto you that my joy might remain in you, and that your joy might be full."

Andrew Murray

4

CHRIST'S LOVE TO US

As the Father hath loved me, so have I loved you: continue ye in my love.
John 15:9

Think of what Christ says: "As the Father hath loved me"—what a divine, everlasting, wonderful love! "Even so have I loved you." It was the same love with which He had loved the Father and that He always bore in His heart, which He now gave into the hearts of His disciples. He yearns that this everlasting love should rest upon us, and work within us, that we may abide in it day by day. What a blessed life! Christ desires every disciple to live in the power of the self-same love of God that He Himself experienced. Do you realize that in your fellowship with Christ in secret or in public, you are surrounded by and kept in this heavenly love? Let your desire reach out to this everlasting love. The Christ with whom you desire fellowship longs unspeakably to fill you with His love.

Andrew Murray

5

BEARING FRUIT

Abide in me, and I in you.
John 15:4

Notice the order of this twofold abiding. The condition of having the Lord dwelling in us is that we ourselves should be dwelling in Him. We must abide in Him if we would have Him abiding in us. The whole chapter sets forth the deep and mysterious truth of the soul's union with Christ. There is a union of life and there is a union of will. Fellowship cannot be known unless the latter, as well as the former, is a reality in our experience.

Another point we must remember is declared in this chapter: Christ is not the root or the stem only; He is the whole vine. He says, "I am the vine." So that what Christ is, covers every branch and every leaf and every tendril of the whole plant. Remember, Paul in another place designates the name "Christ" as given to the whole body (see 1 Cor. 12:12).

The believer is to abide in Christ as the branch abides in the vine. The function of the branch is to maintain connection with the stem, to receive the life-sap at one end and to bear the fruit at the other. The branch cannot *produce* the fruit—its responsibility is to *bear* it.

Evan H. Hopkins

6

TRY LOVING

This is my commandment, that you love one another as I have loved you.
John 15:12, RSV

Only recently have I had any appreciation of what it cost God to love me and I am beginning to see people in a totally different light. It is not a bright light. There is a softness about the light beneath the cross. Photographers know how important shadows and angles are. When I compare my passport picture with the touched up one my mother has on her dresser, it's like looking at two different people. Yes, shadows and angles do a lot to soften people. When we look at people in the light of the cross, we find it casts a shadow across the faults of others, their weaknesses, their stupidities, their dullness, their petty ways—and most mercifully, we find God's love and forgiveness broad enough to cover all of our transgressions and shortcomings as well as theirs.

Not only do we change, but also the people around us change when

August

we start loving them in this revolutionary way. If you want to get along with people, you can. Try loving them, We can never be the same, once we start giving out the love of God.

Betty Carlson

7

DIVINE COMFORTER

But when the Comforter is come, whom I will send unto you from the Father, even the Spirit of truth, which proceedeth from the Father, he shall testify of me: And ye shall bear witness, also because ye have been with me from the beginning.

John 15:26–27

Paul magnified God the Son as being just as consoling as God the Father: "Now our Lord Jesus Christ himself (who) hath given us everlasting consolation and good hope through grace . . ." (2 Thess. 2:16).

His comforting presence and consoling words and works permeate the Gospels, where He is found breaking up funerals, drying tears, raising the dead, healing lepers, casting out devils, dying for a world of sinners lost and ruined by the fall. What a divine Comforter He was—and ever *is!* One of His beatitudes reads, "Blessed are they that mourn; for they shall be comforted" (Matt. 5:4). The afflicted woman, diseased for twelve years, was one who knew, experientially, what it was to be comforted by Him. Touching the hem of His garment, she was healed. After she identified herself to Jesus, He greatly encouraged her by saying, "Daughter, be of good comfort; thy faith hath made thee whole" (Matt. 9:22), and a—

> Peace that passeth all understanding,
> With gladness filled her soul.

Herbert Lockyer

> Be with me when no other friend
> The mystery of my heart can share;

August

And be Thou known, when fears transcend,
By Thy best name of Comforter.

Rawson

8

God's Plan

We must obey God rather than men.　　　　　　　*Acts 5:29*, RSV

Without question the unplanned life is a tragedy. God has made
His plan for us; we should make our plans to conform to His. We
plan everything else—our education, our homes, our household duties, our social affairs. The captain of the ship moves by chart; the
mountain climber employs a guide; the tourist follows his map or
guidebook. The architect plans his house in every detail before he
starts work. The painter plans his picture and every stroke of the
brush is full of meaning. But too often the life itself is unplanned. The
Bible tells us of a foolish man who began building a house without
having counted the cost, and the house was a failure—it was never
completed. Do we want to imitate that man? It is most unwise to leave
God out of our planning.

A. T. Rowe

9

Living in Love

*This is my commandment, that you love one another as I have loved you.
Greater love has no man than this, that a man lay down his life for his
friends.*

John 15:12–13, RSV

The goal of human nature is to be fully human. The glory of Christ
is a person fully alive, reaching full potential, recreated in his image.
Whatever we do to escape our humanness ends up in some form of
inhumanity. Selfishness and self-centeredness make us less than the

August

human beings our Lord intended us to be. The only way to change human nature is to remove the distortions which keep us from true humanness. Our fallen nature is in rebellion against our Creator. We seek to run our own lives with no center of control. This results in the pride, anger, hostility, and competitiveness which are signs of inhumanity. When Christ takes hold of a life, he makes the person more human. It is the devil's game to try to convince us that we should try to escape our humanity. Treeness is the purpose of a tree; the glory of a rose is roseness. And what is the glory of a person? It is wholeness of personhood: a healed, released, loved, and loving person. What we call change in human personality is really liberating that person from those things which cause him or her to be inhuman. True humanness is the result of allowing Christ to love us, daring to love ourselves, and creatively loving others as gifts from him.

Lloyd J. Ogilvie (AHA)

10

Footprints in the Sand

If the world hates you, keep in mind that it hated me first. If you belonged to the world, it would love you as its own. As it is, you do not belong to the world, but I have chosen you out of the world. That is why the world hates you.

John 15:18–19, NIV

There is no need to be depressed over the trials we have to suffer or through fear of persecution. As Christians, I think we sometimes tend to forget that we have a companion in our struggles. It reminds me of a story printed by Ann Landers in her column and repeated across the country in various media:

> One night I dreamed I was walking along the beach with the Lord. Many scenes from my life flashed across the sky. In each scene I noticed footprints in the sand. Sometimes there were two sets of footprints, other times there was only one.
> This bothered me because I noted that during the low periods of my life, when I was suffering from anguish, sorrow, or defeat, I could see only

one set of footprints, so I said to the Lord, "You promised me, Lord, that if I followed you, you would walk with me always. But I have noticed that during the most trying periods of my life there has been only one set of footprints in the sand. Why, when I have needed you most, have you not been there for me?"

The Lord replied, "The times when you have seen only one set of footprints, my child, is when I carried you."

Billy Graham (TA)

11

THE PRE-EMINENT CHRIST

He will glorify me, for he will take what is mine and declare it to you.
John 16:14, RSV

During the brilliant Victorian days in England, when those two great preachers were at their zenith—Parker at the City Temple and Spurgeon at the Metropolitan Tabernacle—the fashion for visitors in London was to hear Parker on Sunday morning and Spurgeon at night. An American visitor followed this procedure. His morning comment was, "My! what wonderful oratory" His evening comment was, "Oh, what a wonderful Savior!" Dear Spurgeon!—with him it was Jesus, Jesus, JESUS, all the time. And that is *always* the distinguishing trait when the Holy Spirit is filling a person or a ministry. The saintly old Dr. F.B. Meyer used to say, "In all real believers Jesus is *present.* In some He is not only present, but *prominent.* In others (all too few) He is not only present and prominent, He is *pre-eminent.*" I wonder which of those three categories you and I belong too—present? or prominent? or pre-eminent?

J. Sidlow Baxter

12

THE CRUCIBLE OF GOD

They said to (Peter), "Are not you also one of his disciples?" He denied it and said, "I am not."
John 18:25, RSV

August

Could this be the same disciple who was surnamed "the rock" by the Lord Himself? Could this be the same Peter who, unafraid, preached to the scribes and Pharisees on the day of Pentecost? The Lord Jesus must have looked deep into Peter's heart beyond the weak human shell which would yield and break, down to the rocklike core of courage which would eventually stand the test. How encouraging it is to think upon Peter when we ourselves become discouraged in our own weakness and failure, for in Peter we have an object lesson of what the Lord can do with even the weakest of men. Once a little maid could make Peter tremble—but in the crucible of God, Peter's character was formed and fashioned until he could courageously die a martyr's death, unafraid and completely victorious in Christ.

Peter persevered—and as Spurgeon once remarked, "By perseverance the snail reached the ark!"

13

THE OBJECT LESSON

Carrying his own cross, he went out to The Place of the Skull (which in Aramaic is called Golgotha). Here they crucified him, and with him two others—one on each side and Jesus in the middle.

John 19:17–18, NIV

My friend and associate, Cliff Barrows, told me this story about bearing punishment. He recalled the time when he took the punishment for his children when they had disobeyed. "They had done something I had forbidden them to do. I told them if they did the same thing again I would have to discipline them. When I returned from work and found that they hadn't minded me, the heart went out of me. I just couldn't discipline them."

Any loving father can understand Cliff's dilemma. Most of us have been in the same position. He continued with the story: "Bobby and Bettie Ruth were very small. I called them into my room, took off my belt and my shirt, and with a bare back, knelt down at the bed. I made them both strap me with the belt ten times each. You should have heard the crying! From them, I mean! They didn't want to do it. But I told them the penalty had to be paid and so through their sobs and tears they did what I told them."

Cliff smiled when he remembered the incident. "I must admit I wasn't much of a hero. It hurt. I haven't offered to do that again, but I never had to spank them again, because they got the point. We kissed each other when it was over and prayed together."

In this infinite way which staggers our hearts and minds, we know that Christ paid the penalty for our sins, past, present, and future. That is why He died on the cross.

Billy Graham (TA)

14

WITH ONE ACCORD

They were all with one accord in one place. . . . And they were all filled with the Holy Ghost. . . .

Acts 2:1, 4

A wrestler gathers up his whole strength and counts upon every member of his body doing its very utmost. In an army at war, with its millions of soldiers, each detachment not only throws its whole heart into the work it has to do, but it is ready to rejoice and take new courage from every example of the bravery and enthusiasm of the far-distant members of the one great army. And is not this what we need in the church of Christ, such an enthusiasm for the King and His kingdom and such a faith in His purpose that His name will be made known to every human being? Should not our prayers rise up every day, with a large-hearted love that grasps the whole body of Christ and pleads for the power of the Holy Spirit on all its members, even to the very weakest?

The strength unity gives is something inconceivable. The power of each individual member is increased to a large degree by the inspiration of fellowship with a large and conquering host. Nothing can so help us to an ever-larger faith as the consciousness of being one body

August

and one spirit in Christ Jesus. It was as the disciples were all with one accord in one place on the Day of Pentecost that they were filled with the Holy Spirit. United prayer brings the answer to prayer.

Andrew Murray

15

Standing Where the Fire Has Been

Since we have now been justified by his blood, how much more shall we be saved from God's wrath through him!

Romans 5:9, NIV

An old preacher in England, who had lived on the American prairies in his youth, was involved in street corner evangelism in the small towns and villages. He attracted an audience with his Wild-West stories describing how the Indians had saved their wigwams from prairie fires by setting fire to the dry grass adjoining their settlement. "The fire cannot come," he explained, "where the fire has already been. That is why I call you to the Cross of Christ."

He continued his graphic analogy by explaining, "Judgment has already fallen and can never come again!" The one who takes his stand at the Cross is saved forevermore. He can never come into condemnation, for he is standing where the fire has been. The saved person is in God's safety zone, cleansed by the blood of Christ.

Billy Graham (TA)

16

Your Inheritance

And now, brethren, I commend you to God, and to the word of his grace, which is able to build you up, and to give you an inheritance among all them which are sanctified.

Acts 20:32

August

When an immigrant first received the title deed of the broad lands made over to him in the far West, he had no conception of what had been conveyed to him by the government. And though acres vast enough to make an English county were in his possession—rich and loamy soil, stored with mines of ore—yet he was not sensibly the richer. For long days he traveled toward his inheritance and presently pitched a flimsy shanty upon its borders. But even though he had reached it, many years would pass before he could understand its value, or compel it to minister to his need.

Child of God, your estate has been procured at the cost of blood and tears; but you do not buy it! Its broad acres have been made over to you by deed of gift. They became yours in the counsel chamber of eternity, when the Father gave Himself to you in Jesus. And they became yours in fact, when you were born at the foot of the cross. As soon as your eyes were opened to behold the crucified Lord, you became all unconsciously heir to the length, breadth, depth, and height of God.

F. B. Meyer

17

I'm Yours, God

Wherefore, O King Agrippa, I was not disobedient to the heavenly vision. . . .

Acts 26:19, RSV

Remember the story of Paul's conversion experience? God struck down the fiery Pharisee as he traveled the Damascus road. Paul's question was, "Who are you, Lord?" (Acts 9:5). From there, men led him into the city, where he stayed in a house for three days. The great ministry of the apostle then unfolds in the succeeding chapters.

Had it been most of us on the road to Damascus, I imagine our question would have been, "Lord, what do you want me to *do?*" We'd rather jump into action than define our relationship. However, somewhere in our growing commitment to Jesus Christ we need to settle the question of being versus doing.

While pondering that question, a phrase from an old love song filtered through my mind: "I'm yours to command." That's the place to start.

I'm yours, God. I'm here. Activities grow out of that. But we start with simply acknowledging who we are and who God is.

A newspaper item I read recently told of a wealthy man who owns homes in California, New York, and Florida. He keeps each home fully staffed. Employees must be ready on three hours' notice to provide total service, including a full-course meal. For the employees of the house in Florida, which he visited less than three weeks last year, this means days and weeks of simply being there, staying ready for action at his command.

As we think of the realm of guidance we need to realize that *presence* precedes *guidance*. God wants to direct our lives and make them useful. But our lives have to be his first.

T. Cecil Meyers

18

ASSURANCE, NOT APPREHENSION

And we know that in all things God works for the good of those who love him, who have been called according to his purpose.

Romans 8:28, NIV

The Scriptures confirm that sometimes God does give direct guidance by the Holy Spirit. But if not, he does not allow "wrong" choices to go unredeemed. It can't be otherwise. If not, who would be willing to choose when faced by two paths at a fork in the road? We would be paralyzed with fear of making the wrong choice. Or having finally made a choice, we would live always with the agonizing possibility that the other path might have been better.

So in grace, God redeems the choices of his children. That is what grace is—undeserved favor. God does not coerce me, manipulate me, or violate my will. He does not play from a stacked deck. He respects the powers which he created within me. As one who loves him and is called according to his purpose, I am free to choose and God elects my choice to be right.

All of which says to me, "Love God, relax, and get on with the business of living!" The principle that God is sovereign over not only my life but my choices liberates me to live with assurance instead of apprehension that I may blow it.

Stan Mooneyham

19

PERSONALIZED FORGIVENESS

Blessed are they whose inquities are forgiven, and whose sins are covered. Blessed is the man to whom the Lord will not impute sin.

Romans 4:7–8

Our days are wintry, frigid and forlorn, no promise of the life and warmth of spring, until we become personally aware of God's forgiveness. To know that "God so loved the world that he gave his Son" is different from knowing that he loves *me* so much that he gave his Son. It's not enough to know with my mind that God forgives men their sins; I must experience his forgiveness of my sins.

We may be cut off from this experience by one of two mindsets. Like Simon, we may be conscious of no need for forgiveness. Or, we may be so conscious of our sins, so overcome by their power, that we see no hope. We can't accept God's love and forgiveness "for such a worm as I."

Those of the first mindset need to hear again Paul's emphasis on the universality of sin: "All have sinned and come short of the glory of God" (Rom. 3:23). Even Jesus said, "There is none good save God." We fool ourselves into thinking that our religious performance will justify us before God. Jesus' parable to Simon erases the line between *righteous* and *sinners*. . . . Yet even in exposing Simon's true situation, Jesus didn't condemn. . . .

Those of the second mindset—"I'm so sinful and so unworthy,

God can never accept me"—need to hear and receive the great promises of the gospel. "The saying is sure and worthy of full acceptance, that Christ Jesus came into the world to save sinners" (1 Tim. 1:15, RSV). "It is not the healthy that need a doctor, but the sick; I have not come to invite virtuous people, but to call sinners to repentance" (Luke 5:31, NEB). "But God shows his love for us, in that while we were yet sinners Christ died for us" (Rom. 5:8, RSV).

Maxie Dunnam

20

THE HUMAN DILEMMA

I do not understand my own actions. For I do not do what I want, but I do the very thing I hate . . . I delight in the law of God, in my inmost self, but I see in my members another law at war with the law of my mind and making me captive to the law of sin which dwells in my members.

Romans 7:15, 22–23, RSV

Here was the graphic conflict between the different I's within. Yet Paul is certain that we can reduce that conflict, that we can bring our different selves into harmony through the Holy Spirit. "Live your whole life in the Spirit and you will not satisfy the desires of your lower nature. For the whole energy of the lower nature is set against the Spirit, while the whole power of the Spirit is contrary to the lower nature. Here is the conflict, and that is why you are not free to do what you want to do. But if you follow the leading of the Spirit, you stand clear of the Law" (Gal. 5:16–18, *Phillips*).

Paul knew what modern psychologists know: we are *many selves*. Our name is "legion" or "mob." We grow in wholeness as we recognize these many selves and bring them into harmony by allowing Christ to be Lord of them all. Christ as Lord of our lives becomes the center around which our many selves move in concert. . . .

When we recognize that we are more than one person, we can begin to identify the various aspects of ourselves, gain some objectivity, and begin to bring these different aspects into harmony around the Lordship of Christ. This is what Paul was saying when he wrote to the

Galatians, "The life I now live is not my life, but the life which Christ lives in me" (Gal. 2:20, NEB).

Maxie Dunnam

21

THE HIGHEST JOY

By whom also we have access by faith into this grace wherein we stand, and rejoice in hope of the glory of God.

Romans 5:2

Confident hope breeds inward joy. The man who knows that his hope of glory will never fail him because of the great love of God, of which he has tasted, that man will hear music at midnight; the mountains and the hills will break forth before him into singing wherever he goes. Especially in times of tribulation he will be found "rejoicing in hope of the glory of God." His profoundest comfort will often be enjoyed in his deepest affliction, because then the love of God will specially be revealed in his heart by the Holy Ghost, whose name is "the Comforter." Then he will perceive that the rod is dipped in mercy, that his losses are sent in fatherly love, and that his aches and pains are all measured out with gracious design. In our affliction God is doing nothing to us which we should not wish for ourselves if we were as wise and loving as God is. O friends! You do not want gold to make you glad, you do not even need health to make you glad; only get to know and feel divine love, and the fountains of delight are unsealed to you—you are introduced to the highest joy!

C. H. Spurgeon

22

THE SEEKING CHRIST

God, sending his own Son in the likeness of sinful flesh and for sin, he condemned sin in the flesh, in order that the just requirement of the law might

181

August

be fulfilled in us, who walk not according to the flesh but according to the spirit.

Romans 8:3–4, RSV

Christ became obedient unto death in order to condemn sin on behalf of the whole human race. He tasted death of the most cruel sort. He fulfilled every detail of the law and thus removed every obstacle in the path of God's forgiveness of sin. He was in every sense the perfect Lamb of God. In mankind's long quest for God, Jesus is the climax. Jesus is God revealed to man. We learn of the nature of God as we know Jesus. What kind of God does Jesus reveal? D. M. Baillie, in his book *God Was in Christ*, says that Jesus reveals "a seeking God, whose very nature is to go the whole way into the wilderness in quest of man." The New Testament teaches that man is reconciled to God through Jesus Christ. "God was in Christ reconciling the world to himself" (2 Cor. 5:19).

It was in the cross that the Son of God became also the Son of man, taking upon himself what is ours and transferring to us what is his, "so that what is his by nature becomes ours by grace." John Calvin says that Jesus Christ acted as a mediator who "had to restore us to divine favor so that children of men could become children of God." In Jesus Christ God provides the means whereby his ceaseless, life-giving power is perpetuated and the means of creation is revealed. A new life and a new nature is offered mankind through the person of Christ.

Frank H. Crumpler

23

BLESSED

Likewise the Spirit also helpeth our infirmities: for we know not what we should pray for as we ought: but the Spirit itself maketh intercession for us with groanings which cannot be uttered.

Romans 8:26

182

August

He prayed for strength that he might achieve;
He was made weak that he might obey.
He prayed for wealth that he might do greater things;
He was given infirmity that he might do better things,
He prayed for riches that he might be happy;
He was given poverty that he might be wise.
He prayed for power that he might have the praise of men;
He was given infirmity that he might feel the need of God.
He prayed for all things that he might enjoy life;
He was given life that he might enjoy all things.
He has received nothing that he asked for—all that he hoped for;
His prayer was answered—he was most blessed.

Author Unknown

24

Praying Hands

For God is my witness, when I serve with my spirit in the gospel of his Son, that without ceasing I mention you always in my prayers. . . .
Romans 1:9, rsv

While I cry to God that I want to pray, I seem to have a lag in my soul that doesn't want to! But as I look back over my life, I see that all the significant, lasting things that have happened have come about through prayer. May God keep me at it!

A fine surgeon and I were having lunch some time ago, and he said to me, "You know, I had a surgery to do that was very delicate. This surgery had been attempted twice before, and it hadn't been successful. I brought in famous people to help me with it. But the thing that made the difference," he said, "was that that morning my wife and I held hands, and we prayed together for that surgery. We asked God to help me and to guide my hands. And it was just marvelous! I was 'way beyond myself.' The surgery was a wonderful success."

And then he said to me, "I don't know why I haven't prayed more often." And all I could do was agree with him.

Peter Deyneka, that famous missionary to the countries surround-

August

ing Russia, says in his accented English, "No prayer, no power; little prayer, little power. Much prayer, much power!"

Raymond C. Ortlund

25

HOPE IN THE FACE OF FATE

And we know that in all things God works for the good of those who love him, who have been called according to his purpose.

Romans 8:28, NIV

When his tired, bruised body began to weaken under the load, the apostle Paul said in triumph, "We know that if the earthly tent we live in is destroyed, we have a building from God, an eternal house in heaven, not built by human hands" (2 Cor. 5:1).

The world called him foolish for his belief that men could become partakers of eternal life through faith. But he jutted out his chin and said exultantly, "I know whom I have believed, and am convinced that he is able to guard what I have entrusted to him for that day" (2 Tim. 1:12).

Every one of these triumphant affirmations rings with the note of hope and the assurance of life immortal. Though the Christian has no immunity from death and no claim to perpetual life on this planet, death is to him a friend rather than a foe, the beginning rather than the end, another step on the pathway to heaven rather than a leap into a dark unknown.

Billy Graham (TA)

26

THE HISTORY OF HOPE

That we through patience and comfort of the scriptures might have hope. . . . The God of hope fill you with all joy and peace in believing, that ye may abound in hope, through the power of the Holy Ghost.

Romans 15:4, 13

A powerful message comes from Ecclesiastes 9:11: "The race is not to the swift, nor the battle to the strong, nor bread to the wise, nor riches to the intelligent, nor favor to men of skill; but time and chance happen to them all"(RSV). Can you believe that? Those with Ph.D.s and those who are smart and who run fastest aren't always going to make it. But you and I who have been passed by in education or skills or money or physical advantages can have something that the Spirit of God can work with—and that's hope. Hope that God gives us about what is and what can yet be.

What can be? I think Teilhard de Chardin in *On Love* said it best, "Some day after we have mastered the winds, the waves, the tides and gravity, we will harness for God the energies of love and then for the second time in the history of the world man will have discovered fire."

Bruce Larson (RC)

27

THE SECRET OF VICTORY

In all these things we are more than conquerors through him that loved us.
Romans 8:37

The secret of victory in the Christian life is found in surrender. To the extent that we abandon ourselves to Christ, to that extent we will find ourselves victorious in Christ in day-by-day living.

As we yield ourselves to His Spirit, we find ourselves led of Him. We discover, in our prayer life, that our praying is guided by His hand. We are even given the words to say. Our prayer burdens are given at His command!

We will be startled to discover new force and vitality in our prayer life. We will find our hearts singing in spite of trial and temptation, in spite of testing from without. We will find ourselves girded with His might in the midst of temptation. We will discover that we are more than *conquerors* in Him.

The secret of victory, then, lies in complete recognition of God's

August

power and might at the disposal of His child. Oh, that today we might realize the tremendous dynamic of faith that we are neglecting—that we might resolve this very day to, first of all, yield ourselves to Him, and secondly, take and use the conquering power He has placed at our command.

28

KNOWING THAT GOD KNOWS

We know that in everything God works for good with those who love him, who are called according to his purpose.

Romans 8:28, RSV

I take several newspapers at my home every day, both from England and the United States. As I glance through them or watch the television news, I am aware of the terrible suffering, terrorism, crime, and injustice that exist in our world and I sometimes cannot help but ask the question "Why?" As the nations of the world are arming as never before in history, as Armageddon looms nearer, it is a comforting thought to know that God is behind everything which touches my life. Things happen to me that I cannot understand, but I never doubt God's love. In the hour of trial I may not be able to see His design, but I am confident it must be in line with His purpose of love.

I may not know His plans, but I know He knows, and that's enough for me.

Billy Graham (TA)

29

PRAYER AND HIS RICHES

For there is no difference between the Jew and the Greek: for the same Lord over all is rich unto all that call upon him.

Romans 10:12

This is a new expression. The Apostle might have said, as we read in Joel 2:13: "He is gracious and merciful, slow to anger, and of great kindness, and repenteth him of the evil." But the apostle means to emphasize the fact that God gives exceedingly abundantly above all that we ask or think, as we read in Ephesians 3:20, so that compared with His gifts, the prayers of those who call upon Him seem poor and modest. Those who call upon Him could make "all grace abound toward you." He therefore is rich when He gives; we are poor when we pray. He is mighty when He grants us our petitions; we are timid and weak when we ask. We do not pray for as much as He can and will give, for we do not pray according to His ability (to give), but far short of His ability, according to our weakness. But he can give only according to His might; therefore He always gives more than we ask for.

Martin Luther

Oswald Smith said: "When we work we work; when we pray, God works."

30

DECISIVE DEDICATION

I appeal to you therefore, brethren, by the mercies of God, to present your bodies as a living sacrifice, holy and acceptable to God, which is your spiritual worship.

Romans 12:1, RSV

One of the miracle lessons to come out of the tragic martyrdom of the five courageous missionaries who sacrificed their lives nearly twenty-five years ago in Ecuador, was the youth of these selfless and devoted men. While still in their late twenties and early thirties, they had all made their "decisive dedication" and were now called upon to present their all on the altar of sacrifice.

Almost prophetically, as we look back upon it, one of them, Jim Elliot, at the age of twenty, wrote, "God, I pray Thee, light these idle sticks of my life and may I burn up for Thee. Consume my life, my God, for it is Thine. I seek not a long life but a full one, like You, Lord Jesus." What would be accomplished if every Christian took this attitude toward life?

August

John Wesley wrote, "If I had three hundred men who feared nothing but God, hated nothing but sin, and were determined to know nothing among men but Jesus Christ, and Him crucified, I would set the world on fire." Am I a match—or a wet blanket?

31

Nor Things to Come

For I am persuaded, that neither death, nor life, nor angels, nor principalities, nor powers, nor things present, nor things to come . . . *shall be able to separate us from the love of God, which is in Christ Jesus our Lord.*

Romans 8:38–39, emphasis mine

This passage has always been a favorite of mine—a shelter in the time of storm, a beacon in darkness, an encouragement in despair. But only recently I rediscovered what I think is one of its most important and most neglected phrases.

Nor things to come.

This is not something to be read only at funerals. It means things to come at any time. After death? Sure. But before death, too. Things like an energy shortage. Inflation. Recession. International turmoil. The feeling we're being outnumbered by lawbreakers, domestic and international. Things that happen in Washington, Moscow, Teheran, Riydah, wherever. Things that happen on our own street, in our own family, on our own job.

Nor things to come.

Words to be written over our fears! Emblazoned over the lintel of tomorrow! Embedded in our hopes!

Things to come, whatever they may be, hold no paralyzing terror for those whose Lord is Christ Jesus. God's love does not come and go. He will not let anything get in its way.

Stan Mooneyham

September

1

THE POSITIVE POWER OF CHRIST

Put ye on the Lord Jesus Christ. . . .   *Romans 13:14*

Do not be content with a negative religion. Be positive. Do not only put off—put on as well. Put off by putting on. It is not enough to doff the robes of night, you must don the armor of light. Cast away the works of the flesh, because you have become encased in that glistening panoply woven out of sunbeams and light. Do not only resist impurity—put on Christ as your purity.

If you put on Christ as your purity, you will have no difficulty in being free of the taint of impurity. Do not simply forbid wrath, anger, malice, but assume Christ's heart of compassion, His kindness, humility, meekness, longsuffering and forbearance. Indeed to cultivate these will make those impossible. You need make no provision for the flesh, not expecting to sin, not living in perpetual fear of its outbreak and solicitations, when once you have put on by faith and in the power of the Holy Spirit, the Lord Jesus Christ.

F. B. Meyer

2

REJOICING IN SUFFERING

Be joyful in hope, patient in affliction, faithful in prayer.
Romans 12:12, NIV

> Before the winds that blow do cease,
>   Teach me to dwell within Thy calm,
> Before the pain has passed in peace,
>   Give me, my God, to sing a psalm.

189

September

Let me not lose the chance to prove
The fullness of enabling love.

When the Holy Spirit of God is having His way in my life, I will be able to sing this victorious song with Amy Carmichael. Though bed-ridden as a result of an accident some twenty years before her death, and in almost constant pain, she continued to minister through her devotional writings and poetry, staying at the heart of the Dohnavur Fellowship in India. Her keen insight and her refreshingly spiritual writings revealed the depth of her walk with Christ. She remains a striking example of a Christian whose physical suffering enabled her to reflect the character of Christ. She lived a life of rejoicing in the midst of tribulation. Her face radiated the love of Christ, and her life epitomized the saintly stature the surrendered Christian can reach if he reacts to suffering by rejoicing in it.

Billy Graham (TA)

3

HILARIOUS MERCY

Having gifts that differ according to the grace given to us, let us use them: . . . prophecy . . . service . . . teaching . . . exhortation . . . liberality . . . acts of mercy, with cheerfulness.

Romans 12:6–8, RSV

Paul challenges us to show mercy with cheerfulness (Rom. 12:8). The word for "cheerfulness" in Greek is *hilarotees*, from *hilaros*, meaning "hilarity." Mercy with cheerful laughter and joy! There's an antidote for a merciless, purgatorial pout!

It's so difficult to give up our right to punish people. We feel we must balance the scales by our reserved feelings and attitudes. Eventually, the anger is turned in on ourselves, and we become anxious and depressed.

But remember that Paul called for hilarious mercy only after he had reminded his readers of the mercies of God. "I beseech you

September

therefore, brethren, by the *mercies* of God, that you present your bodies a living sacrifice, holy, acceptable to God, which is your reasonable service. And do not be conformed to this world (and its lack of mercy!), but be transformed by the renewing of your mind (fresh experiences of God's mercy), that you may prove what is that good and acceptable and perfect will of God." On the basis of that, we can hear the challenge, given to the Christians at Rome, not to think of themselves more highly than they ought to think, "but to think soberly, as God has dealt to each one a measure of faith" (Rom. 12:1–3, parenthetical additions mine).

A sober evaluation of the mercies of God bursts forth in hilarious mercy. When we review how merciful God has been to us, we can't contain the flow of mercy through us. The inflow and outgo become one constant experience.

Lloyd J. Ogilvie (CGB)

4

God Is Faithful

God is faithful, by whom ye were called unto the fellowship of his Son Jesus Christ our Lord.

1 Corinthians 1:9

"How then is God faithful?" I answer: In fulfilling each promise which he has made, to all to whom it is made, all who fulfill the condition of that promise. More particularly, (1) "God is faithful" in that "[he] will not suffer you to be tempted above that ye are able [to bear]" (1 Cor. 10:13). (2) "The Lord is faithful, who shall stablish you, and keep you from evil" (if you put your trust in him); from all the evil which you might otherwise suffer, through "unreasonable and wicked men" (2 Thess. 3:2–3). (3) "Quench not the Spirit; hold fast that which is good; Abstain from all appearance of evil; [and] your whole spirit and soul and body be preserved blameless unto the coming of our Lord Jesus Christ. Faithful is he that calleth you, who also will do it" (1 Thess. 5:19, 21–24). (4) Be not disobedient unto the

September

heavenly calling; and "God is faithful, by whom ye were called . . . [to] confirm you unto the end, that ye may be blameless in the day of our Lord Jesus Christ" (1 Cor. 1:8–9). Yet, notwithstanding all this, unless you fulfill the condition, you cannot attain the promise.

"Nay, but are not 'all the promises, yea and amen'?" They are firm as the pillars of heaven. Perform the condition, and the promise is sure. Believe, and you will be saved.

John Wesley

5

To Do or Not to Do

All things are lawful unto me, but all things are not expedient: all things are lawful for me, but I will not be brought under the power of any. . . . All things are lawful for me, but all things are not expedient: all things are lawful for me, but all things edify not.

1 Corinthians 6:12, 10:23

The difficulty about amusements, where to go and where not to go, is not a new one. It agitated the Christians at Corinth centuries ago as it agitates us; and led to one of the questions which the apostle Paul answered in his first epistle. We must have recreation, times when jaded nerves recuperate themselves, and tired brains turn from their absorbing thoughts to lighter themes. We will perform the serious work of life more successfully if we have seasons of rest. Then the perpetual question arises, "How far is all this amusement lawful and expedient? What should be our attitude as Christians toward amusement?" First, we must never be enslaved by any form of pleasure. Second, we must have an eye to others. Whatever is in harmony with the tender, holy, unselfish, and blessed nature of Jesus, is an amusement which we may gladly become involved in. If it does not leave a bad taste in our mouths, or a feeling of guilt, if it is wholesome and health-giving, it will add to our effectiveness as children of God.

F. B. Meyer

September

6

THE TESTING GROUND

Wherefore let him that thinketh he standeth take heed lest he fall.
1 Corinthians 10:12

The most sensible, the most secure, the most stable saint can fall flat on his face—but read on: "There hath no temptation taken you but such as is common to man: but God is faithful, who will not suffer you to be tempted above that ye are able; but will with the temptation also make a way to escape, that ye may be able to bear it" (1 Cor. 10:13). Notice that the way of escape is not avoidance—but that ye may be able to *bear* it. God does not allow the testing to come into your life that you might be able to *avoid* it, but that you might discover how secure, how stable you are in the midst of the testing. He will only allow things to come into your life that you can cope with in the strength that he gives. Have we heard him speak with authority—and does he have full authority over our lives? This is the key to blessed living.

The life of sensibility, security, and stability is built on the rock. How thankful we should be for the firm foundation in the midst of a world that is floundering and foundering all around us. This is what gives the Christian that extra spark, that added impetus, to face his world with strength and stability when all around him is weak and unstable.

Stuart Briscoe

7

THE WAY TO WORK

Whether therefore ye eat, or drink, or whatsoever ye do, do all to the glory of God.
1 Corinthians 10:31

September

What counts in God's sight is not the work we do, but the way in which we do it. Two men may work side by side in the same factory or store; the one, at the end of the day, shall have put in a solid block of gold, silver, and precious stone, while the other has contributed to the fabric of his life-work an ephemeral, insubstantial addition of wood, hay, and stubble, destined to be burnt. What is the difference between the two? To the eye of man, there is none; to the eye of God, much; because the one has been animated, in the lowest, commonest actions, by the lofty motive of pleasing God, and doing the day's work thoroughly and well, while the other wrought to escape blame, to secure the commendation of man, or to win a large wage. Never be ashamed of honest toil, of labors, however trivial or menial, which you can execute beneath the inspiration of noble aims; but be ashamed of the work which, through it makes men hold their breath in wonder, yet, in your heart, you know to have emanated from earthly, selfish, and ignoble aims.

F.B. Meyer

8

A More Excellent Way

But covet earnestly the best gifts: and yet show I unto you a more excellent way.

1 Corinthians 12:31

In the preceding verses, St. Paul has been speaking of the extraordinary gifts of the Holy Spirit such as healing the sick; prophesying, in the proper sense of the word, that is, foretelling things to come; speading with strange tongues, such as the speaker had never learned; and the miraculous interpretation of tongues. And these gifts the apostle allows to be desirable; yea, he exhorts the Corinthians, at least the teachers among them (to whom chiefly, if not solely, they were wont to be given in the first ages of the church), to covet them earnestly, that thereby they might be qualified to be more useful either to Christians or heathens. "And yet," says he, "I show unto you a more excellent way"—far more desirable than all these put together. Inasmuch as it will infallibly lead you to happiness, both in this world and in the world to come; whereas you might have all those gifts, yea, in the highest degree, and yet be miserable both in time and eternity. That "more excellent way" was the way of love. That is the gift to be sought above all others!

John Wesley

9

Love Rules without a Sword

Hereby perceive we the love of God, because he laid down his life for us. . . .

1 John 3:16

The love of God is as broad in its expanse as the blue sky above. You can look up and appreciate, to a certain extent, the vastness of the sky—but human eyes cannot begin to measure its true extent. In much the same way, you can faintly comprehend the immensity of the sea, but only see part way into its unfathomable depths. The love of God is just as far beyond human understanding—but, thank God, you need not understand it to enjoy it!

That unknown poet was right when he wrote:

> Love rules without a sword,
> Love binds without a cord!

10

The Quiet People

If I speak in the tongues of men and of angels, but have not love, I am a noisy gong or a clanging cymbal (or smoke without fire).

1 Corinthians 13:1, RSV

No smoke. Pure energy.

We do not always, unfortunately, wish simply to love. We would rather have it noticed how loving we are. Not publicizing one's own acts of kindness or generosity is harder than keeping secret another person's sins. Most of us like to send up smoke signals which call attention to what we have done. And when the smoke spirals aloft, first a mere wisp, then a massive column that climbs high enough to mark our presence prominently, spiritual energy is depleted.

Thank God for those who do their jobs quietly and efficiently and dependably with a minimum of public attention, their interest in getting the job done, their loyalty to the Lord whose business it is they are doing. I stood on top of the giant Hoover Dam once, barely conscious of the soft whir beneath me as the powerful turbines generated millions of watts of valuable electricity. Afterwards, at a restaurant a few miles down the road, I was driven nearly to distraction by the flashing lights and ringing bells of two stupid pinball machines.

We Christians need to be more appreciative of the quiet ones, less awed by those who roar down kingdom highways leaving a trail of smoke.

Stan Mooneyham

11

A QUALITY OF KINDNESS

Charity suffereth long, and is kind. . . .   *1 Corinthians 13:4*

The truly kind person is one who does not flinch at the cost of extending kindness. He forgets his own personal preferences to proffer help and healing to another. At the price of inconvenience, labor, and personal privation he goes out quietly and without fanfare to bring pleasure to another. Sensitive to the sorrow and suffering of a struggling society, he undertakes to do what he can to alleviate this suffering. He tries to make the world a better and brighter place for those enmeshed in its pain and pathos.

This is the quality of kindness that characterizes God our Father. He *does* care. He *does* suffer for us. Our heavenly Father does come to us in absolute honesty and openness. He lays down His life for us, and He expends Himself without hesitation to enrich us. He identifies

September

Himself with us in our dilemma. Utterly merciful, totally compassionate, incredibly self-giving, He has our welfare and well-being ever in mind—always.

W. Phillip Keller (GLFS)

12

THE MINISTRY OF SUFFERING

And our hope for you is firm, because we know that just as you share in our sufferings, so also you share in our comfort.
2 Corinthians 1:7, NIV

On the natural level we tend to neglect the privilege of prayer until we encounter suffering or difficulty of some kind. We often need to be driven to real prayer by the circumstances that surround us.

Dwight L. Moody was fond of pointing out that there are three kinds of faith in Jesus Christ: *struggling faith*, which is like a man floundering and fearful in deep water; *clinging faith*, which is like a man hanging to the side of a boat; and *resting faith*, which finds a man safe inside the boat—strong and secure enough to reach out his hand to help someone else.

That is the sort of faith you and I must have in order to be effective as Christians—and such faith may be ours through the ministry of suffering in our lives.

Billy Graham (TA)

13

IS PRAYER EVER UNANSWERED?

What am I to do? I will pray with the spirit and I will pray with the mind also; I will sing with the spirit and I will sing with the mind also.
1 Corinthians 14:15, RSV

. . . there is no such thing as unanswered prayer. What seems to be a delay is a special gift to those of us who want everything yesterday.

September

It gives us the wonderful opportunity to discover the greatest answer to prayer for today. We learn to abide in Christ. He is the answer to prayer. His strength is sufficient. Anything else he gives when the time is right will deepen our trust and heighten our praise. But anything without him is nothing at all!

I will never use the words, "unanswered prayer," again! How about you? Can you join me in confident belief that all prayers are answered? Can we relinquish our furtive pressures on the Lord, relax and trust him? Are we ready to say that we will receive answers when two things are accomplished: the Lord's perfect timing and our willingness to obey what is implicit in an answer? So often unanswered prayer is simply the Lord preparing us for what he's made ready. We and other people can get in the way, but there will be an answer even for that. A part of the commitment to delete "unanswered prayer" from our language is the commitment to spend prolonged time in intelligent, purposeful, devoted contact with the Lord.

Lloyd J. Ogilvie (AHA)

14

HIS GRACE IS SUFFICIENT

Not that we are sufficient of ourselves to claim anything as coming from us; our sufficiency is from God.

2 Corinthians 3:5, RSV

He alone is sufficient. "My grace is sufficient for you." The word sufficient is *arkei* in Greek. It means that the supply is in exact proportion to the need—never too much, never too little, never early, never late. Christ knows our deepest needs. There are times he answers our prayers by not granting our requests. Dr. James Denny said, "A refusal is an answer if it is so given that God and the soul understand one another." But also, a delay in answering our prayers brings us to the realization that our greatest longing is for the Lord himself. Any quick provision which makes us less dependent on consistent fellowship with the Provider is no answer at all!

And now consider the secret which only the school of what seems to be unanswered prayer can teach. "My strength is made perfect in weakness." Don't forget the meaning of "perfect" in the Greek: end, purpose, intended goal. Christ's strength achieves its purpose in our weakness. The purpose of prayer is not just to make the best of things, but to allow the Lord to use them to make the best of us. Trials and problems give us a grand chance to discover the adequacy of Christ's strength in our weakness.

Lloyd J. Ogilvie (AHA)

15

New Life in Christ

I have been crucified with Christ; it is no longer I who live, but Christ who lives in me.

Galatians 2:20, RSV

In our land today we are preoccupied with preserving life. There is a frenzied search for products and practices that will aid us in our attempt to *save* our lives. If we save life for ourselves it will be lost to God. Yet if we lose life for God it will come back to us as life at its best. Those who have forgotten their own selfish concerns and have spent themselves for others have found the real meaning in life. Jesus established the everlasting and practical principle of self-denial. The old man of sin and unbelief dies at conversion. The new man of faith and commitment is born. Immersion symbolizes this experience. According to Paul, by baptism "we were buried therefore with him into death, so that as Christ was raised from the dead by the glory of the Father, we too might walk in newness of life" (Rom. 6:4).

For a Christian this death is more traumatic than physical death. It is death to sin—the death of a self-willed person. New and eternal life begins out of this death; we are resurrected into a new life. For such a believer there will be no interruption when the body dies. Physical death for a Christian will simply be like walking through a doorway

September

into a greater realization of the life already begun in him. This is what Jesus meant when he told Martha, "Whoever lives and believes in me shall never die" (John 11:26). On the cross Jesus gave us the hope of eternal life. The symbol of the cross still speaks his message and reminds us of our task.

Frank H. Crumpler

16

TRANSFORMED BY TRAGEDY

And we, who with unveiled faces all reflect the Lord's glory, are being transformed into his likeness with ever increasing glory, which comes from the Lord, who is the Spirit.

2 Corinthians 3:18 NIV

We aren't always responsible for the circumstances in which we find ourselves. However, we are responsible for the way we respond to them. We can give up in depression and suicidal despair. Or, we can look to a sovereign God who has everything under control, who can use the experiences for our ultimate good by transforming us to the image of Christ.

God engineered circumstances. He used them to prove Himself as well as my loyalty. Not everyone had this privilege. I felt there were only a few people God cared for in such a special way that He would trust them with this kind of experience. This understanding left me relaxed and comfortable as I relied on His love, exercising newly learned trust. I saw that my injury was not a tragedy but a gift God was using to help me conform to the image of Christ, something that would mean my ultimate satisfaction, happiness—even joy.

Joni Eareckson Tada

17

FROM DAY TO DAY

Though our outward man perish, yet the inward man is renewed day by day.

2 Corinthians 4:16

September

There is one lesson all young Christians should learn, namely this—*the absolute necessity of fellowship with Jesus each day*. This lesson is not always taught at the beginning of the Christian life, nor is it always understood by the young convert. He should realize that the grace he has received of the forgiveness of sins, of acceptance as God's child, of joy in the Holy Ghost, can only be preserved by the daily renewal in fellowship with Jesus Christ Himself.

Many Christians backslide because this truth is not clearly taught. They are unable to stand against the temptations of the world, or of their old nature. They strive to do their best to fight against sin, and to serve God, but they have no strength. They have never really grasped the secret: *The Lord Jesus will every day* from heaven continue His work in me. But on one condition—*the soul must give Him time each day* to impart His love and His grace. Time alone with the Lord Jesus each day is the indispensable condition of growth and power.

Andrew Murray

18

THE LORD WILL PROVIDE

And God is able to provide you with every blessing in abundance, so that you always have enough of everything and may provide in abundance for every good work.

2 Corinthians 9:8, RSV

Though troubles assail, and dangers affright,
Though friends should all fail, and foes all unite,
Yet one thing secures us, whatever betide,
The promise assures us, "The Lord will provide."

The birds, without barn or storehouse, are fed;
From them let us learn to trust for our bread;
His saints what is fitting shall ne'er be denied,
So long as 'tis written, "The Lord will provide."

September

No strength of our own, nor goodness we claim;
Our trust is all thrown on Jesus' name;
In this our strong tower for safety we hide;
The Lord is our power, "The Lord will provide."

When life sinks apace, and death is in view,
The word of His grace shall comfort us through;
Not fearing or doubting, with Christ on our side,
We hope to die shouting, "The Lord will provide."

John Newton

19

HANDLING THE THORNS

To keep me from becoming conceited because of these surpassingly great revelations, there was given me a thorn in my flesh, a messenger of Satan, to torment me.

2 Corinthians 12:7, NIV

God allows the fires of tribulation to come into our lives in order to make us, and keep us, humble. He could have delivered Paul from his "thorn in the flesh," but He refused all of Paul's requests for relief and instead promised His grace.

God also does not exempt Christians from suffering because it deepens their prayer life. Nothing will drive us to our knees quicker than trouble. Sometimes in our prayers we wonder why the answer is delayed or does not seem to come at all. Many of God's sufferers are praying for relief, but God's answer seems to be "No." Healing may not come, but God does answer our prayers. He does not always answer them in the way we want. We may not have prayed according to the will of God. In the Garden of Gethsemane as Jesus faced the cross He prayed: "Father, *if thou be willing*, remove this cup from me" (Luke 22:42, italics mine). Our prayers must be in accordance with the will of God for the simple reason that God knows better what is good for us than we know ourselves.

Billy Graham (TA)

September

20

The Rock of Safety

Therefore I take pleasure in infirmities, in reproaches, in necessities, in persecutions, in distresses for Christ's sake: for when I am weak, then am I strong.

2 Corinthians 12:10

When we are weak we are strong, because then we are driven away from self to God. All strength is in God, and it is well to come to the one solitary storehouse and source of might. There is no power apart from God. As long as you and I look to the creature, we are looking to a cracked, broken cistern, that holds no water; but when we know that it is broken, and that there is not a drop of water in it, then we hasten to the great fountain and wellhead. While we rest in any measure upon self, or the creature, we are standing with one foot on the sand; but when we get right away from human nature because we are too weak to have the least reliance upon self whatever, then we have both feet on the rock and this is safe standing.

C. H. Spurgeon

21

Pressed

I am crucified with Christ: nevertheless I live; yet not I, but Christ liveth in me: and the life which I now live in the flesh I live by the faith of the Son of God, who loved me, and gave himself for me.

Galatians 2:20

Pressed out of measure and pressed to all length;
Pressed so intensely it seems, beyond strength;
Pressed in the body and pressed in the soul,
Pressed in the mind till the dark surges roll.
Pressed by foes, and a pressure from friends.
Pressure on pressure, till life nearly ends.
Pressed into knowing no helper but God;

September

Pressed into loving the staff and the rod.
Pressed into liberty where nothing clings;
Pressed into faith for impossible things.
Pressed into living a life in the Lord,
Pressed into living a Christ-life outpoured.

Author Unknown

22

GROWING IN GRACE

I am crucified with Christ: nevertheless I live; yet not I, but Christ liveth in me.

Galatians 2:20

What a noticeable change had come between the time when Paul cried submissively, "Lord, what wilt thou have me to do?" looking to an outside Christ for commandment, and the same Paul crying, "Not I who live, but Christ liveth in me!" rejoicing in the inspiration of an inward Savior. This is a dramatic illustration of what it means to "grow in grace." This was the perfect victory for which Paul was always striving so intensely.

The victory did not come perfectly to him in this world. It cannot to any of us. Dependent as victory is upon the knowledge of Christ by the soul, it cannot be perfect until the soul's knowledge of Christ shall be perfect in heaven. . . .

"That I may know him." Those are Paul's words. How constantly we come back to his large, rounded life, as the picture of what the Christian is and should become.

Phillips Brooks

23

THE FAITH LIFE

The life which I now live in the flesh I live by faith of the Son of God, who loved me, and gave himself for me.

Galatians 2:20

If we were to ask Paul what he meant by saying he no longer lives but that Christ lives in him, what now is his part in living that life, he would give us the answer: *"The life that I now live in the flesh is a life of faith in the Son of God, who loved me and gave himself up for me."* His whole life, day by day, was an unceasing faith in the wonderful love that had given itself for him. Faith was the power that possessed and permeated his whole being and his every action.

Here we have the simple but full statement of the secret of the true Christian life. It is not faith only in certain promises of God, or in certain blessings received from Christ. It is a faith that has a vision of how entirely Christ gives himself to the soul to be, in the very deepest and fullest sense of the word, his life and all that implies for every moment of the day. As essential as continuous breathing is to the support of our physical life is the unceasing faith in which the soul trusts Christ and counts upon Him to maintain the life of the Spirit within us. Faith ever rests on that infinitive love in which Christ gave Himself wholly for us, to be ours in the deepest meaning of the word, and to live His life over again in us.

Andrew Murray

24

PUT ON CHRIST

> . . . *as many of you as have been baptized into Christ have put on Christ.*
> Galatians 3:27
> *Put ye on the Lord Jesus Christ, and make not provision for the flesh, to fulfill the lusts thereof.*
> Romans 13:14

The word that is here translated "put on" is the same that is used in regard to putting on clothes. We have put on "the new man," and we have the new nature as a garment that is worn, by means of which all can see who we are. Paul says of the Christian when he has confessed Christ at baptism, that he has put on Christ. As a man may be recognized by the garment he wears, so the Christian is known as the one who has put on Christ and exhibits Him in his whole life and character.

September

And again he says: "Put on the Lord Jesus"—not alone at conversion, but from day to day. As I put on my clothes each day and am seen in them, so the Christian must daily put on the Lord Jesus, so that he no longer lives after the flesh to fulfill its lusts, but shows forth the image of his Lord and the new man formed in His likeness.

Andrew Murray

25

RAISED UP TOGETHER

(God) hath raised us up together . . . that like as Christ was raised up from the dead by the glory of the Father, even so we also should walk in newness of life.

Ephesians 2:6; Romans 6:4

In the story of the Deluge, the ark bore Noah and his family from the old world, where corruption and sin had reigned, to the new world of resurrection and life, as it emerged from its watery grave; even so the Lord Jesus, the true Ark of Safety, has borne us through His death and resurrection into the world of Life. It is on this thought that the apostle bases the appeal, "If ye then were raised with Christ, seek those things that are above."

This is the beginning of sanctification: to feel that in Jesus we no longer belong to the world that cast out and crucified Him, but to that in which He reigns forevermore; to know that His cross and grave stand between us and the past; to realize the power of His resurrection in its daily detachment from sin and attachment to God.

F.B. Meyer

26

CHOSEN FOR LOVE

According as he hath chosen us in him before the foundation of the world, that we should be holy and without blame before him in love.

Ephesians 1:4

September

God's election points to His love. Men have sometimes thought and spoken of God's "choosing" in such a way as to encourage exclusive and proud conceit—as though God's love were a high wall enclosing a favored few, so that their flower and fruit might be kept from every defiling, pilfering hand. To think this is to misconceive the entire purpose of God.

If a man boasts of his election in an arrogant and exclusive spirit, he shows that he has missed its point and aim, and is certainly outside its scope. The eternal purpose of God reveals itself, not merely in the new-found rapture, but in the new-found love. The love of God proves the election of God. If you do not love, you may prate of election as you will, but you have neither part nor lot in it. But, if we are in Christ, by a living faith, we have been chosen to love, and love must be divinely possible—even easy. God's choice always carries with it an equivalent of power to be and do that for which He has chosen us.

F.B. Meyer

27

LOVE IS LIMITLESS

Wherefore I also, after I heard of your faith in the Lord Jesus, and love unto all the saints.

Ephesians 1:15

Love and faith are inseparable. When there is faith in the Lord Jesus, there will always be love toward all the saints. Because faith is the faculty of taking God into the heart. Faith is God-receptiveness. Faith appropriates the nature of God, as the expanded lungs the mountain air, or as the child the parent's gift. Faith, like a narrow channel, conveys God's ocean fullness into the areas of human need. Wherever, therefore, faith links the believer to the Lord Jesus, His nature, which is love, pure as mountain dew, begins to flow in to the waiting, expectant heart; and then to flow out thence toward all the saints.

The love of God knows no favorite sect. It singles out no special school; but, as the sun and wind of nature, breathes and shines alike on all. It is cosmopolitan and universal. You cannot imprison it within the walls of any one Christian community. It laughs at your restrictions, and with equal grace raises up witnesses and standard-bearers from all parts of the church. Thus, as we become more like God, our love overlaps the barrier of our little pond and passes out to greet all saints, and to expend itself on the great world of men.

F.B. Meyer

28

GRACE—THE FREE GIFT OF GOD

By grace you have been saved through faith; and this is not your own doing, it is the gift of God not because of works, lest any man should boast.
Ephesians 2:8–9, RSV

Grace is the free gift of God, which he bestows, not on those who are worthy of his favor, not on such as are previously holy, and so fit to be crowned with all the blessings of his goodness; but on the ungodly and unholy; on those who till that hour were fit only for everlasting destruction; those in whom was no good thing, and whose only plea was, "God be merciful to me, a sinner!" No merit, no goodness in man precedes the forgiving love of God. His pardoning mercy supposes nothing in us but a sense of mere sin and misery; and to all who see, and feel, and own their wants, and their utter inability to remove them, God freely gives faith, for the sake of him in whom he is always "well pleased."

John Wesley

29

THE POWER WITHIN US

And you hath he quickened, who were dead in trespasses and sins.
Ephesians 2:1

He will do more than just forgive us our sins; He will protect, maintain, and quicken into stronger and healthier growth. The Holy

September

Spirit will take charge of the feebly smoking flax and fan its flickering flame into fire. He who hath begun a good work in you will complete it. There shall be a perfecting of the tender purpose, a blossoming of the fragile bud. Is this not included in that nourishing and cherishing which is predicted of the Lord's body? It might be applied as well to a nurse's or mother's solicitude for some flickering baby-life, that keeps standing still and asking whether or not it should continue. "After two days will he revive us: in the third day he will raise us up, and we shall live in his sight" (Hos. 6:2). The power that raised up Jesus from the dead on the third day, waits to do as much for us, not spasmodically and intermittently, but regularly, certainly, ceaselessly, until it seats us beyond all principality and power beside His own steadfast throne.

F.B. Meyer

30

RAISED UP IN POWER

And hath raised us up together, and made us sit together in heavenly places in Christ Jesus.

Ephesians 2:6

What Canaan was to the Jewish people, that the heavenly places are to us. When the twelve stones were taken from the bed of the Jordan and placed on the farther side, the whole people were deemed to have entered upon the possession of their inheritance. This in spite of the fact that two-and-a-half tribes elected to settle on the farther side, and their wives and children would probably never cross the Jordan at all. So when Jesus passed to the throne, we passed with Him.

Was He raised? So were we. Was He made to sit at the Father's right hand? *That* is our place. Was every foe made His footstool? Then not one of them can overcome us so long as we are in abiding fellowship with our risen Lord. If the "together" of the inner life is maintained, the "together" of victory is secure. Oh, to tread in the power of the Holy Spirit in these high places!

F.B. Meyer

October

1

CALLED OF GOD

I, therefore, the prisoner of the Lord, beseech you that ye walk worthy of the vocation wherewith ye are called.

Ephesians 4:1

The simplest words are the deepest. Take, for instance, the word *call*. It is constantly on our lips. The mother calls her child. The businessman calls his friend. And God appropriates it in His dealing with men. He speaks to every soul of man, once, twice, many times, as when He said, "Samuel, Samuel," or "Saul, Saul." In some solemn hour of decision, in a moment of awful crisis, by human voice or written word, or by the pleading and remonstrance of conscience, God's voice may be heard calling men to Himself to heaven and to a saintly life. On that call the apostle bases his argument for holiness. Act worthily of the love which summoned you, and of the goal to which you have been called. Stand still and ask yourself before you speak, or act, or decide—is this worthy of that great ideal which God has conceived for me, when He called me from the rest of men to be His priest, His son, His saint? If not, avoid it like the plague!

F. B. Meyer

2

EXCEEDING ABUNDANTLY

(He) is able to do exceeding abundantly above all that we ask or think, according to the power that worketh in us.

Ephesians 3:20

"Exceeding abundantly." Here Paul coins a word for his own peculiar use. It seems as though at times the Holy Spirit crowded such great and radiant revelations in the apostle's mind and heart that even the rich vocabulary at his disposal was not sufficient to express them. But when ordinary language fails, Paul employs his own. There was no superlative at hand which could describe his sense of the over-whelming ability of God, and so he just constructed a word of his own, the intensity of which can only be suggested in our English phrase "exceeding abundantly." The power flows up, and out, and over! It is a spring, and therefore incalculable.

We can measure the resources of a cistern; we can tell its capacity to a trifle. We can register the contents of a reservoir; at any moment we can tell how many gallons it contains. But who can measure the resources of a spring? It is to this springlike quality in the divine power, the exceeding abundance, the immeasurable quantity, that the apostle refers.

We can bring our little vessels to the spring and take them away filled to overflowing, and the exceeding abundance remains. The "doing" of our God is an inexhaustible well.

J. H. Jowett

3

THE DIMENSIONS OF HIS LOVE

May be able to comprehend with all saints what is the breadth, and length, and depth, and height [of the love of Christ].

Ephesians 3:18

Its *breadth*. It is as broad as the race of man. It is like the fabled tent which, when opened in a courtyard, filled it; but when unfurled in the tented field, it covered an army. It claims all souls.

Its *length*. It is timeless and changeless. It never began; it will never stop. It cannot be tired out by our exactions or demands upon its patience.

Its *height*. Stand by the cradle, or lower yet, at the cross, and you behold it, like Jacob's ladder, reaching to the throne of God. A spiral staircase by which the guiltiest may climb from the dark dungeon into the palace.

October

Its *depth*. There is no sin so profound, no despondency so low, no misery so abject, but the love of Christ is deeper. Its everlasting arms are always underneath.

As we consider these things, we can almost hear the voice of God speaking to us as to Abraham: "Lift up now thine eyes, and look from the place where thou art, northward and southward, and eastward and westward; for all the land which thou seest, to thee will I give it, and to thy seed forever. Arise, walk through the land in the length of it, and in the breadth of it; for I will give it unto thee" (Gen. 13:14–15, 17). When we separate ourselves from our Lots, this land is ours. It is an undiscovered continent on which we are settled; but every year we may push our fences outward to enclose more of its infinite extent.

F. B. Meyer

4

RICH IN MERCY

. . . be kind to one another, tenderhearted, forgiving one another, as God in Christ forgave you.

Ephesians 4:32, RSV

What a marvelous thing it is to be a Christian in a society with problems, knowing you are God's means of rectifying the problems. Jesus said, "Blessed are the merciful: for they shall obtain mercy" (Matt. 5:7). A Christian is merciful; he is kind. A practicing Christian goes the extra mile and turns the other cheek. Why? Because his God is rich in mercy. If there were no other call given in Scripture, I would expect Christians to be merciful people for this very simple reason: Our God is a merciful God. Grace is God giving us what we don't deserve. Mercy is God withholding from us what we *do* deserve. Merciful kindness is seeing someone reap the results of his rash actions, and being heartbroken over their pain. It's the opposite of the one who gloats over the misfortunes of others.

The church of Jesus Christ is supposed to be full of kind people, reproduced by a merciful God. Are you and I known as kind people? Or are we mainly interested in our own small world, our own concerns, our own tiny circle? A kind person will be characterized by concern more for others than for himself. He will stand out from the crowd because of his concern. This world does not like different people. But the world needs the kindness you and I can bring because our roots are in our merciful God.

Stuart Briscoe

5

SUFFERING PROVIDES STRENGTH

Glory and honor are in his presence; strength and gladness are in his place.

1 Chronicles 16:27

Cyrus Albertson tells of a violin maker who searched all his life for wood that would make violins with a certain haunting sound of beauty. At last he found what he wanted in wood cut right at the timberline on a high mountain. Timberline in the Rockies is the last strand of trees, often twelve thousand feet above sea level. Up there winds blow so fiercely that even bark has no chance to grow on the windward side. All the branches point in one way. A tree must stay on its knees to live at all. But the wood in these trees is found to be the most resonant in the world. It makes wonderful violins and they in turn make music to stir men's souls. But these trees live on their knees. So must we. You who suffer, through your experience, can be turned to joy, usefulness, and beauty of character, if you trust God and love him with all your heart. In his power suffering can be transformed, and you can become much more than you are.

T. Cecil Meyers

6

SUNSHINE AND STORM

Children, obey your parents in the Lord for this is right.

Ephesians 6:1, RSV

213

October

How much is involved in this little word, "in"? Look at it this way: Would we ever see a rainbow if it were not revealed by the sunlight? Would we ever see the true beauty of autumn colors unless they were illuminated by God's sunlight? This is the secret of the Christian life as well. If we look upon everything that happens as being "*in* the Lord," we will be much happier in spite of what seems to be a difficult experience. "*In* Christ" lies the key that opens the door to all that is best. He is the Way. As we realize this, we will discover new richness in what might otherwise become the merely routine.

Dr. Richard Halverson says: "In His providence, God knows how much joy and sorrow, how much pleasure and pain, how much prosperity and poverty is proper for His child. He knows the correct balance of sunshine and storm, the precise mixture of darkness and light it takes to perfect a son."

7

THE FOES WE FIGHT

For we wrestle not against flesh and blood, but against principalities, against powers, against the rulers of the darkness of this world, against spiritual wickedness in high places.

Ephesians 6:12

Never in this life can we escape from temptation. The holier we get, the more subtle and vehement will be the assaults of the dark legions, though they may wear white over their gray armor. The nearer we get to our Prince in thought and fellowship, the more we will be assaulted. It is from under the opened heaven that we are driven to the wilderness to be tempted. There is no such fighting as in the heavenly places themselves. Here we wrestle not against flesh and blood, but against the world-rulers of this darkness. But the issue cannot be doubtful. In the thought of God, and in the Ascension of our blessed Lord, they are beneath our feet and conquered; and He waits to realize His purpose in the weakest of His saints. "Having done all, *stand*"; God will fight for you, and you shall hold your peace.

F. B. Meyer

October

8

CALLED TO REST

Therefore take the whole armor of God, that you may be able to withstand in the evil day, and having done all, to stand.

Ephesians 6:13, RSV

We Americans are said to have a short crisis attention span. We want to deal with the boat people or the earthquake victims quickly and move on to something else. But it is not enough to initiate a relief effort, come up with great ideas, get something started. It quickly becomes a question of who will stay by for the long haul. Whose faithfulness, commitment, and gentleness are deep enough to keep them going when the newness has worn off, when the task seems endless and the excitement has degenerated into hard, slogging work?

Some of the lines of a hymn have stayed with me from childhood:

> I weary of the journey set before me,
> Grow footsore 'ere I reach the mountain crest.

I know the feeling and I expect you know it, too. But then comes the rest of that unforgettable stanza:

> But, lo! I hear a soft voice gently calling,
> Come unto Me and I will give you rest.

Rest comes at the end of the journey. When we reach home. And we're not home yet!

Stan Mooneyham

9

THE CHRISTIAN'S ARMOR

So put on God's armor now! Then when the evil day comes, you will be able to resist the enemy's attacks; and after fighting to the end, you will still hold your ground.

Ephesians 6:13, TEV

October

Paul tells us, "For though we live in the world we are not carrying on a worldly war, for the weapons of our warfare are not worldly but have divine power to destroy strongholds" (2 Cor. 10:3–4, RSV). With weapons such as these, how can we help but win! We should be thankful that our resources are in God, not man!

Thomas Carlyle once said, "You cannot fight the French merely with red uniforms. There must be men inside them!" Paul here gives us a description of a well-equipped soldier, able to stand against every foe. But the weapons of the soldier are on the inside! The Christian soldier is "strong in the Lord in the strength of his might" (Eph. 6:10, RSV. The Christian soldier draws his resources from God Himself. His weapons are truth, righteousness, plus faith and prayer—not a bomb or a cannon, which can fail.

10 _____

SWORDS CAN BE DANGEROUS

Take the helmet of salvation and the sword of the Spirit, which is the word of God.

Ephesians 6:17, NIV

This single offensive weapon in the Christian's inventory needs to be handled carefully, gently, even gingerly. Unless your hands are covered with tough, unfeeling callouses, grasping the sword bare-handed will mean blood on your own fingers—your own motives weighed, your own actions judged. And anyone who has become calloused in the use of the Word of God is in a dangerous spiritual condition.

Nothing about the sword of the Spirit allows me the reckless impunity of the handle while it gives you the hazard of the blade, or vice versa. "God will judge you in the same way you judge others," the Bible says, "and he will apply to you the same rules you apply to others" (Matt. 7:2, TEV).

That ought to make us a little slower to reach for the sword, a little more meticulous in its use. "For the word of God is living and active, sharper than any two-edged sword, piercing to the division of soul and spirit, of joints and marrow, and discerning the thoughts and intentions of the heart" (Heb. 4:12). *My* heart, too. *My* joints and marrow. *My* soul and spirit.

Stan Mooneyham

11

SEEING HIS SALVATION

And take the helmet of salvation, and the sword of the Spirit, which is the word of God.

Ephesians 6:17

The Christian warrior must know God's salvation in his own experience. He must be saved from the guilt and penalty of sin before he can proclaim the plentitude of God's forgiveness to the chief of sinners. He must know the gospel as the follower of God unto salvation from the dominion of sin in his own heart. He must be anticipating the consummation of God's purpose in the redemption of the body. As the helmet glistens in the sunshine, so must the crown of the Christian's experience point upward to heaven and onward to the glory yet to be revealed. He must speak that which he knows, and declare what he has seen and heard. It is when we are experiencing the power of God's salvation that we can declare it to others, with a freedom and a power that needs no further collaboration. And it is when men see the salvation of God exemplified in our own lives and characters, that they will be prepared to accept it as indeed the Word of God.

F. B. Meyer

12

PAUL'S CALL TO PRAYER

Praying always with all prayer and supplication in the Spirit, and watching thereunto with all perseverance, and supplication for all saints.

Ephesians 6:18

October

Paul expects believers to be so filled with the consciousness of their being in Christ, and through Him united consciously to the whole body, that in their daily life and all its involvements, their highest aim would ever be the welfare of the Body of Christ of which they had become members. He counted upon their being filled with the Spirit, so that it would be perfectly natural to them, without the thought of burden or constraint, to pray for all who belong to the Body of Jesus Christ. As natural as it is for each member of my body to be ready every moment to do what is needful for the welfare of the whole, even so, where the Holy Spirit has entire possession, the consciousness of union with Christ will ever be accompanied by consciousness of the union and the joy and the love of all the members.

Is not this just what we need in our daily life, that every believer who has yielded himself undividedly to Christ Jesus will, day by day, every day and all the day, live in the consciousness that he is one with Christ and His Body? The saints of God are to live for Christ their King, and also for all the members of that Body of which He is the Head. May God's people be willing to make this sacrifice of prayer and intercession at all times and for all saints!

Andrew Murray

13

Love with Faith

Peace be to the brethren, and love with faith, from God the Father and the Lord Jesus Christ.

Ephesians 6:23

God's love passes into human hearts. "Love with faith, from God the Father and the Lord Jesus Christ." The stream issues from the common throne of God and of the Lamb; from thence it flows downward to redeemed hearts and through them to a dying world.

Love and faith are inseparable. We trust before we love. We love and find it easy to trust. Faith is the open channel down which God's love passes into our nature; and love in its passage hollows out the channel down which it came. Like burnished mirrors that face each other, they flash the sunbeams to and fro. And thus as we live near

October

God we are filled with love, not ours, but His—His love reflected back on Himself—His love flung toward men.

F. B. Meyer

14

THE POWER OF LOVE

And this I pray, that your love may abound yet more and more in knowledge and in all judgment.

Philippians 1:9

The law of love works whether it be in marriage, between parents and children, friends, business associates, even countries, but we have to work at it continuously and in complete faith that together we can solve problems and experience life at its best. No person can adequately live alone. Try to separate ourselves as we will, we cannot. Like the warp and woof of a rug, our lives are woven together by innumerable, intricate relationships.

Love! What a tremendous word. How many persons critically ill, given up by doctors, have been brought back to health by the love of parents, children, a husband or wife, a love that supplies unfathomable strength? The number would be astonishing if such data were available. How many persons whose lives have been marred by complete failure, crime, attempted suicide, have literally been loved back to victory and accomplishments? Only God knows. Where there is great love, there are great miracles. Never underrate the power of love.

Harold Rogers

15

THE LIFE THAT WINS

For to me to live is Christ, and to die is gain. *Philippians 1:21*

Certain Swiss peasants not very long ago were feeding their flocks on one of the lofty upland valleys. On one side of the pasture stood a

219

number of chalets, or wooden huts, in which they were accustomed to living during the summer, poor shelters which were left as soon as the winter set in. One day they heard a strange rumbling up in the lofty Alps, and they understood what it meant; that a mass of rock or snow had fallen, and would soon come crushing down in the form of an avalanche. In a brief space their fears were realized, for they saw a tremendous mass come rushing from above, bearing destruction in its course.

What did it destroy? Only the old, crazy chalets; that was all. Every man of the shepherds was safe, and untouched; the event was rather to them a matter which caused a *Te Deum* to be sung in the village church below than a subject for mourning and sorrow. They said, "The avalanche is terrible, but it has not slain the aged mother, nor crushed the babe in its cradle; it has injured none of us, but only buried a few hovels which we can soon rebuild."

Their case is a picture of ours. The avalanche of death will fall; but O saints, when it comes this is all it will do for you—your earthly house will be dissolved! Will you fret over so small a loss? No evil will come to you; the poor hut of the body will be buried beneath the earth, but as for yourself, what will you have to do but to sing an everlasting *Te Deum* unto Him who delivered you from death and danger, and raised you to His own right hand?

C. H. Spurgeon

16

The Gift of Suffering

For it has been granted to you that for the sake of Christ you should not only believe in him but also suffer for his sake.
Philippians 1:29, RSV

The special gift of suffering is that it exposes all secondary satisfactions. We live in a world that has made a false god out of quantity rather than quality. It measures greatness by how long we live and not how well we live, in the number of breaths we breathe instead of the breathtaking experiences we enjoy. The passion for trouble-free health has robbed us of a passion for God when it is interrupted. Our false idea of happiness anesthetizes us from finding joy. We cannot tolerate any infractions of our prescribed agendas where everyone lives to be a hundred, is happily married, has perfect children, makes a good living, and retires to trouble-free leisure where the only problem is how to battle boredom. We find ourselves unable to tolerate the imperfect, the incomplete, the inconsistent.

But those secondary expectations are not God's pattern for us. It is only as we come to know "life's smoothness turned rough," that we find a deeper reason for our existence. And that follows the heart-cry, "My soul pants for Thee, O God, my soul thirsts for God, the living God."

Suffering had given the psalmist a precious gift: an intimacy with God greater than the happiness of joining the procession to the Temple, better than the festival celebration in historic ritual of the acts of God in the past. When despair finally brought him to the wrenching prayer of trust, his previous experiences of the God of the past were replaced by the penetrating experience of God in the present. The purpose of the night was to move from the soliloquy of self-centered pity to the dialogue of God-centered praise. God did not waste the tragedy. He used it to give more than answers; he became the Answer.

Lloyd J. Ogilvie (AHA)

17

SACRIFICED SERVANT

But made himself of no reputation, and took upon him the form of a servant, and was made in the likeness of men.

Philippians 2:7

Our world is in revolt. Wars and rumors of wars surround us, as they have since the distant past. Conflict exists between man and himself, man and his fellow man, and man and God. Is there no help?

October

Cannot God bring peace and good will into these troubled scenes? Yes, for Paul says that "God also hath highly exalted him [Jesus], and given him a name which is above every name: that at the name of Jesus every knee should bow, of things in heaven, and things in earth, and things under the earth" (Phil. 2:9–10). Thus, God will be glorified and become all in all.

But notice the process by which this consummation will be secured. Our Lord Jesus will effect it without the aid of much that we expected, and through means that we do not expect. He will become a servant and a sacrifice, through which He will manifest the love of God in the most conspicuous and convincing manner; that He might bear away the guilt of the world, and might work out and bring in an everlasting righteousness. Therefore, He is exalted and bears evermore the name of Jesus—the Savior.

F. B. Meyer

18

God and Our Questions

For God is at work in you, both to will and to work for his good pleasure.
Philippians 2:13, RSV

Actually, I am convinced God is the author of, as well as the answer to our aching questions. It is because he is at work in us that we even dare to question! Honest intellectual questioning is a sign of growth, not denial. God wants us to get in touch with the questions which have kept us from growing spiritually. Our questions reflect our inbred, divine desire to grow. God knows that if we dare to think, eventually our questions will lead us to him, and into the profound relationship with him for which we were created.

Essentially, I believe life's biggest questions are the result of the fact that our concept of God has been too small, our vision of him too limited. Therefore, the only antidote to our quandary of questions is to learn to fully acknowledge God's greatness. That was Paternus's advice to his son: "First of all, my child, think magnificently of God.

Magnify His providence; adore His power; pray to Him frequently and incessantly. Bear Him always in your mind; teach your thoughts to reverence Him in every place, for there is no place where He is not. Therefore, my child, fear and worship, and love God; first and last, think magnificently of God."

Lloyd J. Ogilvie (AHA)

19

THE PEACE OF GOD

And the peace of God, which passeth all understanding, shall keep your hearts and minds through Christ Jesus.

Philippians 4:7

Peace is the most precious of all the gifts and graces of the Spirit; so precious indeed is peace that it was the one legacy left us by our departing Lord. "Peace I leave with you, my peace I give unto you: not as the world giveth, give I unto you. Let not your heart be troubled, neither let it be afraid." Joy may be more exciting but peace is more sustaining.

It is the "peace of God." It is not peace with God which comes to us with forgiveness and salvation, but is the very peace of God Himself, His own calm, restful heart possessing ours and filling us with His divine stillness.

It is a "peace which passeth all understanding." There is no rational explanation for it. It does not come to us by reasoning things out and seeing our way clear, but it is often most profound when all the circumstances of our life are most perplexing and distressing. It contradicts all conditions and constantly proves its heavenly origin and its supernatural birth.

It is the peace that saves us from anxious care. Its watchword is "Be careful for nothing." It simply crowds out all our corroding anxieties and fills us with such satisfaction that there is really nothing that we can fear.

It is a peace that fills the heart with constant thankfulness and the

October

lips with praise. A life of peace leads to a life of praise, and a life of praise in turn leads to a life of peace.

A.B. Simpson

20

STAND AT THE BOW!

I press toward the mark for the prize of the high calling of God in Christ Jesus.

Philippians 3:14

Paul is telling us: Always stand at the bow! Leave the stern with its backward look and make for the bow. To spend time in sad review of past sins and failures is not to put them to the best account. Confess them, and believe that for Christ's dear sake they are absolutely forgiven! Failure often provides the material for success, and our dead selves may become the stepping-stones to better things. Did not our Lord say to His disciples: "Sleep on now and take your rest" —the past is irreparable—but immediately added: "Arise, let us be going!"—the future is available. Therefore, leave the stern with its backward look, and move forward to the bow.

Look out to the vast circle of the horizon, and prepare for the new lands to be explored, the wonderful discoveries that await us, the great missions hidden in the future which are waiting to be fulfilled. Never doubt that the clouds will break. Never dream that wrong will triumph. Never count yourself God-forsaken or forgotten. The Master may seem to be asleep on His pillow, oblivious and uncaring, but His hand is on the helm. He guides your course. He rules the waves and they obey Him.

21

WINNING THE PRIZE

So I run straight toward the goal in order to win the prize, which is God's call through Christ Jesus to life above.

Philippians 3:14, RSV

October

One of my heroes as a college student, and later on as a young businessman, was Jim Elliot, probably the most eloquent of the five young missionaries so brutally martyred in Ecuador many years ago. A real student leader, he was an upperclassman when I attended Wheaton College. What a discerning evaluation he had of the truly valuable in life! As a youth of 22, he wrote, "One of the great blessings of Heaven is the appreciation of Heaven on earth. *He is no fool who gives what he cannot keep to gain what he cannot lose.*"

Jim Elliot had learned the same lesson as the apostle Paul. The goal of life is eternal life, not the empty rewards of this earth. Thus, earthly life, sought for its own sake, becomes valueless and purpose-less. On the other hand, if life is lived with eternity's values in view, it takes on a whole new aura of meaning. Paul also wrote, "The preaching of the cross is to them that perish, foolishness," another and equally discerning evaluation. But to us who believe, he went on, "It is the power of God unto salvation." Another wise man once wrote, "In this world, it is not what we take up, but what we give up, that makes us rich."

22

THE DAWN OF A NEW DAY

I press on toward the goal. . . .   Philippians 3:14, RSV

Those servants who refuse to get bogged down in and anchored to the past are those who pursue the objectives of the future. People who do this are seldom petty. They are too involved in getting a job done to be occupied with yesterday's hurts and concerns. Very near the end of his full and productive life, Paul wrote: "I have fought the good fight, I have finished the course, I have kept the faith" (2 Tim. 4:7). What a grand epitaph! He seized every day by the throat. He relentlessly pursued life.

I know human nature well enough to realize that some people excuse their bitterness over past hurts by thinking, "It's too late to change. I've been injured and the wrong done against me is too great for me ever to forget it. Maybe Paul could press on—not me!" A person with this mindset is . . . determined not to change because

October

"life has dealt him or her a bad hand." But when God holds out hope, when God makes promises, when God says, "It can be done," there are *no exceptions.* With each new dawn there is delivered to your door a fresh, new package called "today." God has designed us in such a way that we can handle only one package at a time . . . and all the grace we need will be supplied by Him as we live out that day.

Charles R. Swindoll (IYS)

23

STRENGTH IN STRESS

I can do all things in him who strengthens me.   Philippians 4:13, RSV

Stress is a part of life. It goes with the territory. The challenge is to turn it into what Dr. Hans Selye, founder of the Institute of Stress, calls "eustress." The "eu" comes from the Greek for *good.* Dr. Selye suggests that there can be a constructive or healthy stress which not only tests the fiber of our character, it also teaches us to know and depend on inner resources. The question is how to find equalizing strength from within for the stress which bombards us from without.

Only Christ can give us that. What stabilizers are to a ship in a strong sea, his indwelling presence is to the Christian in the gales of life. He uses the stress that hits us to show us his ability in our disability.

Lloyd J. Ogilvie (AHA)

24

GETTING TO KNOW GOD

I want to know Christ and the power of his resurrection and the fellowship of sharing in his sufferings, becoming like him in his death. . . .
Philippians 3:10, NIV

As a young man of twenty-three, Jim Elliott wrote, "Oh the fullness, pleasure, sheer excitement of knowing God on earth. I care not if I ever raise my voice again for Him if only I may love Him, please Him." If only we, with the apostle Paul and this young martyred missionary, could realize that God and His Son should have our greatest love and devotion. It should be greater even than our desire to serve Him. If we realized this, how much happier our Christian experience would be—and how much richer our fellowship with Him. If our first purpose in life were to get to know the Lord better—and better and better—all of the various aspects of our service would fall into their proper place and perspective.

Our love for Him, and I write this carefully, that it might not be misunderstood, *is more important to Him than our service.* "What do you do during the day?" a friend asked an elderly Scotch woman who lived alone. "Well," she said, "I get my hymn book and sing. Then I get the Bible and let the Lord speak to me. When I get tired of reading and cannot sing anymore, I just sit still and let the Lord love me!"

25

OF WINGS AND BOUGHS

And my God will supply every need of yours according to his riches in glory in Christ Jesus.

Philippians 4:19, RSV

We may as well admit it. By ourselves, in our own strength, we simply can't cope. Life is too complicated, too overwhelming. The boughs upon which we think to rest securely prove too fragile. Savings. Investments. Relationships. Community. Nation. Which of them is substantial enough to carry our weight? Inflation erodes the savings of a lifetime. High interest rates make it difficult to buy—or sell—a home. There is lessening personal security; nowadays, thieves do more than break through and steal. They terrorize whole cities.

As a nation, we appear to be placing our trust increasingly in armaments, a bough that milleniums of world history have repeatedly demonstrated to be very insecure indeed. Family and personal relationships shatter. Children leave home or return home after their own

October

breakups. Health deteriorates. Loved ones die. Things don't work out as we anticipated.

When the boughs break, if there are no wings, there is nothing. Martin Luther, who knew something about standing on the promises, expressed it another way: "I have held many things in my hands, and I have lost them all; but whatever I have placed in God's hands, that I still possess."

Stan Mooneyham

26

STARS AND SUNLIGHT

My God will meet all your needs according to his glorious riches in Christ Jesus.

Philippians 4:19, NIV

What a promise this is for the Christian! The source is God—"my God," the apostle calls Him. The supply is exhaustless—"according to his glorious riches." And the Savior is the channel through whom these riches come to us. The equation is totally in my favor. *My* needs are balanced over against *His* riches. There is no way I could improve upon that arrangement. No matter what my need, He is more than able to meet it. We are not to treat God as the anonymous writer puts it: "Some people treat God like they do a lawyer; they go to Him only when they are in trouble."

I find that I need Christ just as much, and sometimes more, in my more exalted hours as I do in the times of difficulties, troubles, and adversity. Many times we make the mistake of thinking that Christ's help is needed only for sickrooms or in times of overwhelming sorrow and suffering. This is not true. Jesus wishes to enter into every mood and every moment of our lives. He went to the wedding at Cana as well as to the home of Mary and Martha when Lazarus died. He wept with those who wept and rejoiced with those who rejoiced. Someone has said, "There are just as many stars in the sky at noon as at midnight, although we cannot see them in the sun's glare."

Billy Graham (TA)

October

27

THE MAGNET OF CHRIST

To them God chose to make known how great among the Gentiles are the riches of the glory of this mystery, which is Christ in you, the hope of glory.
Colossians 1:27, RSV

The story is told of one who underwent operation after operation for the removal of a small piece of broken needle which had lodged in his eye. Each operation had driven that little irritating object deeper into the sensitive organ until the man was in danger of losing his sight.

Finally a young doctor thought of a new way to handle the case. Leaving his probes and other delicate instruments in his bag, he used a small but powerful magnet, holding it as close to the eye as he dared. Immediately the small piece of steel needle began to move outward toward the magnet, soon leaving the wounded eye and relieving the sufferer.

This method was as simple as it was successful. By a single touch, the eye was saved and the trouble overcome. In just the same way, the power and attraction of Christ works in the life of the sinner, removing the irritation of the old life and providing power to live the new life.

28

GOD'S BLANK CHECK

But my God shall supply all your need according to his riches in glory by Christ Jesus.
Philippians 4:19

To really believe in the all-sufficiency of God means to believe that He is actually at liberty to do for us all that we need a God for, and that we have a right to take Him for everything for which we are unequal and insufficient. It means that He has promised all things necessary for life and godliness, that He has provided all things, and

October

that we have a right to come to Him for all things, presenting without question the mighty check on the bank of heaven, "My God shall supply all your need according to his riches in glory by Christ Jesus."

It means that we have a God who is equal to our salvation and the salvation of any sinner, however lost and however long he has resisted the mercy and grace of God. It means that God is equal to your sanctification and the sanctification of any temperament, no matter how impracticable; the counteracting of any habit no matter how confirmed; the overcoming of any defect, infirmity, and sin, no matter how deeply rooted and aggravated; victory over any and every temptation that may come, and a life made holy through and through and preserved blameless unto the coming of the Lord Jesus Christ.

A.B. Simpson

> There is such strength, my soul doth ask no greater,
> For Christ, in me, a work hath now begun
> And I have all the strength of earth's Creator!
> 'Tis not my strength but Christ's, and we are one!

Connie Calenberg

29

Hymn of Trust

But my God shall supply all your need according to his riches in glory by Christ Jesus.

Philippians 4:19

> O Love Divine, that stooped to share
>   Our sharpest pang, our bitterest tear,
> On Thee we cast each earth-born care,
>   We smile at pain while Thou art near!
>
> Though long the weary way we tread,
>   And sorrow crown each lingering year,
> No path we shun, no darkness dread,
>   Our hearts still whispering, Thou art near!

October

When drooping pleasure turns to grief,
  And trembling faith is changed to fear,
The murmuring wind, the quivering leaf,
  Shall softly tell us, Thou art near!

On Thee we fling our burdening woe,
  O Love Divine, forever dear,
Content to suffer while we know,
  Living and dying, Thou art near!

Oliver Wendell Holmes

30

FORGIVE AND FORGET

Be gentle and ready to forgive; never hold grudges. Remember the Lord forgave you, so you must forgive others.

Colossians 3:13, TLB

Clara Barton, founder of the American Red Cross, was once reminded of an especially cruel thing that had been done to her years before. But Miss Barton seemed not to recall it.

"Don't you remember it?" her friend asked.

"No," came the reply, "I distinctly remember forgetting that incident. . . ."

Chances are the wounds we pause to lick and the scars we aim to perpetuate aren't worth the time and effort it takes to nurture them in the first place. Anyway I've heard that only little people get hurt by little things and big people are tall enough to look over them. Have you heard this, too? Do you live by it?

Somehow it's always been very difficult for me to forget the little and big hurts of yesteryear. With time, some of them which were only seeds spring up like weeds and ruffle me to the point of desperation. That's when (I'm ashamed to admit it) I bang doors and yip at unsuspecting victims. Mother used to remind me that unless I had completely forgotten an insult to my pride or dignity, I had not forgiven it. I'm getting more forgetful all the time about things I want to remember. And I'm really trying to get forgetful about the not-want-to-remember things. Certainly there are enough beautiful things to think about that we need not keep twirling the ugly ones around. Need we?

Phyllis C. Michael

31

SEEING GOD

He is the image of the invisible God, the first-born of all creation; for in him all things were created, in heaven and on earth, visible and invisible, whether thrones or dominions or principalities or authoritiesall things were created through him and for him. He is before all things, and in him all things hold together. . . . For in him all the fullness of God was pleased to dwell.

Colossians 1:15–17,19, RSV

God is the supreme Light, the source of all light, for he is the Creator of the universe, the sun and moon and stars and all the light in the universe, especially the light of human understanding. Modern science has helped us to realize that we only see light when it is reflected off an object. Light moves so fast that our eyes cannot keep pace with it. This is also why we cannot see God. Our minds cannot keep pace with him. But out of sheer love, he has incarnated his light into human form so that we could see him in his fullness. He encounters us as a person and speaks to us face to face. Christ, the light of the world, is the eternal light of God slowed down for human comprehension and observation. From the fullness of God, we have received a revelation with nothing left out! Christ is the "freeze-frame" of God's magnificence for us to behold with awe and wonder. . . . When we think magnificently of God, our thoughts begin in Christ, God's light in the world, and they return unendingly to him.

Lloyd J. Ogilvie (AHA)

November

1

Do It to It!

Whatsoever ye do, do it heartily, as to the Lord.   Colossians 3:23

I was talking to a salesman the other day, and he was discouraged because he was making only fair sales. He said, "It's so hard for me to sell these tires. I'm not genuinely sold on them myself."

A lot of us call ourselves Christians, but we make poor salesmen because we readily give the impression we're not genuinely sold ourselves. A basic Christian teaching is this: "Whatsoever ye do, do it heartily, as to the Lord, and not unto men." Paul, who wrote that, did not sit around and only write letters telling other people what they should and should not do. Everything he taught, he attempted to put into practice. I am sure he would be the first to admit that he fell on his face a few times. He lived very much an overcoming sort of life; but what delights me about Paul—he did all things heartily unto his Lord.

Betty Carlson

2

Grace and Glory

The Lord will give grace and glory.   Psalm 84:11

Bounteous is Jehovah in His nature; to give is His delight. His gifts are beyond measure precious, and are as freely given as the light of the sun. He gives grace to His elect because He wills it, to His redeemed because of His covenant, to the called because of His promise, to believers because they seek it, to sinners because they need it.

November

He gives grace abundantly, seasonably, constantly, readily, sovereignly—doubly enhancing the value of the boon by the manner of its bestowal. Grace in all its forms He freely renders to His people: comforting, preserving, sanctifying, directing, instructing, assisting grace, He generously pours into their souls without ceasing, and He always will do so, whatever may occur. Sickness may befall, but the Lord will give grace; poverty may happen to us, but grace will light a candle at the darkest hour. Reader, how blessed it is as years roll 'round, and the leaves begin again to fall, to enjoy such an unfading promise as this, "The Lord will give grace."

The little conjunction "and" in this verse is a diamond rivet binding the present with the future; grace and glory always go together. God has married them, and none can divorce them. The Lord will never deny a soul glory to whom He has freely given grace. Glory, the glory of heaven, the glory of eternity, the glory of Jesus, the glory of the Father, the Lord will surely give to His chosen. Oh, rare promise of a faithful God!

C. H. Spurgeon

3

On Faith and Politics

Again, the devil took him to a high mountain and showed him all the kingdoms of the world and their splendor. "All this I will give you," he said, "if you will bow down and worship me." Jesus said to him, "Away from me, Satan! For it is written: 'Worship the Lord your God, and serve him only.' "
Matthew 4:8–10, NIV

I am as frightened of an evangelical power bloc as I am of any other. Worldly power in religious hands—Islamic or Christian—has hardened into more than one inquisition. That God has delivered us from the hands of zealous, but misguided, saints is all that at times has saved us.

Although it is not impossible to harmonize the two in some situations, there is actually a basic conflict between Christian commitment and political power. The strength of faith is in its avalanche of

November

powerlessness, its tidal force of love. If politics is the art of achieving the possible, faith is the art of achieving the impossible. Politics says, "Destroy your enemies." Christian faith says, "Love your enemies." Politics says, "The end justifies the means." Christian faith says, "The means validate the end." Politics says, "The first shall be first." Christian faith says, "The last shall be first."

I shall certainly continue to participate in the political process, and I hope you will. I will vote with care and a sense of responsibility, and I believe you will. That is all that either of us has the right, as Christians, to request of the other.

And when I go to church, I expect to be looking up at the pulpit for a pastor, teacher, friend. Not for a ward heeler.

Stan Mooneyham

4

PRAYER PURIFIES

Continue in prayer. . . . *Colossians 4:2*

The more praying there is in the world the better the world will be, the mightier the forces against evil everywhere. Prayer, in one phase of its operation, is a disinfectant and a preventive. It purifies the air; it destroys the contagion of evil. Prayer is no fitful, shortlived thing. It is no voice crying unheard and unheeded in the silence. It is a voice which goes into God's ear, and it lives as long as God's ear is open to holy pleas, as long as God's heart is alive to holy things.

God shapes the world by prayer. Prayers are deathless. The lips that uttered them may be closed in death, the heart that felt them may have ceased to beat, but the prayers live before God, and God's heart is set on them and prayers outlive the lives of those who uttered them; outlive a generation, outlive an age, outlive a world.

Prayer is the keynote of the most sanctified life, of the holiest ministry. He does the most for God who is the highest skilled in prayer. Jesus Christ exercised His ministry after this order.

E.M. Bounds

November

5

Praying People

Pray without ceasing.   *1 Thessalonians 5:17*

Praying men mean much more than men who say prayers; much more than men who pray by habit. It means men with whom prayer is a mighty force, an energy that moves heaven and pours untold treasures of good on earth. The number and efficiency of the laborers in God's vineyard in all lands is dependent on the men of prayer. The mightiness of these men of prayer increases, by the divinely arranged process, the number and success of the consecrated labors. Prayer opens wide their doors of access, gives holy aptness to enter, and holy boldness, firmness and fruitage. Praying men are needed in all fields of spiritual labor.

E. M. Bounds

I can take my telescope and look millions and millions of miles into space, but I can lay it aside and go into my room, shut the door, get down on my knees in earnest prayer, and see more of heaven and get closer to God than I can assisted by all the telescopes and material agencies on earth.

Sir Isaac Newton

6

Unceasing Intercession

Pray without ceasing.   *1 Thessalonians 5:17*

"Pray without ceasing." Let us take that word in a large faith, as a promise of what God's Spirit will work in us, of how close and intimate our union to the Lord Jesus can be, and our likeness to Him, in His ever blessed intercession at the right hand of God. Let it become to us one of the chief elements of our heavenly calling, to be consciously the stewards and administrators of God's grace to the world around us.

November

As we think of how Christ said, "I in them, and thou in me," let us believe that just as the Father worked in Him, so Christ *the interceding High Priest will work and pray in us.* As the faith of our high calling fills our hearts, we will begin literally to feel that there is nothing on earth for one moment to be compared with the privilege of being God's priests, walking without intermission in His holy presence, bringing the burden of the souls around us to the footstool of His throne, and receiving at His hands the power and blessing to dispense to our fellowmen.

This is indeed the fulfillment of the word of old, "Man created in the likeness and the image of God."

Andrew Murray

7

PRAY WITHOUT CEASING

Pray without ceasing.   *1 Thessalonians 5:17*

What does it mean to "pray without ceasing"? It is given him "always to pray, and not to faint." Not that he is always in the house of prayer; though he neglects no opportunity of being there. Neither is he always on his knees, although he often is, or on his face, before the Lord his God. Nor yet is he always crying aloud to God, or calling upon him in words; for many times "the Spirit maketh intercession for him with groans that cannot be uttered." But at all times the language of his heart is this: "Thou brightness of the eternal glory, unto thee is my heart, though without a voice, and my silence speaketh unto thee." And this is true prayer, and this alone. But his heart is ever lifted up to God, at all times and in all places. In this he is never hindered, much less interrupted, by any person or thing. In retirement or company, in leisure, business, or conversation, his heart is ever with the Lord. Whether he lie down or rise up, God is in all his thoughts; he walks with God continually, having the loving eye of his mind still fixed upon him, and everywhere "seeing him that is invisible."

John Wesley

November

8

THIS I KNOW

Pray without ceasing. In every thing give thanks: for this is the will of God in Christ Jesus concerning you.

                                          1 Thessalonians 5:17–18

> I know not by what methods rare,
> But this I know, God answers prayer.
> I know that He has given His Word,
> Which tells me prayer is always heard,
> And will be answered, soon or late.
> And so I pray and calmly wait.
>
> I know not if the blessing sought
> Will come in just the way I thought;
> But leave my prayers with Him alone,
> Whose will is wiser than my own,
> Assured that He will grant my quest,
> Or send some answer far more blest.
>
>   Eliza M. Hickok

9

THE SECRET OF CONTENTMENT

But godliness with contentment is great gain.   *1 Timothy 6:6*

Negatively, contentment delivers from worry and fretfulness, from avarice and selfishness. Positively, it leaves us free to enjoy what God has given us.

Contentment is the product of a heart resting in God. It is the soul's enjoyment of that peace which passes all understanding. It is the outcome of my will being brought into subjection to His will. It is the blessed assurance that God does all things well, and is, even now, making all things work together for my ultimate good. This experience has to be "learned" by "proving what is that good, and acceptable, and perfect, will of God" (Rom. 12:2). Contentment is possible

238

only as we cultivate and maintain that attitude of accepting everything which enters our lives as coming from the Hand of Him who is too wise to err, and too loving to cause one of His children a needless tear.

Let our final word be this: real contentment is only possible by being much in the presence of the Lord Jesus. It is only by cultivating intimacy with that One who was never discontent that we will be delivered from the sin of complaining. It is only by daily fellowship with Him who always delighted in the Father's will that we will learn the secret of contentment.

10

The Spirit of Love

But the fruit of the Spirit is love.   *Galations 5:22*

For God hath given us the spirit of love.   *2 Timothy 1:7*

When God, according to promise, writes His law in our hearts, the summing up of that law is love. It governs the life of the man wholly devoted to God, and controls his thoughts and actions. This divine love in the heart of man is as a little sanctuary, whence the child of God receives power, in obedience to the inner law of love, to live always in the love of God. This holy love includes fellowship with God, union with Christ, and love to the brethren.

How can we attain to this experience? Through faith alone. The chief sign of faith in the blind and the lepers who came to Christ to be healed was the knowledge of their own impotence and inability to help themselves. When our eyes have been opened, and we realize that the love of God has already been shed abroad in our hearts by His Spirit, enabling us to keep His commandments and to love the brethren—then let us bow in stillness of soul before God and adore the love which has taken possession of our hearts until our faith can firmly say: God has indeed given me the spirit of love in my heart. *In the power of the Spirit I can and will love God and my fellowship.*

Andrew Murray

November

11

THE PLUS FACTOR

For God did not give us a spirit of timidity but a spirit of power and of love and self-control.

2 *Timothy 1:7*, RSV

In a real way Paul was saying to his young friend Timothy, "Realize your plus factor. Start now. Don't be afraid. Reach out for accomplishment, health, and a life of service and opportunity. If you are governed by fears and a sense of failure, that is exactly what life will deal to you—rejection and disappointment. If you center your attention on the true gift God has given you—power and calm courage—you may reach out and claim the good that is already yours. If you have ability and talent, use it with vigor so that both others and you may profit by it. Always keep this plus factor uppermost in your mind. Launch out and do whatever God has given you to do. If you have never quite made it before, forget it. Perhaps you were concentrating too much on the minus factor. Remember, it is your plus factor that God wants you to use. If this factor controls you, you are on the way."

Harold Rogers

12

COMBINING PRAYER AND THANKSGIVING

Continue in prayer, and watch in the same with thanksgiving.

Colossians 4:2

In John 11:41 Jesus sets a beautiful example for His followers in this matter of combining prayer and thanksgiving. In fact, here Jesus expresses His thanks to the Father for answering a prayer He had not even prayed. Looking at the passage, we cannot find His petition that Lazarus be raised even recorded. All we have is His eloquent expression of praise to the Father that His "unspoken request" was granted. After this, in verse 43, He commands Lazarus to come forth—and

He does so dramatically, a startling example of death defeated at its own game.

If Jesus, divine Son of God, expressed thanksgiving in prayer, shouldn't we? And our thanks are not to be a complacent expression of self-satisfaction as was the Pharisee's prayer, "I thank thee that I am not as other men—such as this publican"! No, our prayers are to be *humble* expressions of our praise, not arrogant demands on God's bounty, as if He owed us anything at all. Jesus here does not really *ask* for anything. He just thanks God for prayer already answered. Do you and I ever do that? In Matthew 11:25 Jesus gives us another capsule "model prayer": "I thank thee, O Father, Lord of heaven and earth, because thou hast hid these things from the wise and prudent, and hast revealed them unto babes." Let's follow His blessed example. With Christina Rosetti, recognize this truth: "Were there no God, we would be in this glorious world with grateful hearts: and no one to thank!"

13

LOVE WILL SURVIVE

For God hath not given us the spirit of fear; but of power, and of love, and of a sound mind.

2 Timothy 1:7

There's beauty in the world. It is a startling thought that however horrible the circumstances, no war, no atrocities, no seaminess, no brutality, no pain can destroy the beauty of a rosy dawn, the glory of a flaming sunset, the song of a mockingbird at three in the morning, the loveliness of a deed of mercy, the look in a mother's face as she bends over a sick child. Viscount Gray heard Campbell McInness sing some of Handel's music in 1914 when Europe was being torn apart. He wrote: "Europe is in the most terrible trouble it has ever known in civilized times, and no one can say what will be left at the end. But Handel's music will survive." Believe that. Love will survive. Hope will. Truth will. Beauty will. We are to be eradicators of the ugly and establishers of the beautiful.

T. Cecil Meyers

November

14

On Meekness and Weakness

Put them in mind to be subject to principalities and powers, to obey magistrates, to be ready to every good work, to speak evil of no man, to be no brawlers, but gentle, showing all meekness unto all men.

Titus 3:1–2

Meek men are not weak men. The meek are gracious, congenial individuals who are easy to get along with. These genial, good-natured souls win friends on every side because they refuse to shove, push, and throw their weight around. They do not win their wars with brutal battles and fierce fights. They win their way into a hundred hearts and homes with the passport of a lowly, loving spirit.

Their unique genius is their gentleness. This quality of life does not come from a position of feeble impotence, but rather from a tremendous inner strength and serenity. Only the strong, stable spirit can afford to be gentle. It is the sublime Spirit of the living God who bestows upon us the capacity to express genuine concern and compassion for others. His selfless self-giving enables us to treat others with courtesy and consideration. This quality is much more than a thin veneer of proper propriety or superficial politeness. . . . Rather, it is the epitome of a laid-down life, poured out, laid out, lived out on behalf of others.

W. Phillip Keller (GLFS)

15

A Perspective on Trouble

For the grace of God that brings salvation has appeared to all men. It teaches us to say "No" to ungodliness and worldly passions, and to live self-controlled, upright and godly lives in this present age, while we wait for the blessed hope—the glorious appearing of our great God and Savior, Jesus Christ, who gave himself for us to redeem us from all wickedness and to purify for himself a people that are his very own, eager to do what is good.

Titus 2:11–14, NIV

November

I seriously doubt if we will ever understand our trials and adversities until we are safely in heaven. Then when we look back we are going to be absolutely amazed at how God took care of us and blessed us even in the storms of life. We face dangers every day of which we are not even aware. Often God intervenes in our behalf through the use of His marvelous angels. I do not believe that anything happens to an obedient Christian by accident. It is all in God's purpose. "We know that in all things God works for the good of those who love him, who have been called according to his purpose" (Rom. 8:28).

The apostle Paul again said, "All this is for your benefit, so that the grace that is reaching more and more people may cause thanksgiving to overflow to the glory of God. Therefore we do not lose heart. Though outwardly we are wasting away, yet inwardly we are being renewed day by day. For our light and momentary troubles are achieving for us an eternal glory that far outweighs them all" (2 Cor. 4:15–17). He again wrote to the Corinthians, "All things are yours, whether . . . the world or life or death or the present or the future— all are yours" (1 Cor. 3:21–22).

Billy Graham (TA)

16

A PLACE IN GOD'S LOVE

But when the time came for the kindness and love of God our Savior to appear, then he saved us—not because we were good enough to be saved, but because of his kindness and pity—by washing away our sins and giving us the new joy of the indwelling Holy Spirit.

Titus 3:4–5, TLB

If only we could realize that we do not have to accomplish great things or be something we are not to have a place in God's love. All we have to do is to be ourselves where we are and listen. Regardless of our station in life, we have the ability to grow in a vital and wonderful way because the spirit of God is within us.

Our Lord said, "The kingdom of God is within you" (Luke 17:21). His kingdom is joy, peace and security in the Holy Spirit, but to

November

have this sense of his presence we must prepare a place and keep it worthy of him. For that he gave direction when he said, "If a man loves me, he will keep my word and my Father will love him and we will come to him and make our home with him" (John 14:23).

This is the best news we can have. We are not alone, not hunting an elusive spirit. He is with us and wants to be recognized even more than we may want to recognize Him. He has a divine plan for every life based on the divine order of the universe. The plan he has for us will not harm another, will in no way move another from his or her rightful place, but it will blend us in harmony and purpose if we let it. His plan has been thought out well in advance. His Spirit is in us to administer that plan, but he must have our willingness. When he has that, he will supply all the power in the universe.

Harold Rogers

17

THE LORD MY HELPER

The Lord is my helper, and I will not fear what man shall do unto me.
Hebrews 13:6

The writer to the Hebrews is expressing a vital spiritual truth here. Surprisingly enough, it does not receive too much attention elsewhere in the Scriptures, except in the Psalms. A quick look at these verses helps to put the concept into perspective: "Thou art the helper of the fatherless" (10:14); "Lord be thou my helper" (30:10); "Behold, God is mine helper" (54:4); "For he shall deliver. . . him that hath no helper" (72:12).

The first three of these Psalms are attributed to David, the last to his illustrious son, Solomon. David learned his lesson of dependence upon the Lord during his years as a shepherd and warrior, and his first-person expression reflects that personal experience. Solomon, on the other hand, seems to speak academically, in the third person. A glance at other passages in Psalms reveals that David often prayed to his God to "help" him and thanked Him for that help.

November

All of us know what it means to need help. When our work is piled mountain high around us, the only answer is prayer. Many great people of God, people who accomplished great things for Him, have written that the greater their responsibility, the more time they needed to spend in prayer. David would echo a hearty "Amen" to that practice for it was his practice, too.

If God is our Helper, we need not worry no matter how great the task, no matter how outspoken the opposition. When we pray, we release the floodgates of power from on high that will buoy us up and over the greatest obstacle, lift us above and beyond those difficulties and dangers that press in upon us. Thank God, He is our Helper, and we need not fear what man can do to us!

18

CHRIST OUR HIGH PRIEST

For we have not an high priest which cannot be touched with the feeling of our infirmities; but was in all points tempted like as we are, yet without sin. Let us therefore come boldly unto the throne of grace, that we may obtain mercy, and find grace to help in time of need.

Hebrews 4:15–16

As we ponder these wonderful verses, we notice that Christ as our High Priest has obtained for us access to and acceptance with God, and on this account we may and must be courageous in our confession. But He also possesses sympathy, and on this account we must and should have confidence in approaching Him. His greatness inspires our courage, and His sympathy elicits our confidence.

W. H. Griffith-Thomas

> Lord, what a change within us one short hour
> Spent in Thy presence will avail to make!
> What heavy burdens from our bosoms take!
> What parched grounds refresh as with a shower!
> We kneel, and all around us seem to lower;
> We rise, and all, the distant and the near,

November

Stands forth in sunny outline, brave and clear;
We kneel, how weak; we rise, how full of power!
Why, therefore, should we do ourselves this wrong,
Or others—that we are not always strong—
That we are sometimes overborne with care—
That we should ever weak or heartless be,
Anxious or troubled—when with us is prayer,
And joy and strength and courage are with Thee!

Richard Chenevix Trench

19

Of Prayer and Grace

Let us therefore come boldly (into the presence of God), that we may obtain mercy, and find grace to help in time of need.

Hebrews 4:16

Come boldly into the presence of God, as the writer to the Hebrews expressed it.

Only do not try to bring all your baggage with you.

We are too prone, in the Western world, to bring all our problems to God. We regard prayer as a time for untangling the messes we have made. We think of it as a ouija board for reaching difficult decisions.

Try leaving everything behind.

Be like the Basque sheepherder who always prayed, "Lord, here is John."

Afterwards, or near the end of prayer, the disordered ends of your existence will fall more easily into place. Decisions will be easier to make.

But during the prayer itself, simply steep your soul in God. Let him roll over you like the waves of the ocean. Drift with him this way and that. Become one with him. As Annie Dillard puts it:

Experiencing the present
purely is being emptied and hollow.
you catch grace as a man
fills his cup under a waterfall.

John Killinger

November

20

THE QUALITY OF OUR SACRIFICE

By faith Abraham, when he was tested, offered up Isaac, and he who had received the promises was ready to offer up his only son.

Hebrews 11:17, RSV

Our heavenly Father is not as much interested in the *quantity* of our devotion to Him as He is in the *quality* of our love. Abraham could have sacrificed a calf or a lamb and not even missed it, but what kind of love would that have expressed? How deep would his devotion have been, if expressed as lightly as that? No, God wants our very best, our most prized possession. If I give Him part of myself, but keep back a portion for my own personal pleasures, I have not measured up to His standard, for He gave His best for me.

With the unknown poet we should reply:

> Sculptor of souls! I lift to Thee,
> Encumbered heart and hands;
> Spare not the chisel, set me free,
> However dear the bands.

21

OUR CELESTIAL ADVOCATE

. . . he is able to help for all time to save those who draw near to God through him, since he always lives to make intercession for them.

Hebrews 7:25, RSV

How encouraging is the thought of the Redeemer's never-ceasing intercession for us. When we pray, He pleads for us; and when we are *not* praying, He is advocating our cause, and by His supplications shielding us from unseen dangers. We little know what we owe to our Savior's prayers. When we reach the hilltops of heaven, and look back upon all the way whereby the Lord our God has led us, how we shall praise Him who, before the eternal throne, has pleaded our cause against our unseen enemies. *"But I have prayed for thee*, that thy faith fail not."

If any one should ask me for an epitome of the Christian religion, I should say, it is in that one word—*prayer*. If I should be asked, "What will take in the whole of Christian experience?" I should answer, "Prayer." A man must have been convinced of sin before he could pray; he must have had some hope that there was mercy for him before he could pray. All the Christian virtues are locked up in the word *prayer*.

C. H. Spurgeon

22

ABRAHAM IS FAITH

By faith Abraham, when he was called to go out into a place which he should after receive for an inheritance, obeyed.

Hebrews 11:8

Whither he went, Abraham knew not; it was enough for him to know that he went with God. He leaned not so much upon the promises as upon the Promiser. He looked not on the difficulties of his lot, but on the King—eternal, immortal, invisible, the only wise God, who had deigned to appoint his course, and would certainly vindicate Himself. O glorious faith! This is your work, these are your possibilities: contentment to sail with sealed orders, because of unwavering confidence in the love and wisdom of the Lord High Admiral: willing to rise up, leave all, and follow Christ because of the glad assurance that earth's best cannot bear comparison with heaven's least.

F. B. Meyer

23

A THANKSGIVING PSALM

I will sing unto the Lord, because he hath dealt bountifully with me.

Psalm 13:6

November

As the trees shake off their leaves and lift their branches to heaven;
  So my soul sheds its cares and its thoughts of the world and
    reaches up to Thee in adoration;
As the geese, flying southward before the winter wind,
  Seek the warmth of the sun,
So my soul flies to the warmth of Thy love.
  As the black bulbs lie in the warm earth awaiting the spring,
So do I rest in Thy love and Thy law, awaiting Thy bidding to service;
  As the harvest is gathered into the barns against the winter,
So into my soul is gathered Thy bounty and Thy provision.
  Therefore will I praise Thee and will offer thanks in Thy
    sanctuary;
Every day will I bless Thy holy name and sing a hymn of praise;
  I will thank Thee for Jesus, Thy Son, my Savior. Amen.

Author Unknown

24

Spiritual Sponges

But be ye doers of the word, and not hearers only, deceiving yourselves.
James 1:22, RSV

With some reasonableness we pilgrims can argue that we have arrived at this point in our faith only with much struggle, and who is to say when we know enough, have enough, believe enough to return something to the reservoir? So we go back to the same seminars and lectures (repeaters even get a discount) year after year for more input.

In our zeal for spiritual self-improvement (nothing wrong with that, per se), we soak it all up, trying to hold every drop, absorbing until we're positively dripping, bloated, always taking without giving back. Being a "disciple"—a learner—was never intended to turn Christians into one-way sponges.

Still we pray, "Lord, fill me." I don't recall ever hearing, "Lord, empty me." The thought of being emptied is not a pleasant one, but emptying is what makes a sponge good for something. It's not bad to feel "all wrung out" if you know where to get filled up again.

Taking without giving back. We don't like it when people do it to us. "Sponging" is what we call it. Scripture has something to say

November

about spiritual sponges. After wisely advising, "Each of you must be quick to listen," James soon adds, "Only be sure you act on the message and do not merely listen" (James 1:19, 22, NEB). In my copy, I have underlined *act*.

Stan Mooneyham

25

THE WONDERFUL GIFT OF WISDOM

But the wisdom from above is first pure, then peaceable, gentle, open to reason, full of mercy and good fruits, without uncertainty or insincerity.
James 3:17, RSV

The secret of Solomon's wisdom is given in Proverbs 1:7. He says pointedly, "The fear of the Lord is the beginning of wisdom." Here fear means awe and wonder, dependence and praise. The first three chapters of Proverbs eloquently describe the wonderful gift of wisdom. The way to wisdom is found in Proverbs 3:5–7: "Trust in the Lord with all your heart, and lean not on your own understanding. In all your ways acknowledge Him, and He shall direct your paths. Do not be wise in your own eyes; fear the Lord and depart from evil" (NJKV).

In the New Testament, wisdom is sublimely focused in Jesus Christ. Paul clearly describes him as the incarnate wisdom of God, "Christ the power and the wisdom of God" (1 Cor. 1:24) "Who was made to us wisdom from God" (1 Cor. 1:30). In Colossians the apostle boldly asks that his fellow believers in Colossae be filled with the knowledge of God's will "in all wisdom and spiritual understanding" (Col. 1:9). He also identified wisdom as one of the gifts of the Holy Spirit (1 Cor. 12:8).

What this means to us is that God has revealed his wisdom in Jesus Christ. When we ask for wisdom in our doubts, we are drawn into closer union with Christ himself. The more we know of him, the more we will be able to find answers to our questions and resolution of our doubts.

Lloyd J. Ogilvie (AHA)

26

PAST, PRESENT, AND FUTURE

Perseverance must finish its work so that you may be mature and complete, not lacking anything.

James 1:4, NIV

Thinking about the activity of God in her life, Joni Eareckson Tada learned a powerful lesson in practical faith. She talks about her pilgrimage: "I saw God continually 'working out my salvation.' He helped me deal with my past, for which He had forgiven me through Christ's death and resurrection. Then I saw Him effectively at work in the present. Although still apprehensive, I knew God was working in my life to save me not only from the past penalty of sin, but from its present power. Finally, I knew His Spirit was busy within me, trying to create a Christlike character in my life. Therefore, I could trust Him for the future and the full expression of His redemption which I would realize in the life to come."

This reminds me of a poem by an unknown poet, contrasting faith and doubt:

> Doubt sees the obstacles,
> Faith sees the way;
> Doubt sees the blackest night,
> Faith sees the day;
> Doubt dreads to take a step,
> Faith soars on high;
> Doubt questions, "who believes?"
> Faith answers, "I!"

27

THE KNOWLEDGE OF GOD

And this is life eternal, that they might know thee.   John 17:3

Brother Lawrence had a great longing to know God, and for this purpose went into a monastery. His spiritual advisers gave him prayer

November

books to use, but he put them aside. It helps little to pray, he said, if I do not know the God to whom I pray. And he believed that God would reveal Himself. He remained a long time in silent adoration, to come under the full influence of the presence of this great and holy Being. He continued in this practice, until later he lived consciously and constantly in God's presence and experienced His blessed nearness and keeping power. As the sun rising each morning is the pledge of light through the day, so the quiet time waiting upon God, to yield ourselves for Him to shine on us, will be the pledge of His presence and His power resting with us all the day. Be sure that the sun has risen upon your soul.

Learn this great lesson that the sun each day proclaims: As the sun on a cold day shines on us and imparts its warmth, believe that the living God will work in you with His love and His almighty power. God will reveal Himself as life and light and joy and strength to the soul that waits upon Him.

"Lord, lift thou up the light of thy countenance upon us" (Ps. 4:6).

"Be still, and know that I am God" (Ps. 46:10).

Andrew Murray

28

Prayer and Faith

Is any one of you in trouble? He should pray. Is any one happy? Let him sing songs of praise.

James 5:13, NIV

Joni Eareckson Tada knows about the prayer of faith. She says, "Wisdom is *trusting* God, not asking, 'Why, God?' Relaxed and in God's will, I know He is in control. It is not a blind, stubborn, stoic acceptance, but getting to know God and realize He is worthy of my trust. Although I am fickle and play games, God does not; although I have been up and down, bitter and doubting, He is constant, everloving.

"James, the apostle, wrote to people who were being torn apart by lions. Certainly their lot was far worse than mine. If this Word was sufficient for their needs, it can definitely meet mine."

November

Apparently, Dwight L. Moody must have learned the same lesson, for he writes, "I prayed for faith and thought it would strike me like lightning. But faith did not come. One day I read, 'Now faith comes by hearing, and hearing by the Word of God.' I had closed my Bible and prayed for faith. I now began to study my Bible and faith has been growing ever since."

29

MULTIPLIED PEACE

May grace and peace be multipled to you. . . .　　　　Peter 1:2, RSV

These two words, *grace* and *peace*, contain in them the whole sum of Christianity. Grace contains the remission of sins: peace, a quiet and joyful conscience. When the grace and peace of God are in the heart, then is man strong. Then he can neither be cast down by adversity nor puffed by prosperity, but walks on evenly, keeping to the highway. It is in the spirit that you find the paradise of grace and peace.

Martin Luther

Some unknown wise man put it well when he said, "Before we can enjoy the peace of God we must know the God of peace." How thankful I should be that I serve a God of grace and peace!

30

PASSION IN PRAYER

Elijah was a man subject to like passions as we are, and he prayed earnestly that it might not rain: and it rained not on the earth by the space of three years and six months.

James 5:17

When we read that Elijah was a man subject to the same passions as we, we are apt to suppose that here lies the driving force of his life. But the scripture makes it clear that it was not his passion, but his

November

prayer which achieved the wonderful results. He prayed earnestly that it might not, or that it might, rain, and his prayers had power over the very course of nature.

We need have no difficulty in accepting the fact of this great miracle. One commentator says that he can see no difference between a man asking a fellow man to water his lawn than to ask God to send rain. In each case the will of a man must operate on the will of another; and if it can operate on the will of man, why should it not operate also on the will of our heavenly Father? This, however, is not the main thought before us, but that Elijah, though capable of the same earnestness with which we are all endowed, refused to accomplish his life work by the employment of these lower energies. Rather, he set himself to obtain the results he sought through prayer. He was a man of like passions with ourselves, but he prayed earnestly. He turned his passion into prayer.

F. B. Meyer

December

1

SEASONS OF THE HEART

The Lord shall preserve thee from all evil: he shall preserve thy soul. The Lord shall preserve thy going out and thy coming in from this time forth, and even for evermore.

Psalm 121:7–8

As night follows day, so winter follows summer. It, too, has a beauty, a deep sense of rest, though I must admit I much prefer the warmer seasons.

Often, while we were living in the Black Hills, we would go out on a winter night. If there was a moon, the shadows on the snow were like etchings and we would wonder about the various designs and wish we were artists so that we might capture some of their ethereal beauty.

Yet there comes a time, summer or winter, to go indoors, close the drapes and remember there is one who keeps eternal vigilance while we sleep.

Harold Rogers

2

THE FRAGRANCE OF SWEET WINE

That the trial of your faith, being much more precious than of gold that perisheth, though it be tried with fire, might be found unto praise and honor and glory at the appearing of Jesus Christ.

1 Peter 1:7

Trials test, but they also deepen and intensify the spiritual temper of the believer just as the furnace strengthens steel, and the fire

December

purifies gold. Testing inevitably produces a better person—or a bitter person. In a sense, the outcome is up to the individual and his attitude toward testing.

The courageous quadriplegic, Joni Eareckson Tada, exemplifies the proper reaction to pressure. One person, under pressure, can react as does a marble—splintering into shards of glass, hurting anyone with whom he comes in contact. Or one can handle pressure as does the grape—yielding sweet and refreshing wine as the pressure is applied. That's the way Joni handles it.

In our scripture today, Peter goes on to give the secret of reacting like the grape. In verse 8, referring to Jesus Christ, he says, "Whom having not seen, ye love; in whom, though now you see him not, yet believing, ye rejoice with joy unspeakable and full of glory." This is the secret of being a "grape" Christian. If we can rejoice under trial, if we can yield submissively under pressure, we can give forth the sweetest fragrance and the sweetest wine.

3

GIFT OF GLOVES

But he said to me, "My grace is sufficient for you, for my power is made perfect in weakness." I will all the more gladly boast of my weaknesses, that the power of Christ may rest upon me.

2 Corinthians 12:9, RSV

Recently, I rushed to the airport to take a plane to Detroit. Forgetting that all the country does not enjoy the mild winter weather of California, I neglected to take along an overcoat, muffler, and gloves. Totally unequipped, I arrived in a Detroit blizzard. There was nothing to do but go to a department store and buy what I needed.

Perhaps it was because I had not worn gloves often in the past ten years that I was fascinated by the illustration my new gloves gave me. Without the insertion of my hand, the gloves were listless, inanimate, motionless. When they received my hand, the gloves were alive, vital, energized. Our self is like an empty glove. It is meant to be filled in order to fulfill its purpose. When we invite Christ to fill our self with himself, we become confident and bold. We no longer need to say with William E. Henley, "I am the master of my fate, I am the captain of my soul," but are able to say,

> I cannot do without Thee
> I cannot stand alone;
> I have no strength or goodness
> Nor wisdom of my own.
> But Thou, beloved Savior
> Art all in all to me
> And perfect strength in weakness
> Is theirs who lean on Thee.

Author Unknown

Lloyd J. Ogilvie (AHA)

4

THE MILK OF THE WORD

As newborn babes, desire the sincere milk of the word, that ye may grow thereby.

1 Peter 2:2

See what a charming parable the Lord has given us here in the mother's milk. Out of her own life does the mother yield food and life to her child. The feeding of the child is the work of the tenderest love, in which the child is pressed to the breast, and is held in the closest fellowship with the mother. And the milk is just what the weak child requires, food gentle and yet strong.

Even so is there in the Word of God the very life and power of God. His tender love will through the Word receive us into the gentlest and most intimate fellowship with Himself. His love will give us out of the Word what is, like warm soft milk, just fitted for our weakness. Let no one suppose that the Word is too high or too hard for him. For the disciple who receives the Word, and trustfully relies on Jesus to teach him by the Spirit, the Word of God shall practically prove to be gentle milk for newborn infants.

Andrew Murray

December

5

THINKING ABOUT THORNS

Live such good lives among the pagans that, though they accuse you of doing wrong, they may see your good deeds and glorify God on the day he visits us.

1 Peter 2:12, NIV

The apostle Paul, by firsthand experience, knew what it meant to suffer. As he was telling the people of Corinth about some of his exalted personal experiences with the risen Lord, he confessed that he had a real physical problem: "To keep me from becoming conceited because of these surpassingly great revelations, there was given me a thorn in my flesh, a messenger of Satan, to torment me" (2 Cor. 12:7).

We don't know exactly what that "thorn in the flesh" was, but it must have been a physical ailment. It may have been some type of eye disease or epilepsy; or, as Sir William Ramsay thought most likely, a malarial fever. Some have suggested it might have been chronic insomnia—though I think it unlikely. However, we do know how he handled his problem and what his subsequent attitude toward it was (see 2 Cor. 12:8–10).

Certainly Paul did not like that thorn in the flesh. But when he knew that it was not possible to get rid of it, he stopped groaning and began glorifying. He knew it was God's will and that the affliction was an opportunity for him to prove the power of Christ in his life.

Billy Graham

6

HARMONY IN HUMILITY

Finally, all of you have unity of spirit, sympathy, love of the brethren, a tender heart and a humble mind.

1 Peter 3:8, RSV

December

Peter speaks here of something more than mere unison—this is harmony. The essence of harmony can best be illustrated by the marvelous music made by a large modern symphony orchestra. If all the instruments merely played in unison, how "lifeless" their contribution would be. But when each member plays his own instrument, with a variety of scores combining to make rich and beautiful harmony, that's something different! The same is true of a field of wild flowers—the greater the variety of color, the more overwhelming the result to the eyes. This is the way it should be among Christians —each one performing his or her God-given task in harmony with others—harmony built on common faith in an uncommon Lord.

The apostle Paul was talking about the interrelationships among people when he instructed us to "Do nothing from selfishness or conceit, but in humility count others better than yourself" (Phil. 2:3).

7

THE MASTER'S TOUCH

If we confess our sins, he is faithful and just and will forgive us our sins and purify us from all unrighteousness.

1 John 1:9, NIV

There is a well-known story of some fishermen in Scotland who had spent the day fishing. That evening they were having tea in a little inn. One of the fishermen, in a characteristic gesture to describe the size of the fish that got away, flung out his hands just as the little waitress was getting ready to set the cup of tea at his place. The hand and the teacup collided, dashing the tea against the whitewashed walls. Immediately an ugly brown stain began to spread over the wall. The man who did it was very embarrassed and apologized profusely, but one of the other guests jumped up and said, "Never mind." Pulling a pen from his pocket, he began to sketch around the ugly brown stain. Soon there emerged a picture of a magnificent royal stag with his antlers spread. That artist was Landseer, England's foremost painter of animals.

December

This story has always beautifully illustrated to me the fact that if we confess not only our sins but our mistakes to God, He can make out of them something for our good and for His glory. Somehow it's harder to commit our mistakes and stupidities to God than it is our sins. Mistakes and stupidities seem so dumb, whereas sin seems more or less to be an outcropping of our human nature. But Romans 8:28 tells us that if they are committed to God He can make them work together for our good and His glory.

Billy Graham (HBBA)

8

ACCEPTING GOD'S LOVE

If we confess our sins, he is faithful and just to forgive us our sins, and to cleanse us from all unrighteousness.

1 John 1:9

Acknowledging oneself as a sinner and becoming personally aware of God's forgiveness is the central event that makes a person a Christian. Paul described it this way: "For the love of Christ leaves us no choice, when once we have reached the conclusion that one man died for all and therefore all mankind has died. His purpose in dying for all was that men, while still in life, should cease to live for themselves, and should live for him who for their sake died and was raised to life" (2 Cor. 5:14–15). This is not a halfway sort of thing. God doesn't do things partially.

Is this why, even as professing Christians, we are still unfree? Do we think God has only partly forgiven us? We have a tough time loving him because our attention is still upon our sin. We spend our energy wrestling with our guilt. A personal conviction has to come to us at the core of our being. It overcomes all other temporary feelings or reversals into guilt and self-condemnation: Christ has forgiven me. My sin is no longer the issue. I am being made new. I will not be uptight over my sins. I will stand tall in God's forgiveness and allow him to mold me after his likeness.

Maxie Dunnam

9

DIVINE ADVOCATE

My little children, I am writing this to you so that you may not sin; but if any one does sin, we have an advocate with the Father, Jesus Christ the righteous; and he is the expiation for our sins, and not for ours only but also for the sins of the whole world.

1 John 2:1–2, RSV

A certain missionary was struggling with the language of the natives among whom he labored. When he came to *Advocate* ("Comforter") in John 14:16, he tried to translate it into a word or phrase expressing the meaning to the native mind, but was baffled. Calling to his native assistant, he said, "Come over to my side and help me with this word." Thus, all at once, the missionary had his translation, "one called alongside to help."

During His earthly ministry, Jesus had been God's Advocate with men, pleading God's cause with them, seeking to win them for His Father. He was ever at the call of saint and sinner alike who needed His help. He was going away, however, and both He and the Father would see to it that their own would not be left without another Advocate on the earth. This further heavenly Comforter would not be recognized by an unspiritual world, but all true believers would know and welcome Him (John 14:16, 19, 25, 26; 15:26; 16:7).

Herbert Lockyer

10

ADORATION

Behold, what manner of love the Father hath bestowed upon us, that we should be called the sons of God.

1 John 3:1

I love my God, but with no love of mine,
  For I have none to give;

December

I love Thee, Lord, but all the love is Thine
 For by Thy love I live.
I am as nothing, and rejoice to be
Emptied and lost and swallowed up in Thee.

Thou, Lord, alone art all Thy children need,
 And there is none beside;
From Thee the streams of blessedness proceed,
 In Thee the blest abide—
Fountain of life and all-abounding grace,
Our source, our center, and our dwelling place.

Madame Guyon

11

THE EVERLASTING ARMS

The eternal God is thy refuge, and underneath are the everlasting arms.
Deuteronomy 33:27

One of the sweetest passages in the Bible is this one: "Underneath are the everlasting arms."

We often sink low under the weight of sorrows. Sudden disappointments can carry us, in an hour, from the heights down to the very depths. Props that we leaned upon are stricken away. What God means by it very often is just to bring us down to "the everlasting arms." We did not feel our need of them before. We were "making flesh our arm," and relying on human comforts or resources.

There is something about deep sorrow that tends to wake up the child-feeling in all of us. A man of giant intellect becomes like a little child when a great grief strikes him, or when a grave opens beneath his fireside.

One great purpose in all affliction is to bring us down to the everlasting arms. What new strength and peace it gives us to feel them underneath us! We know that, far as we may have sunk, we cannot go any farther. Those mighty arms cannot only hold us, they can lift us up. They can carry us along. Faith, in its essence, is simply a resting on the everlasting arms. It is trusting them, and not our own weakness. The sublime act of Jesus as our Redeemer was to descend to the lowest depths of human depravity and guilt, and to bring up His redeemed ones from that horrible pit in His loving arms. Faith is just the clinging to those arms, and nothing more.

Theodore L. Cuyler

12

HUMBLE HEARTS

Hereby perceive we the love of God, because he laid down his life for us: and we ought to lay down our lives for the brethren.

1 John 3:16

It is a straightforward case of cause and effect, not some complicated formula or technique. In fact, not until the impact of the laid-down life of Christ comes crashing through the crust around our hard, self-centered hearts will humility ever displace our despicable self-preoccupation. Then and only then will the expulsive power of humility's presence displace our selfishness enabling us to go out into a broken, shattered, bleeding, wounded world as suffering servants.

The humility of Christ, the meekness of His gracious Spirit, the gentleness of our God can only be known, seen, felt, and experienced by a tough world in the lives of God's people. If the society of our twentieth century finds God at all they will have to find Him at work in the garden of His children's lives. It is there His fruits should flourish and abound. It is there they should be readily found.

W. Phillip Keller (GLFS)

13

HOME—WHERE LOVE LIVES

I will walk within my house with a perfect heart. Psalm 101:2

Home is the holy of holies of a man's life. There he withdraws from all the world, and, shutting his door, is alone with those who are

December

his own. It is the reservoir of his strength, the restorer of his energies, the resting place from his toil, the brooding place for his spirit, the inspiration for all his activities and battles.

Home is where love lives. Not where it boards, nor pays occasional visits, even long visits, nor even where it may be a sort of permanent guest, with familiar access to certain rooms and cozy corners. But where it owns the front-door key, sits by the glow of a hearthfire of its own kindling, and pervades the whole house with its presence. It may be a king's spacious, luxurious palace. It may be the poor man's narrow-walled cottage, or anywhere in between these two extremes.

There may be present the evidences of wealth and culture and of the sort of refinement that these give, and even the higher refinement they can't give, and yet the place not be a home. And there may be the absence of all this, except the real refinement that love always breeds, and yet there may be a home in the sweet, strong meaning of that word.

S. D. Gordon

14

The Lord Our Keeper

The Lord is thy keeper: the Lord is thy shade upon thy right hand.
Psalm 121:5

I remember one time my little girl was teasing her mother to get her a muff, and so one day her mother brought a muff home, and although it was storming, she very naturally wanted to go out to try her new muff. So she tried to get me to go out with her. I went out with her, and I said, "Emma, better let me take your hand." She wanted to keep her hands in her muff, and so she refused to take my hand. Well, by and by she came to an icy place, her little feet slipped, and down she went. When I helped her up she said, "Papa, you may give me your little finger." "No, my daughter, just take my hand." "No, no, papa, give me your little finger." Well, I gave my finger to her, and for a little way she got along nicely, but pretty soon we came to another icy place, and again she fell. This time she hurt herself a

December

little, and she said, "Papa, give me your hand," and I gave her my hand, and closed my fingers about her wrist, and held her up so that she could not fall. Just so God is our keeper. He is wiser than we.

D. L. Moody

15

PORTRAIT OF A SERVANT

. . . if someone who is supposed to be a Christian . . . sees a brother in need, and won't help him—how can God's love be within him?
1 John 3:17, TBL

True servants are merciful. They care. They get involved. They get dirty, if necessary. They offer more than pious words.

And what do they get in return? What does Christ promise? ". . . *they shall receive mercy*." Those who remain detached, distant, and disinterested in others will receive like treatment. But God promises that those who reach out and demonstrate mercy will, in turn, receive it. Both from other people as well as from God Himself. We could paraphrase this beatitude: "O the bliss of one who identifies with and assists others in need—who gets inside their skin so completely he sees with their eyes and thinks with their thoughts and feels with their feelings. The one who does that will find that others do the same for him when he is in need."

That is exactly what Jesus, our Savior, did for us when He came to earth. By becoming human. He got right inside our skin, literally. That made it possible for Him to see life through our eyes, feel the sting of our pain, and identify with the anguish of human need. He understands. Remember those great words:

"But Jesus the Son of God is our great High Priest who has gone to heaven itself to help us; therefore let us never stop trusting him. This High Priest of ours understands our weaknesses, since he had the same temptations we do, though he never once gave way to them and sinned" (Heb. 4:14–15, TBL).

Charles R. Swindoll (IYS)

December

16

Love and Faith

And this is his commandment, that we should believe on the name of his Son Jesus Christ, and love one another, as he gave us commandment.

1 John 3:23

The church must learn not only to preach the love of God in redemption; it must go further and teach Christians to show that the love of Christ is in their hearts, by love shown to the brethren. Our Lord called this a new commandment: a badge by which the world should recognize His disciples!

There is great need for this preaching of love. God sometimes allows bitterness to arise between Christians that they may view the terrible power of sin in their hearts and shrink back at the sight. How greatly a minister and his people should feel the importance of Christ's command: "Love one another." A life of great holiness will result if we really love each other as Christ loves us.

May the reading of this passage help us to understand the two manifestations of love: the wonderful love of God in Christ to us, and the wonderful love in us, through the Holy Spirit, to Him and to our brethren.

Andrew Murray

17

Separate, Yet Penetrating

In this was manifested the love of God toward us, because that God sent his only begotten Son into the world, that we might live through him.

1 John 4:9

How can we help our bent world? We must practice two concepts which, first considered, seem opposite and unreconcilable: we must be willing to withdraw ourselves and be separate from our world, but, conversely, we must have the courage to penetrate it. Both of these avenues are lined with critics.

December

Looking at Jesus and John the Baptist will serve to illustrate. John was a recluse—a monk, a hermit. He scorned the gayer life of the cities and spent his years, short as they were, in eroded washes and canyons of the Jordan, lonely and apart. Jesus, on the other hand, went where the action was. He came preaching in the cities, Decapolis, Jerusalem, Jericho. He went to weddings and dinner parties. He did not traffic in sin but he trafficked with sinners.

Both Jesus and John received harsh criticism. John was criticized for his asceticism. People said that John "had a devil." He would have to be crazy, they reasoned, to stalk around the Jordan jungles in haircloth, munching grasshoppers. Of Jesus they said, "Look, he is a gourmand and an alcoholic!" If neither Jesus nor John the Baptist could escape criticism for these two principles, we must expect to receive it also.

Calvin Miller

18

THE JOY OF LOVING

If we love one another, God dwelleth in us, and his love is perfected in us.
1 John 4:12

Now, will anyone be so hardy as to say that love is misery? Is it misery to love God, to give him my heart who alone is worthy of it? Nay, it is the truest happiness; indeed, the only true happiness which is to be found under the sun. So does all experience prove the justness of that reflection which was made long ago, "Thou hast made us for thyself; and our heart cannot rest, until it resteth in thee." Or does anyone imagine, the love of our neighbor is misery; even the loving every man as our own soul? So far from it, that, next to the love of God, this affords the greatest happiness of which we are capable. Therefore,

> Let not the Stoic boast his mind unmoved,
> The brute philosopher, who ne'er has proved
> The joy of loving, or of being loved.

John Wesley

December

19

THE HIGHEST LOVE

If we love one another, God abides in us, and his love is perfected in us.
1 John 4:12, RSV

Our loves need to be converted and harmonized. Much of the tension in our lives is the conflict of our loves. Stanley Jones has helped me most here. In his cryptic way, he says, "The highest in God is the deepest in us—the urge to love and to be loved. . . . So the deepest in man and the highest in God do not conflict—they coincide! To be converted in love, then, is to be converted to the homeland of the soul. . . . All coming to Jesus has the feel of homecoming about it."

Wholeness, then, is not a matter of getting rid of our desires, but a redemption of our desires. "The desire to get rid of desire is desire." The only way to get rid of one desire is to replace it by a higher desire. Here is the ministry of Christ to our loves. Through Christ, "God's love has been poured into our hearts through the Holy Spirit which has been given to us" (Rom. 5:5, RSV). When we open ourselves to the power of the Holy Spirit, our loves are brought into harmony with God's love. Accepting his love, and loving him, we love ourselves and our neighbor. Our other loves become servants to this ultimate love of God, neighbor, and self.

Maxie Dunnam

20

THREE IN ONE

For there are three that bear record in heaven, the Father, the Word, and the Holy Ghost: and these three are one.

1 John 5:7

As strange as it may seem, in requiring you to believe, "there are three that bear record in heaven, the Father, the Word, and the Holy Ghost: and these three are one," you are not required to believe any

December

mystery. Nay, that great and good man, Dr. Peter Browne, sometime Bishop of Cork, has proved at large that the Bible does not require you to believe any mystery at all. The Bible barely requires you to believe such facts—not the manner of them. Now the mystery does not lie in the *fact,* but altogether in the *manner.*

For instance: "God said, Let there be light: And there was light." I believe it: I believe the plain *fact:* There is no mystery at all in this. The mystery lies in the *manner* of it. But of this I believe nothing at all; nor does God require it of me.

Again: "The Word was made flesh." I believe this fact also. There is no mystery in it; but as to the *manner* how he was made flesh, wherein the mystery lies, I know nothing about it; I believe nothing about it; it is no more the object of my faith, than it is of my understanding.

To apply this to the case before us: "There are three that bear record in heaven: and these three are one." I believe this *fact* also (if I may use the expression), that God is Three and One. But the *manner how* I do not comprehend; and I do not believe it. Now in this, in the *manner,* lies the mystery; and so it may; I have no concern with it. It is no object of my faith: I believe just so much as God has revealed, and no more. But this, the *manner,* he has not revealed; therefore, I believe nothing about it. But would it not be absurd in me to deny the *fact* because I do not understand the *manner?* That is, to reject *what God has revealed,* because I do not comprehend *what he has not revealed?*

John Wesley

21

DIVINE LOVE

And this is love, that we walk after his commandments.   *2 John 6*

What is love if not locally expressed? What is vocation if not something done in a specific place? What is faith if its object is not singular, if it does not tie us to a given fellowship?

God's love is the model—a love that came down to earth, that got

December

all tangled up in the particularities of our history. For God did not choose to save us by writing in the sky, but by the gift of a child, a man, a cross, and an empty tomb. Let us trust our sample of life. We haven't got it all, but no one has. Let us run not some imagined, ideal race, but as the writer of Hebrews put it, "the race that is set before us"—helps, hindrances, and all (Heb. 12:1).

Prayer

O Thou who didst not disdain to set
Thy love and do Thy work in the midst of men,
keep us faithful to the gospel where we are;
lest in dreaming of times and places more ideal
we should fail Thee here and now.
As Thou hast loved, so may we love.
Through Jesus Christ our Lord.

Amen.

Ernest T. Campbell

22

THE OTHER SIDE OF LOVE

And the angels that did not keep their own position but left their proper dwelling have been kept by him in eternal chains . . . until the judgment of the great day.

Jude 6, RSV

God's keeping power operates negatively as well as positively. Notice what happens to those angels who kept not their first estate. Whatever else it means, it must mean that they had the potential for high possibilities of service for which they were fitted—yet they forfeited it, and the very power by which they might have served became the chain by which they were enwrapped. Do not presume on the divine keeping power, for there is always the dread possibility of neutralizing it. Keep yourselves therefore in the love of God. Have you the light? Follow the gleam. Are you in the midcurrent? Don't get turned off into a side stream. Are you being used? Keep under your

270

body and bring it to subjection, lest having preached to others you may yourself become rejected.

There is One who is able to keep us from falling, not only from within, but from without. We are of value to Christ for His saving and redemptive purposes. We are greater than worlds or suns, greater than time or space, greater than the universe in which we are found. We are "kept for Jesus Christ"; let us not be unmindful or ungrateful, for through the ages, this prayer continues to rise from the heart of our Redeemer: "I pray, not that thou shouldest take them out of the world, but that thou shouldest keep them from the evil."

F. B. Meyer

23

PREPARING THE WAY

Prepare ye the way of the Lord.   *Isaiah 40:3*

These were the words of "the voice of him that crieth in the wilderness." When seven hundred years afterward, John the Baptist was preaching repentance "in the wilderness of Judea," the evangelist Matthew said that "this is he that was spoken of by the prophet."

Now, nearly two thousand years have passed since the Baptist's voice was heard saying, "Repent" and "Prepare ye the way of the Lord," and yet this preparation is not fully completed. Thank God it has been completed in the hearts and lives of millions! But there are millions more to whom we still must cry: "Prepare ye the way of the Lord!" He is anxious not merely to come *to* us, but to come *in* us— to come in the fullness of His grace into our hearts and lives. But He cannot do this until we have "prepared the way." We must put away and lay aside everything which is of the nature of a stumbling block in His way.

"Prepare ye the way of the Lord," so that He may come triumphantly right into the heart, and there set up His throne and reign with undisputed sway. This is *His* desire; may it, too, be mine.

John Roberts

December

24

THE GIFT OF GOD

Thanks be unto God for his unspeakable gift.   2 Corinthians 9:15

The one great work of God's love for us is, He gives us His Son. In Him we have all. Hence the one great work of our heart must be to receive this Jesus who has been given to us, to consider Him and use Him as ours. I must begin every day anew with the thought, *I have Jesus to do all for me.* In all weakness or danger or darkness, in the case of every desire or need, let your first thought always be, *I have Jesus to make everything right for me, for God has given Him to me.* Whether your need be forgiveness or consolation or confirmation, whether you have fallen, or are tempted to fall, in danger, whether you know not what the will of God is in one or another matter, or know that you have not the courage and the strength to do His will, let this always be your first thought, *the Father has given me Jesus to care for me.*

Some unknown thinker has reminded us: "Don't let the abundance of God's gifts make you forget the Giver in your satisfaction over the gifts."

Andrew Murray

25

THE WORD BECAME FLESH

And the Word became Flesh, and dwelt (or tabernacled) among us, and we beheld His glory, glory as of the only begotten from the Father, full of grace and truth.

John 1:14, NASB

That word *tabernacle* is an interesting one; it comes out of the Old Testament. Remember when God ordered his people to have a temporary worship place while they were in the wilderness? Moses was given directions for building the tabernacle. It was a beautiful tent in which to house the very Presence of God.

December

Why does John 1 say that Christ tabernacled among us? Well, there are many similarities. The tabernacle was rough on the outside, but gloriously beautiful on the inside, with God's hidden presence. Our Lord Jesus Christ seemed poor and rough, but inside the poverty of that body there was the glory. "We beheld His glory," said John, referring to the Transfiguration of Jesus, the one time when that inner glory was allowed to be exposed. The tabernacle in the wilderness was a place where God would meet with his people. And when Jesus tabernacled on earth, it was so that man could meet with God.

The Old Testament tabernacle was among the people of Israel for only about thirty-five years. So was our Lord.

The tabernacle didn't stay in one place like a permanent temple, but it went wherever the people went. And Jesus didn't even have a place to lay his head. He was a man on the move, for the people's sake. He tabernacled among us; he had no permanent dwelling place. He didn't make people come to him; he went to them.

God among us! What a miracle! It had been planned for all eternity. It was for your redemption, and for mine. The ramifications of that birth are enormous and are by no means all worked out yet. "God was in Christ, reconciling the world unto Himself."

Raymond C. Ortlund

26

The Place of Prayer

Behold, I stand at the door, and knock: if any man hear my voice, and open the door, I will come in to him, and will sup with him, and he with me.
Revelation 3:20

I doubt that I know of a passage in the whole Bible which throws greater light upon prayer than this one does. It is, it seems to me, the key which opens the door into the holy and blessed realm of prayer.

This teaches us, in the first place, that it is not our prayer which moves the Lord Jesus. It is Jesus who moves us to pray. He knocks. Thereby He makes known His desire to come in to us. Our prayers are always a result of Jesus' knocking at our hearts' doors.

December

From time immemorial prayer has been spoken of as the breath of the soul. And the figure is an excellent one indeed.

The air which our body requires envelops us on every hand. The air of itself seeks to enter our bodies and, for this reason, exerts pressure upon us. It is well known that it is more difficult to hold one's breath than it is to breathe. We need but exercise our organs of respiration, and air will enter forthwith into our lungs and perform its life-giving function to the entire body.

The air which our souls need also envelops all of us at all times and on all sides. God is round about us in Christ on every hand, with His many-sided and all-sufficient grace. All we need to do is to open our hearts.

Prayer is the breath of the soul, the organ by which we receive Christ into our parched and withered hearts.

He says, "If any man open the door, I will come in to him." Notice carefully every word here. It is not our prayer which draws Jesus into our hearts. Nor is it our prayer which moves Jesus to come in to us. All He needs is access. He enters in wherever He is not denied admittance.

O. Hallesby

27

LIFE'S UPS AND DOWNS

Then I heard a loud voice in heaven say: "Now have come the salvation and the power and the kingdom of our God, and the authority of his Christ. For the accuser of our brothers, who accuses them before our God day and night, has been hurled down. They overcame him by the blood of the Lamb and by the word of their testimony; they did not love their lives so much as to shrink from death."

Revelation 12:10–11, NIV

"Why can't I seem to solve my problems?" This question reminds me of a Peanuts cartoon. It pictures Lucy in her psychiatrist's booth giving counsel to Charlie Brown. Charlie has lost another ball game and feels depressed and defeated. Lucy, the psychiatrist, is explaining

to him that life is made of ups and downs. Charlie goes away scream-
ing, "But I hate downs, all I want is ups."

I'm afraid that often those of us who teach the Christian message
give the impression that once we have accepted Jesus Christ we will
never again have any problems. This isn't true, but we do have Someone to help us face our problems. I have a paraplegic friend who has
been that way for over thirty years. In spite of overwhelming problems for which there is no solution, she has learned not only to live
with her condition, but to be radiant and triumphant, blessing and
winning others to Christ.

Billy Graham (HBBA)

28

POSITIVE SUFFERING

*God himself will be with them, he will wipe away every tear from their
eyes, and death shall be no more, neither shall there be mourning nor crying,
nor pain any more for the former things have passed away.*
Revelation 21:4, RSV

When we hear someone say, "All suffering is the will of God," we
should ask, "What do you mean by the 'will of God'?" If one means
God's permissive, circumstantial will, then I agree. If one means
God's perfect or intentional will, then I would have to disagree. Most
suffering is God's will only in the sense that He *permits* it to come.
Notice the use of the word *most*. *Most* has to be used, not only
because of the suffering that comes as a result of natural catastrophes
that we do not understand, but also I do not believe any person has
the wisdom or the right to say how God will always operate. . . .

If we understand that most suffering is simply permitted by God,
will you not agree that we will no longer tend to blame the Lord for
our suffering? Our main question will not be, "Who did sin?" or,
"Why suffering?" but instead, "What will God do for me and for
others in and through my sufferings?"

T. B. Maston

December

29

BLESSED BLOOD

And they overcame him by the blood of the Lamb. . . .

Revelation 12:11

No religion that ignores this elemental fact in human consciousness is destined to permanence. To say with Buddha, "You can wipe out your sins with good deeds," or with Mohammed, "God is good, and will not be hard on you," is not enough. The religious creed that deals most radically and drastically with sin is the one which will ever appeal most strongly to the human heart, and it is because Jesus Christ has not treated sin lightly, but has loosed men from it by His blood, that He shall be enthroned forever when the names of all other teachers shall have faded as stars at noon.

Whatever else the blood of Christ may mean, it means that Christ has viewed our sin as of tremendous gravity. With Him it is no slight illness to be cured by a regimen of diet and exercise. It is deep-seated, radical, perilous, endangering the fabric of our soul's health and the scope of our soul's outlook on the future. This is He who came by water and blood; not by water only, but by water and blood. He has loosed us from our sins in His own blood. And He is coming again to take us unto Himself forever!

F. B. Meyer

30

THE INSPIRED WORD

And if any man shall take away from the words of the book of this prophecy, God shall take away his part out of the book of life, and out of the holy city, and from the things which are written in this book.

Revelation 22:19

What is there in Scripture that invested it, in Christ's judgment, with such unique authority? What are the Scriptures? It would be difficult to find a reply more satisfactory and scriptural than that given by the late A. J. Gordon: "Literature is the letter; Scripture is the letter inspired by the Spirit." What Jesus said of the new birth is equally applicable to the doctrine of inspiration: "That which is born of the flesh is flesh, and that which is born of the Spirit is spirit." Educate, develop, and refine the natural man to the highest possible point, yet he is not a spiritual man till, through the new birth, the Holy Spirit renews and indwells him. So of literature; however elevated its tone, however lofty its thought, it is not Scripture. Scripture is literature indwelt by the Spirit of God. The absence of the Holy Spirit from any writing constitutes the impassable gulf between it and Scripture. "*In fine*, the one fact which makes the Word of God a unique book, standing apart in solitary separateness from other writings, is that which also parts the man of God from common men—the indwelling of the Holy Spirit."

F. B. Meyer

31

A NEW START

As we have therefore opportunity, let us do good unto all men, especially unto them who are of the household of faith.

Galatians 6:10

A new year is opening before us, and there is some satisfaction in feeling that this will give us an opportunity for a brand new start. Each true heart in which there is a spark of the divine life turns eagerly toward the unblemished page, the untrodden way, the new year. We turn not with wonder simply, or with hope, but with the fervent resolve to let the past bury its dead, and to live a nobler, fuller, sweeter life in the days that remain for us.

But it is of little purpose merely to wish and to resolve. We must deal with mistakes and sins which have dogged our footsteps in the past. If we could turn our backs upon these, and make a new start, we could then expect the coming year to make us better people.

F. B. Meyer

Contributors

Contributors

Titles

Titles

Titles

Acknowledgments

The following titles are used by permission of Word Books, Publisher, Waco, Texas. The compiler expresses deep appreciation to these authors for permission to excerpt portions of their books:

Briscoe, D. Stuart. *Tough Truths for Today's Living.* Copyright © 1978. (Formerly *Now for Something Totally Different.*)
Campbell, Ernest T. *Locked in a Room with Open Doors.* Copyright © 1974.
Crumpler, Frank H. *The Invincible Cross.* Copyright © 1977.
Dunnam, Maxie. *Barefoot Days of the Soul.* Copyright © 1975.
Graham, Billy. *Till Armageddon.* Copyright © 1981.
Graham, Billy. *How to Be Born Again.* Copyright © 1977.
Keller, W. Phillip. *David.* Copyright © 1985.
Keller, W. Phillip. *Elijah.* Copyright © 1980.
Keller, W. Phillip. *A Gardener Looks at the Fruits of the Spirit.* Copyright © 1979.
Keller, W. Phillip. *Salt for Society.* Copyright © 1981.
Larson, Bruce. *Risky Christianity.* Copyright © 1976.
Mooneyham, Stan. *Traveling Hopefully.* Copyright © 1984.
Ogilvie, Lloyd J. *Ask Him Anything.* Copyright © 1981.
Ogilvie, Lloyd J. *Congratulations—God Believes in You!* Copyright © 1980.
Ortlund, Raymond C. *Intersections.* Copyright © 1979.
Richards, Larry. *When It Hurts Too Much to Wait.* Copyright © 1985.
Rogers, Dale Evans. *God in the Hard Times.* Copyright © 1984.
Swindoll, Charles R. *Dropping Your Guard.* Copyright © 1983.
Swindoll, Charles R. *Improving Your Serve.* Copyright © 1981.
Swindoll, Charles R. *Strengthening Your Grip.* Copyright © 1982.

A special thanks to Joni Eareckson Tada for *Joni* (Grand Rapids, MI: Zondervan, 1976).